ITALO CALVINO

Why Read the Classics?

Italo Calvino's works include *Numbers in the Dark*, *The Road to San Giovanni*, *Six Memos for the Next Millennium*, *The Baron in the Trees*, *If on a Winter's Night a Traveler*, *Invisible Cities*, *Marcovaldo*, and *Mr. Palomar*. Calvino died in 1985.

Also by ITALO CALVINO

Why Read the Classics?

ITALO CALVINO

Translated from the Italian by

MARTIN McLAUGHLIN

VINTAGE BOOKS
A Division of Random House, Inc.
New York

FIRST VINTAGE BOOKS EDITION, DECEMBER 2000

Translation copyright © 1999 by Jonathan Cape

The Library of Congress has cataloged the Pantheon edition as follows:
Calvino, Italo.
[Perché leggere i classici. English]
Why read the classics? / Italo Calvino;
translated from the Italian by Martin McLaughlin.
p. cm.
ISBN 0-679-41524-6.
1. Canon (Literature) 2. Literature—History and criticism. I. Title.
PN81.C25513 1999
809—dc21 99-21535
CIP

Vintage ISBN: 0-679-74349-9

www.vintagebooks.com

Printed in the United States of America
10 9 8 7 6 5 4 3

Contents

Translator's Introduction

Eleven of the thirty-six essays in this book have appeared in English before.[1] The justification for retranslating those eleven pieces stems from the desire to provide an integral English version that corresponds exactly to the important posthumous anthology *Perché leggere i classici* (Milan: Mondadori, 1991). That volume represents a personal collection of essays on Calvino's classics, selected in consultation with the author's widow, and based on material that the author had set aside for some such future publication. Calvino's English readers now not only have access to a substantial and coherent sample of his literary criticism but can also gain an insight into what amounts to his personal canon of great classics. Some of the essays appearing here for the first time in English translation will be of particular interest to Calvino's readers in the Anglo-American world: no fewer than seven of them deal with major authors of texts in English (Defoe, Dickens, Conrad, Stevenson, Twain, James, Hemingway), while others contain substantial references to writers such as Sterne (Diderot), Shakespeare (Ortes), Dickens (Balzac) and Kipling (Hemingway).

One of several other insights that this collection offers is the omnivorous nature of Calvino's tastes in reading. Apart from the seven essays on texts in English, Italian literature naturally enjoys pride of place with ten essays, but there are no fewer than nine devoted to French works, four to classical authors from the ancient world, and two each to Russian and Hispanic writers.

The volume also provides an idea of how one of the twentieth century's greatest fiction writers developed as a literary critic, starting with early essays from his militant Communist period in the 1950s (on Conrad,

Hemingway, Defoe, Pasternak), covering his prolific and varied literary interests in the 1970s (English, Russian, French and Greco-Roman writers), right down to some of his final and finest essays written in the 1980s. The essays chart the development of an increasingly sophisticated literary critic, who was anything but provincial in his literary tastes: on the evidence of these essays, even if he had not become an internationally renowned fiction writer, Calvino would have been one of the most interesting essayists and critics of the twentieth century.

Why Read the Classics? also mirrors the fiction writer's own creative evolution, from neorealist to postmodernist, from Conrad and Hemingway to Queneau and Borges. Right from the outset he was particularly interested in literature in English: Stevenson and Kipling had been favourite authors in his childhood, and his university thesis on Conrad (completed while he was writing his first novel, in 1946–47) was a precocious study of the ideas, characters and style of the author of *Lord Jim*. As a writer of neorealist fiction, he was naturally deeply indebted to Hemingway, so it is no surprise to find that these two authors are the subjects of the earliest essays in this collection. During the 1950s, as his own fiction shifts from neorealism towards fantasy, Calvino moves away from twentieth-century authors: the essay on *Robinson Crusoe* is almost exactly contemporary with his longest, and most 'Robinsonian' novel, *The Baron in the Trees* (1957), and many of the episodes highlighted in Calvino's essay on Defoe resurface intertextually in his novel.

The 1963 essay on Gadda was written just at the time when a new literary avant-garde emerged in Italy which also had a profound effect on Calvino. Gadda's sense of the complexity of the world suited perfectly the mood of the author, who at that stage was turning his back on traditional realist fiction and embarking on the cosmicomical tales that were to confirm his international reputation as a major fantasist. These cosmic interests are reflected in the essays on Cyrano and Galileo: the latter, Calvino claimed in a famous polemic in the 1960s, was one of the most important Italian prosewriters ever.

Many of the 1970s essays in this collection are introductions to novellas or long short stories by authors such as James, Twain, Tolstoy, Stevenson and Balzac. This was part of an attractive initiative undertaken by Calvino in those years, the series he launched with Einaudi entitled 'Centopagine'. He always held a high aesthetic regard for brief texts (of no more than one hundred pages) which avoided the complexity and length of the novel. His often declared admiration for eighteenth-century Enlightenment values is reflected in the essays on Diderot, Voltaire and Ortes, while his enthusiasm for classic nineteenth-century fiction is evident in the substantial contributions on Stendhal and Flaubert, and in the detailed analysis of *Our Mutual Friend*, which displays particular sensitivity to Dickens' style and to the comparative efficacy of rival Italian translations of the novel.

One final trend also evident here is worth noting: in the 1970s and 1980s not only does Calvino turn back to Italian classics such as Ariosto, but he also rereads a number of ancient texts, such as Homer, Xenophon, Ovid and Pliny. His creative writing in this period is also informed by this new aspiration towards classical qualities: in the central section of *Invisible Cities*, for instance, the city of Baucis explicitly recalls the myth in the central book of Ovid's *Metamorphoses*, discussed at length in the essay in this volume. Similarly the central definition of Pliny in the 1982 essay ('the measured movement of [Pliny's] prose . . . is enlivened by his admiration for everything that exists and his respect for the infinite diversity of all phenomena') throws interesting light on the creative work Calvino was composing at this same time: in one sense *Mr Palomar* (1983) is a modern, or post-modern, Pliny, its smooth prose encompassing his interest in all flora and fauna. Calvino's appetite for French literature also embraces contemporary writers such as Ponge and Queneau, the essay on the latter reflecting the Italian author's interest in that innovative blend of literature and mathematics that was characteristic of the French author and his friends in the OULIPO (Ouvroir de Littérature Potentielle); while Ponge's defamiliarisation of quotidian objects echoes Mr Palomar's attempt to see the universe with fresh eyes, whether it be waves on a beach, the sky at night, or the blades of grass in a lawn. The collection as a whole thus offers a kind of rear view into the everyday workshop of a great creative writer: what Calvino read was often metamorphosed creatively, intertextually, into what Calvino wrote.

Despite the variety of texts discussed here, and their suggestion of the author's evolution, there are important constants. There is an extraordinary consistency in his appreciation of those works that celebrate the practicality and nobility of human labour, a line that Calvino traces from Xenophon to Defoe and Voltaire before reaching Conrad and Hemingway. On the stylistic side, these essays demonstrate how Calvino consistently appreciated the five literary qualities that he regarded as essential for the next millennium: lightness (Cyrano, Diderot, Borges), rapidity (Ovid, Voltaire), precision (Pliny, Ariosto, Galileo, Cardano, Ortes, Montale), visibility (Stendhal, Balzac, Flaubert), multiplicity or potential literature (Borges, Queneau). Perhaps, then, a further definition of what a classic is could be added to the fourteen definitions put forward in the elegant title essay, 'Why Read the Classics?': 'A classic is a work which (like each of Calvino's texts) retains a consciousness of its own modernity without ceasing to be aware of other classic works of the past.'

Any quotations from non-English original texts about which Calvino is writing are my own translations, either based on the original 'classic' text or on the translation used by Calvino. Given the wide-ranging nature of these essays I have of course been helped by a number of experts to whom I here express my deep gratitude: Catriona Kelly, Howard Miles, Jonny Patrick, Christopher Robinson, Nicoletta Simborowski, Ron Truman.

Christ Church, Oxford   Martin McLaughlin

Notes

1. They appeared in Italo Calvino, *The Literature Machine. Essays*, translated by Patrick Creagh (London: Secker and Warburg, 1987), with the following titles: 'Why Read the Classics?'; 'The Odysseys Within *The Odyssey*'; 'Ovid and Universal Contiguity'; 'Man, the Sky, and the Elephant'; 'The Structure of *Orlando Furioso*'; 'Cyrano on the Moon'; '*Candide*: an Essay on Velocity'; 'The City as Protagonist in Balzac'; 'Stendhal's Knowledge of the "Milky Way"'; 'Guide to *The Charterhouse of Parma* for the Use of New Readers'; 'Montale's Rock'.

Preface

In a letter dated 27 September 1961 Italo Calvino wrote to Niccolò Gallo: 'As for collecting essays as occasional and disparate as my own, one should really wait until the author is either dead or at least in advanced old age.'

Despite this, Calvino did begin to collect his non-fiction in 1980, with the volume *Una pietra sopra* (*Closing the Door*), followed in 1984 by *Collezione di sabbia* (*Collection of Sand*). Subsequently he authorised for his overseas readership a selection which was the English, American and French equivalent of *Una pietra sopra*, but which was not identical to the Italian original: it included the essays on Homer, Pliny, Ariosto, Balzac, Stendhal and Montale, as well as the title essay of the present volume. Later still he modified some of the titles of these essays – and in one case, the article on Ovid, he added another page which he left in manuscript form – with a view to publishing them in a subsequent Italian collection.

In this volume the reader will find most of the essays and articles by Calvino on 'his' classics: the writers, poets and scientific authors who had meant most to him, at different stages of his life. In the case of twentieth-century authors, priority has been given to the essays on those writers and poets whom Calvino held in particular esteem.

Esther Calvino

Why Read the Classics?

Let us begin by putting forward some definitions.

1. *The classics are those books about which you usually hear people saying: 'I'm rereading . . .', never 'I'm reading . . .'*

At least this is the case with those people whom one presumes are 'well read'; it does not apply to the young, since they are at an age when their contact with the world, and with the classics which are part of that world, is important precisely because it is their first such contact.

The iterative prefix 're-' in front of the verb 'read' can represent a small act of hypocrisy on the part of people ashamed to admit they have not read a famous book. To reassure them, all one need do is to point out that however wide-ranging any person's formative reading may be, there will always be an enormous number of fundamental works that one has not read.

Put up your hand anyone who has read the whole of Herodotus and Thucydides. And what about Saint-Simon? and Cardinal Retz? Even the great cycles of nineteenth-century novels are more often mentioned than read. In France they start to read Balzac at school, and judging by the number of editions in circulation people apparently continue to read him long after the end of their schooldays. But if there were an official survey on Balzac's popularity in Italy, I am afraid he would figure very low down the list. Fans of Dickens in Italy are a small elite who whenever they meet start to reminisce about characters and episodes as though talking of people they actually knew. When Michel Butor was teaching in the United States a number of years ago, he became so tired of people asking him about

Émile Zola, whom he had never read, that he made up his mind to read the whole cycle of Rougon-Macquart novels. He discovered that it was entirely different from how he had imagined it: it turned out to be a fabulous, mythological genealogy and cosmogony, which he then described in a brilliant article.

What this shows is that reading a great work for the first time when one is fully adult is an extraordinary pleasure, one which is very different (though it is impossible to say whether more or less pleasurable) from reading it in one's youth. Youth endows every reading, as it does every experience, with a unique flavour and significance, whereas at a mature age one appreciates (or should appreciate) many more details, levels and meanings. We can therefore try out this other formulation of our definition:

2. *The classics are those books which constitute a treasured experience for those who have read and loved them; but they remain just as rich an experience for those who reserve the chance to read them for when they are in the best condition to enjoy them.*

For the fact is that the reading we do when young can often be of little value because we are impatient, cannot concentrate, lack expertise in how to read, or because we lack experience of life. This youthful reading can be (perhaps at the same time) literally formative in that it gives a form or shape to our future experiences, providing them with models, ways of dealing with them, terms of comparison, schemes for categorising them, scales of value, paradigms of beauty: all things which continue to operate in us even when we remember little or nothing about the book we read when young. When we reread the book in our maturity, we then rediscover these constants which by now form part of our inner mechanisms though we have forgotten where they came from. There is a particular potency in the work which can be forgotten in itself but which leaves its seed behind in us. The definition which we can now give is this:

3. *The classics are books which exercise a particular influence, both when they imprint themselves on our imagination as unforgettable, and when they hide in the layers of memory disguised as the individual's or the collective unconscious.*

For this reason there ought to be a time in one's adult life which is dedicated to rediscovering the most important readings of our youth. Even if the books remain the same (though they too change, in the light of an altered historical perspective), we certainly have changed, and this later encounter is therefore completely new.

Consequently, whether one uses the verb 'to read' or the verb 'to reread' is not really so important. We could in fact say:

4. *A classic is a book which with each rereading offers as much of a sense of discovery as the first reading.*

5. *A classic is a book which even when we read it for the first time gives the sense of rereading something we have read before.*

Definition 4 above can be considered a corollary of this one:

6. *A classic is a book which has never exhausted all it has to say to its readers.*

Whereas definition 5 suggests a more elaborate formulation, such as this:

7. *The classics are those books which come to us bearing the aura of previous interpretations, and trailing behind them the traces they have left in the culture or cultures (or just in the languages and customs) through which they have passed.*

This applies both to ancient and modern classics. If I read *The Odyssey*, I read Homer's text but I cannot forget all the things that Ulysses' adventures have come to mean in the course of the centuries, and I cannot help wondering whether these meanings were implicit in the original text or if they are later accretions, deformations or expansions of it. If I read Kafka, I find myself approving or rejecting the legitimacy of the adjective 'Kafkaesque' which we hear constantly being used to refer to just about anything. If I read Turgenev's *Fathers and Sons* or Dostoevsky's *The Devils* I cannot help reflecting on how the characters in these books have continued to be reincarnated right down to our own times.

Reading a classic must also surprise us, when we compare it to the image we previously had of it. That is why we can never recommend enough a first-hand reading of the text itself, avoiding as far as possible secondary bibliography, commentaries, and other interpretations. Schools and universities should hammer home the idea that no book which discusses another book can ever say more than the original book under discussion; yet they actually do everything to make students believe the opposite. There is a reversal of values here which is very widespread, which means that the introduction, critical apparatus, and bibliography are used like a smoke-screen to conceal what the text has to say and what it can only say if it is left to speak without intermediaries who claim to know more than the text itself. We can conclude, therefore, that:

8. *A classic is a work which constantly generates a pulviscular cloud of critical discourse around it, but which always shakes the particles off.*

A classic does not necessarily teach us something that we did not know already; sometimes we discover in a classic something which we had always known (or had always thought we knew) but did not realise that the classic text had said it first (or that the idea was connected with that text in a particular way). And this discovery is also a very gratifying surprise, as is always the case when we learn the source of an idea, or its connection with a text, or who said it first. From all this we could derive a definition like this:

9. *Classics are books which, the more we think we know them through hearsay, the more original, unexpected, and innovative we find them when we actually read them.*

Of course this happens when a classic text 'works' as a classic, that is when it establishes a personal relationship with the reader. If there is no spark, the exercise is pointless: it is no use reading classics out of a sense of duty or respect, we should only read them for love. Except at school: school has to teach you to know, whether you like it or not, a certain number of classics amongst which (or by using them as a benchmark) you will later recognise 'your' own classics. School is obliged to provide you with the tools to enable you to make your own choice; but the only choices which count are those which you take after or outside any schooling.

It is only during unenforced reading that you will come across the book which will become 'your' book. I know an excellent art historian, an enormously well-read man, who out of all the volumes he has read is fondest of all of *The Pickwick Papers*, quoting lines from Dickens' book during any discussion, and relating every event in his life to episodes in Pickwick. Gradually he himself, the universe and its real philosophy have all taken the form of *The Pickwick Papers* in a process of total identification. If we go down this road we arrive at an idea of a classic which is very lofty and demanding:

10. *A classic is the term given to any book which comes to represent the whole universe, a book on a par with ancient talismans.*

A definition such as this brings us close to the idea of the total book, of the kind dreamt of by Mallarmé. But a classic can also establish an equally powerful relationship not of identity but of opposition or antithesis. All of Jean-Jacques Rousseau's thoughts and actions are dear to me, but they all arouse in me an irrepressible urge to contradict, criticise and argue with him. Of course this is connected with the fact that I find his personality so uncongenial to my temperament, but if that were all, I would simply avoid reading him; whereas in fact I cannot help regarding him as one of my authors. What I will say, then, is this:

11. *'Your' classic is a book to which you cannot remain indifferent, and which helps you define yourself in relation or even in opposition to it.*

I do not believe I need justify my use of the term 'classic' which makes no distinction in terms of antiquity, style or authority. (For the history of all these meanings of the term, there is an exhaustive entry on 'Classico' by Franco Fortini in the *Enciclopedia Einaudi*, vol. III.) For the sake of my argument here, what distinguishes a classic is perhaps only a kind of resonance we perceive emanating either from an ancient or a modern work, but one which has its own place in a cultural continuum. We could say:

12. *A classic is a work that comes before other classics; but those who have read other classics first immediately recognise its place in the genealogy of classic works.*

At this point I can no longer postpone the crucial problem of how to relate the reading of classics to the reading of all the other texts which are not classics. This is a problem which is linked to questions like: 'Why read the classics instead of reading works which will give us a deeper understanding of our own times?' and 'Where can we find the time and the ease of mind to read the classics, inundated as we are by the flood of printed material about the present?'

Of course, hypothetically the lucky reader may exist who can dedicate the 'reading time' of his or her days solely to Lucretius, Lucian, Montaigne, Erasmus, Quevedo, Marlowe, the *Discourse on Method*, Goethe's *Wilhelm Meister*, Coleridge, Ruskin, Proust and Valéry, with the occasional sortie into Murasaki or the Icelandic Sagas. And presumably that person can do all this without having to write reviews of the latest reprint, submit articles in the pursuit of a university chair, or send in work for a publisher with an imminent deadline. For this regime to continue without any contamination, the lucky person would have to avoid reading the newspapers, and never be tempted by the latest novel or the most recent sociological survey. But it remains to be seen to what extent such rigour could be justified or even found useful. The contemporary world may be banal and stultifying, but it is always the context in which we have to place ourselves to look either backwards or forwards. In order to read the classics, you have to establish where exactly you are reading them 'from', otherwise both the reader and the text tend to drift in a timeless haze. So what we can say is that the person who derives maximum benefit from a reading of the classics is the one who skilfully alternates classic readings with calibrated doses of contemporary material. And this does not necessarily presuppose someone with a harmonious inner calm: it could also be the result of an impatient, nervy temperament, of someone constantly irritated and dissatisfied.

Perhaps the ideal would be to hear the present as a noise outside our window, warning us of the traffic jams and weather changes outside, while we continue to follow the discourse of the classics which resounds clearly and articulately inside our room. But it is already an achievement for most people to hear the classics as a distant echo, outside the room which is pervaded by the present as if it were a television set on at full volume. We should therefore add:

13. *A classic is a work which relegates the noise of the present to a background hum, which at the same time the classics cannot exist without.*

14. *A classic is a work which persists as background noise even when a present that is totally incompatible with it holds sway.*

The fact remains that reading the classics seems to be at odds with our pace of life, which does not tolerate long stretches of time, or the space for humanist *otium*; and also with the eclecticism of our culture which would never be able to draw up a catalogue of classic works to suit our own times.

Instead these were exactly the conditions of Leopardi's life: living in his father's castle (his 'paterno ostello'), he was able to pursue his cult of Greek and Latin antiquity with his father Monaldo's formidable library, to which he added the entirety of Italian literature up to that time, and all of French literature except for novels and the most recently published works, which were relegated to its margins, for the comfort of his sister ('your Stendhal' is how he talked of the French novelist to Paolina). Giacomo satisfied even his keenest scientific and historical enthusiasms with texts that were never exactly 'up to date', reading about the habits of birds in Buffon, about Frederik Ruysch's mummies in Fontenelle, and Columbus' travels in Robertson.

Today a classical education like that enjoyed by the young Leopardi is unthinkable, particularly as the library of his father Count Monaldo has disintegrated. Disintegrated both in the sense that the old titles have been decimated, and in that the new ones have proliferated in all modern literatures and cultures. All that can be done is for each one of us to invent our own ideal library of our classics; and I would say that one half of it should consist of books we have read and that have meant something for us, and the other half of books which we intend to read and which we suppose might mean something to us. We should also leave a section of empty spaces for surprises and chance discoveries.

I notice that Leopardi is the only name from Italian literature that I have cited. This is the effect of the disintegration of the library. Now I ought to rewrite the whole article making it quite clear that the classics help us understand who we are and the point we have reached, and that consequently Italian classics are indispensable to us Italians in order to compare them with foreign classics, and foreign classics are equally indispensable so that we can measure them against Italian classics.

After that I should really rewrite it a third time, so that people do not believe that the classics must be read because they serve some purpose. The only reason that can be adduced in their favour is that reading the classics is always better than not reading them.

And if anyone objects that they are not worth all that effort, I will cite Cioran (not a classic, at least not yet, but a contemporary thinker who is only now being translated into Italian): 'While the hemlock was being prepared, Socrates was learning a melody on the flute. "What use will that be to you?", he was asked. "At least I will learn this melody before I die." '

[1981]

The Odysseys Within *The Odyssey*

How many Odysseys does *The Odyssey* contain? The Telemachia at the beginning of the poem is really the search for a story that does not exist, the story that will become *The Odyssey*. The bard Phemius in Ithaca's palace already knows the *nostoi* (poems of return from Troy) of the other heroes. There is only one he does not know: the *nostos* of his own king; that is why Penelope does not want to hear him sing any more. And Telemachus sets off in search of this story and heads for the Greek veterans of the Trojan war: if he can get hold of the story, whether it has a happy or sad ending, Ithaca will at last emerge from the disordered, timeless, lawless situation in which it has languished for so many years.

Like all veterans, Nestor and Menelaus have lots to tell; but not the tale that Telemachus is looking for. At least until Menelaus comes out with his tale of fantastic adventure: after disguising himself as a seal, he captured 'the old man of the sea', Proteus of the thousand metamorphoses, and forced him to tell him both the past and the future. Proteus certainly already knew *The Odyssey* inside out: he starts narrating the adventures of Ulysses from the very point at which Homer starts, with the hero on Calypso's island; then he stops. At that point Homer can take over and provide the rest of the tale.

When he arrives at the court of the Phaeacians, Ulysses listens to a blind bard just like Homer who is singing the adventures of Ulysses; the hero bursts into tears; then he decides to start narrating himself. In his own account, he journeys as far as Hades to interrogate Tiresias, and Tiresias tells him the rest of his story. Then Ulysses meets the singing Sirens: what are they singing? Once more *The Odyssey*, possibly identical to the poem we are reading, possibly very different. This 'story of Ulysses' return' already exists even before the return has been completed: it predates the actual events it narrates. Already in the Telemachia section we encounter the expressions 'to think of the return', 'to speak of the return'. Zeus did not 'think of the return' of the Atrides, Agamemnon and Menelaus (3. 160); Menelaus asks Proteus' daughter to 'tell [him] the story of the return' (4. 379) and she explains how to force her father to tell him (390), so that Menelaus can capture Proteus and ask him: 'Tell me how I can return over the sea teeming with fish?' (470).

The return must be sought out and thought of and remembered: the danger is that it can be forgotten before it even happens. In fact one of the first stops in the voyage recounted by Ulysses, amongst the Lotus-eaters, carries the risk of memory loss after eating the sweet fruit of the lotus. That the danger of forgetting should occur at the beginning of Ulysses' journey rather than at the end might seem odd. But if after coming through so many trials, and having borne so many afflictions Ulysses had then forgotten everything, his loss would have been even greater: he would not have derived any experience from his sufferings, or any lesson from what he lived through.

But on closer examination, this risk of forgetfulness is one which is threatened several times in books 9–12: first in the invitation of the Lotus-eaters, then in Circe's drugs, then again in the Sirens' song. On each occasion Ulysses must take care, if he does not want to forget in an instant . . . Forget what? The Trojan War? The siege? The Trojan horse? No: his home, his return voyage, the whole point of his journey. The expression used by Homer on these occasions is 'to forget the return'.

Ulysses must not forget the road he has to travel, the shape of his destiny: in short, he must not forget *The Odyssey*. But even the bard who composes an improvised poem, or the rhapsode who recites from memory sections of poems that have already been sung by others, must not forget if they want to 'tell of the return'; for someone who sings poems without the support of a written text, 'to forget' is the most negative verb in existence; and for them 'to forget the return' means forgetting the epic poems called *nostoi*, the highlight of their repertoire.

On this theme of 'forgetting the future', I wrote a few thoughts some years ago (in the *Corriere della sera*, 10 August 1975) which ended: 'What Ulysses saves from the power of the lotus, from Circe's drugs, and from the Sirens' song, is not just the past or the future. Memory truly counts – for an individual, a society, a culture – only if it holds together the imprint of the past and the plan for the future, if it allows one to do things without forgetting what one wanted to do, and to become without ceasing to be, to be without ceasing to become.'

That article of mine elicited a response by Edoardo Sanguineti in *Paese sera* (now in his *Giornalino 1973–1975*, Turin: Einaudi, 1976), followed by a succession of further responses from each of us. Sanguineti objected in these terms:

> *We must not forget that Ulysses' journey is not a voyage out but a return journey. So we need to ask ourselves for a moment, just what kind of future is he facing? In fact the future that Ulysses is looking to is also in reality his past. Ulysses overcomes the seduction of a Regression because he is heading full tilt towards a Restoration.*
>
> *Of course one day, out of spite, the real Ulysses, great Ulysses, became the Ulysses of his Last Journey, for whom the future is not at all a kind of past, but rather the Realisation of a Prophecy – or even the realisation of a Utopia. Whereas Homer's Ulysses reaches a destination which is the recovery of his past as a present: his wisdom is Repetition, and this can be recognised by the Scar which he bears and which marks him forever.*

In reply to Sanguineti I pointed out (in the *Corriere della sera*, 14 October 1975) that 'in the language of myth, as in that of folktales and popular romances, every enterprise which restores justice, rights wrongs, and rescues people from poverty, is usually represented as the restoration of an ideal order belonging to the past; the desirability of a future that we must conquer is thus guaranteed by the memory of a past we have lost'.

If we examine folktales, we shall see that they present two types of social transformation, both with a happy ending: either from riches to rags then back to riches again; or simply from rags to riches. In the first type it is the prince who because of some misfortune is reduced to being a swineherd or some other lowly person, only to recover his royal status in the end; in the second type there is usually a youth who is born with nothing, a shepherd or peasant, someone who maybe even lacks courage as well, but who either through his own resources or helped by magic beings manages to marry the princess and become king.

The same schemes apply to fables with female protagonists: in the first kind the girl falls from a royal or at least privileged condition to being poor through a stepmother's or stepsisters' jealousy (like Snow White and Cinderella respectively), until a prince falls in love with her and returns her to the top of the social ladder; in the second type there is a real shepherdess or country girl who overcomes all the disadvantages of her humble origins and ends up marrying royalty.

You might think that it is the second type of folktale that articulates most directly the popular desire for a reversal of roles and of individual destinies in society, while those of the first kind filter them into a more attenuated form, as the restoration of a hypothetical preceding order. But on closer reflection, the extraordinary fortunes of the shepherd or shepherdess reflect merely a consolatory miracle or dream, which will be broadly taken up by popular romances. Whereas the misfortunes of the prince or the queen connect the idea of poverty with the idea of *rights that have been trampled on*, of an injustice that must be avenged. In other words this second kind of tale establishes (on the level of fantasy, where abstract ideas can take the form of archetypal figures) something that will become a fundamental point for the whole social conscience of the modern age, from the French Revolution onwards.

In the collective unconscious the prince in pauper's clothing is the proof that every pauper is in reality a prince whose throne has been usurped and who has to reconquer his kingdom. Ulysses or Guerin Meschino or Robin Hood are kings or sons of kings or noble knights overtaken by misfortune who, when they eventually triumph over their enemies, will restore a just society in which their true identity will be recognised.

But is this still the same identity as before? The Ulysses who returns to Ithaca as an old beggar whom nobody recognises is maybe not the same person as the Ulysses who set out for Troy. It was no accident that he had saved his own life by changing his name to Nobody. The only one who instantly recognises him unprompted is his dog Argos, as if to suggest that the continuity of the individual is only evident in signs recognisable by an animal's eye.

For his old nurse the proof of Ulysses' identity is the scar made by a boar's tusk, for his wife it is the secret of the marriage bed made from the root of an olive tree, for his father it is a list of fruit trees: all signs that have nothing to do with the kingly, but rather link him with a hunter, a carpenter, a gardener. On top of these signs there is his physical prowess and his ruthless attack on his enemies; and above all the evidence of the favour of the gods, which is what convinces even Telemachus, though only by an act of faith.

Conversely the unrecognisable Ulysses, on awakening in Ithaca, does not recognise his homeland. Athena herself has to intervene to reassure him that Ithaca really is Ithaca. There is a general identity crisis in the second half of *The Odyssey*. Only the tale guarantees that the characters and the places are the same characters and places as before. But even the tale changes. The story that Ulysses tells first to the shepherd Eumaeus, then to his rival Antinous and Penelope herself, is another, completely different Odyssey: it is a tale of wanderings which have brought the fictitious character which he pretends to be from Crete all the way to Ithaca, a tale of shipwrecks and pirates which is much more credible than the one Ulysses himself had told the King of the Phaeacians. Who is to say that this tale is not the real Odyssey? But this new Odyssey leads on to another Odyssey still: on his travels the Cretan wanderer had met Ulysses. What we have here then is Ulysses telling a tale about Ulysses wandering through countries where the real *Odyssey*, the one we regard as genuine, never says he wandered.

That Ulysses is a great mystifier is something that is well known long before *The Odyssey*. Was he not the person who came up with the famous trick of the Trojan horse? And at the beginning of *The Odyssey*, the first mentions of him occur in two flashbacks about the Trojan war narrated one after another by Helen and Menelaus: and they are two tales of deception. In the first he steals into the besieged city in disguise and carries out a slaughter; in the second he is inside the horse with his comrades and manages to prevent Helen from forcing them to speak and thus to reveal their presence.

(In both episodes Ulysses encounters Helen, first as an ally who is an accomplice in his disguise, but in the second she is an enemy, who impersonates the voices of the Achaeans' wives in a bid to get them to betray their presence. Helen's role is thus contradictory, but it always involves deception. By the same token Penelope too is presented as a deceiver, in her stratagem with the tapestry; Penelope's tapestry is a stratagem which is symmetrical to the Trojan horse, and which like the latter is a product of manual skill and counterfeit: thus the two qualities which distinguish Ulysses are also characteristic of his wife.)

If Ulysses is a deceiver, the whole tale he tells the King of the Phaeacians could be a tissue of lies. In fact these maritime adventures of his, packed into four central books of *The Odyssey*, and containing a rapid series of encounters with fantastic beings (which appear in the folktales of all countries and epochs: the ogre Polyphemus, the four winds trapped in the wineskin, Circe's spells, the Sirens and sea-monsters) contrast with the rest of the poem, which is dominated by more serious tones, psychological tension, and the exciting climax that leads towards the conclusion: Ulysses' recovery of his kingdom and his wife from the clutches of the Suitors. Even in these other parts we find motifs common to folktales, such as Penelope's tapestry and the contest to shoot the bow, but we are closer to modern criteria of realism and verisimilitude: supernatural interventions here are limited to the appearance of the Olympian deities, and even they are usually concealed in human guise.

However, we must remember that these same adventures (notably the one with the Cyclops Polyphemus) are evoked in other parts of the poem. So Homer himself confirms their authenticity; not only that, but even the gods discuss them on Mount Olympus. Nor should we forget that Menelaus too, in the Telemachia, recounts a story (the encounter with the old man of the sea) of the same folktale-type as those narrated by Ulysses. All we can do is to attribute this diversity of fantasy styles to that fusion of traditions of different origin which were handed down by the ancient bards and came together in Homer's poem. The most archaic level of narrative would thus be in Ulysses' first-person account of his adventures.

Most archaic? According to Alfred Heubeck the opposite might have been the case. (See Omero, *Odissea*, Libri I–IV, introduction by Alfred Heubeck, text and commentary by Stephanie West (Milan: Fondazione Lorenzo Valla/Mondadori, 1981).)

Ulysses had always been an epic hero, even before *The Odyssey* (and also before *The Iliad*), and epic heroes, such as Achilles and Hector in *The Iliad*, do not have folktale adventures of that type with monsters and magic spells. But the author of *The Odyssey* has to have Ulysses absent from home for ten years: as far as his family and former comrades in arms are concerned he has vanished and can no longer be found. To do this he has to make him disappear from the known world, to cross over into another geographical space, into a world beyond the human one, into the Beyond (not for nothing do his travels culminate in a visit to the Underworld). For this voyage beyond the bounds of the epic the author of *The Odyssey* turns to traditions (which certainly are more archaic) such as the deeds of Jason and the Argonauts.

So the novelty of *The Odyssey* resides in having an epic hero like Ulysses pitted against 'witches and giants, monsters and eaters of men', that is in situations that belong to a more archaic kind of saga, whose roots are to be found 'in the world of ancient fable, and even in the world of primitive magic and Shamans'.

It is in this that the author of *The Odyssey* shows us, according to Heubeck, his true modernity, which makes him seem close to us, even our contemporary: if traditionally the epic hero had been a paradigm of aristocratic, military virtues, Ulysses is all these things but in addition he is the man who withstands the harshest of experiences, labours, pain, solitude. 'Certainly he too carries his audience into a mythical world of dreams, but this dream world becomes at the same time the mirror image of the real world in which we all live and which is pervaded by need and anguish, terror and pain, and in which man is immersed without escape.'

In this same volume Stephanie West, though she starts from entirely different premisses from Heubeck, ventures a hypothesis that would appear to confirm his argument: the hypothesis that there was an alternative *Odyssey*, another journey of return, preceding Homer's. Homer (or whoever the author of *The Odyssey* was), she argues, finding this tale of voyages too thin and pointless, replaced it with the fabulous adventures, but preserved traces of the earlier version in the account of the disguised Cretan. And in fact in the opening lines there is one verse which ought to epitomise the whole of the poem: 'He saw the cities and came to know the thoughts of many men.' What cities? What thoughts? This line seems to apply more to the voyages of the false Cretan . . .

However, as soon as Penelope has identified her husband in the bedroom which he has now repossessed, Ulysses starts talking again of the Cyclops, the Sirens . . . Perhaps *The Odyssey* is the myth of all voyages? Perhaps for Ulysses-Homer the distinction between truth and falsehood did not exist; he simply recounted the same experience now in the language of reality, now in the language of myth, just as for us even today each journey we undertake, big or small, is still an *Odyssey*.

[1983]

Xenophon's *Anabasis*

Reading Xenophon's *Anabasis* today is the nearest thing to watching an old war documentary which is repeated every so often on television or on video. The same fascination that we experience when watching the black and white of a faded film, with its rather crude contrasts of light and shade and speeded-up movements, emerges almost spontaneously from passages such as this:

> *They completed another fifteen parasangs in three days, every day through deep snow. The third day was particularly terrible, because of the North wind blowing against them as they marched: it raged all over the area, destroying everything and freezing their bodies . . . During the march, in order to defend their eyes from the glare of the snow, the soldiers put something black in front of them: against the danger of frostbite the most useful remedy was to keep moving the feet, never staying still and especially removing one's boots at night . . . A group of soldiers, who had been left behind because of these difficulties, saw not far off, in a valley in the middle of the snow-covered plain, a dark pool: melted snow, they thought. In fact the snow had melted there, but because of a spring of natural water, which rose nearby, sending vapours up to the sky.*

But it is difficult to quote from Xenophon: what really counts is the never-ending succession of visual details and action. It is difficult to locate a passage which epitomises entirely the pleasing variety of the text. Maybe this one, from two pages before:

Some Greeks, who had moved away from the camp, reported having seen in the distance what looked like a massive army, and many fires lit in the night. When they heard this, the commanders thought it unsafe to remain bivouacked in separate quarters, and once more made the soldiers regroup. The soldiers then all camped together again, especially as the weather seemed to be improving. But unfortunately, during the night so much snow fell that it covered the men's armour, the animals, and the men themselves huddled on the ground: the animals' limbs were so stiff with the cold that they could not stand up; the men delayed before standing up because the unmelted snow lying on their bodies was a source of heat. Then Xenophon bravely got up, stripped and started to chop wood with an axe; seeing his example, one of the men got up, took the axe from his hand and continued with the chopping; others got up and lit a fire; and all of them greased their bodies, not with oil, but with unguents found in the local village, an oil made from sesame-seeds, bitter almonds and turpentine, and lard. There was also a perfumed oil made of the same substances.

The rapid shift from one visual representation to another, and from those to an anecdote, and from there again on to a description of exotic customs: this is the texture of the backdrop to a continuous explosion of exciting adventures, of unforeseen obstacles blocking the way of the itinerant army. Every obstacle is overcome, usually, by some piece of cunning on Xenophon's part: every fortified city that has to be captured, every enemy that takes the field to oppose the Greeks in open battle, every fjord to be crossed, every bit of bad weather – all of these require a piece of brilliance, a flash of genius, some cleverly thought-out stratagem on the part of this narrator-protagonist-mercenary leader. On occasions Xenophon appears to be one of those heroes from children's comics, who in every episode manage to survive against impossible odds; in fact, just as in those children's comics, there are often two protagonists in each episode: the two rival officers, Xenophon and Cheirisophus, the Athenian and the Spartan, and Xenophon's solution is always the more astute, generous and decisive one.

On its own the subject matter of *The Anabasis* would have been ideally suited to a picaresque or mock-heroic tale: ten thousand Greek mercenaries are hired under false pretences by a Persian prince, Cyrus the Younger, for an expedition into the hinterland of Asia Minor, whose real aim was to oust Cyrus' brother, Artaxerxes II; but they are defeated at the battle of Cunaxa, and now leaderless and far from their native land, they have to find a way back home amidst very hostile peoples. All they want is to go back home, but everything they do constitutes a public menace: there are ten thousand of them, armed, but without food, so wherever they go they ravage and destroy the land like a swarm of locusts, and carry in their wake a huge following of women.

But Xenophon was not the type of writer either to be tempted by the heroic style of the epic or to have a taste for the grim and grotesque aspects of a situation such as that. His is a precise record written by an army officer, a kind of log-book containing all the distances covered, geographical reference points and details of the vegetable and animal resources, as well as a review of the various diplomatic, strategic and logistical problems and their respective solutions.

The account is interspersed with 'official statements' from high command, and speeches by Xenophon either to the troops or to foreign ambassadors. My classroom memory of these rhetorical excerpts was one of great boredom but I think I was wrong. The secret in reading *The Anabasis* is not to skip anything, to follow everything point by point. In each of those speeches there is a political problem, regarding either foreign policy (the attempts to establish diplomatic relations with the princes and leaders of the territories through which the Greeks have to pass) or internal politics (the discussions between the Greek leaders, with the predictable rivalry between Athenians and Spartans etc.). And since the work was written as a polemic against other generals, about the responsibilities of each person in managing that retreat, then this background of overt or merely covert polemic can only be elicited from those rhetorical pages.

As an action writer Xenophon is a model. If we compare him with the contemporary writer who is his nearest equivalent – Col. T. E. Lawrence – we see how the skill of the English writer consists in surrounding events and images with an aura of aesthetic and even ethical wonder that lies like a palimpsest beneath the factual surface of the prose; whereas in the Greek there is nothing beneath the exactness and dryness of the narration: the austere military virtues mean nothing other than austere military virtues.

Of course there is a kind of pathos in *The Anabasis*: it is the anxiety of the soldiers to return home, the bewilderment of being in a foreign land, the effort not to get separated, because as long as they are still together they carry their own country within them. This struggle of an army to return home after being led to defeat in a war that was not of their making and then left to their own devices, a struggle which is now only to carve out a way home away from their former allies and former enemies, all of this makes *The Anabasis* similar to one strand in recent Italian literature: the memoirs written by Italian Alpini troops on their retreat from Russia. This analogy is no recent discovery: as far back as 1953 Elio Vittorini, launching what was to be a classic of this type of literature, *Il sergente nella neve* (*The Sergeant in the Snow*) by Mario Rigoni Stern, defined it as 'a little *Anabasis* in dialect'. And in fact, the chapters about the retreat through the snow from Xenophon's *Anabasis* (the source of the passages quoted above) are full of episodes which could have been taken entirely from Rigoni Stern's book.

One characteristic of Rigoni Stern and of the best Italian writing on the retreat from the Russian front is that the narrator-protagonist is a fine soldier, just as Xenophon was, and he discusses military action with competence and commitment. For them, as for Xenophon, in the general collapse of the more pompous ambitions, military virtues go back to being virtues of practicality and solidarity against which can be measured the ability of each man to be useful not only to himself but also to the others. (It is worth recalling here Nuto Revelli's *La guerra dei poveri* (*The War Declared by the Poor*) for the passion and frenzy of the disillusioned officer; as well as another fine book, unjustly forgotten, *I lunghi fucili* (*The Long Rifles*) by Cristoforo M. Negri.)

But the analogies stop there. The memoirs of the Alpini stem from the clash between an Italy that was now humble and had come to its senses, and the madness and massacres of all-out war. In the memoirs of a general from the fifth century BC, the contrast is between the role of locust-like parasites to which the Greek army of mercenaries had been reduced and the exercise of the classical virtues – philosophical, civic, military virtues – which Xenophon and his men try to adapt to these new circumstances. And in the event this contrast has none of the heart-rending tragedy of Rigoni Stern's book: Xenophon seems to be sure of having succeeded in reconciling the two extremes. Man can be reduced to a locust but can apply to this condition of locust a code of discipline and decorum – in a word, 'style' – and consider himself satisfied; man is capable of not even discussing for a minute the fact that he is a locust but only the best way of being one. In Xenophon we find already delineated, with all its limitations, the modern ethic of perfect technical efficiency, of 'being up to the job', of 'doing your job well' quite independently of what value is put on one's actions in terms of universal morals. I continue to call this ethic modern because it was modern when I was young, and it was the lesson we derived from so many American films, as well as from Hemingway's novels, and I was caught between adherence to this totally 'technical', 'pragmatic' ethic, and awareness of the void that lay beneath it. But even today, when it seems so different from the spirit of our times, I find that it did have its positive aspects.

Xenophon has the great merit, in moral terms, of never mystifying or idealising his or his men's position. If he often displays an aloofness or aversion towards 'barbarian' customs, it must also be said that 'colonialist' hypocrisy is completely foreign to him. He is aware of being at the head of a horde of parasites in a foreign land, and that the 'barbarian' peoples whose lands they have invaded are in the right not his men. In his exhortations to his soldiers he never fails to remind them of their enemies' rights: 'You have to bear in mind something else. Our enemies will have time to rob us, and will have good reason for ambushing us since we are occupying their property . . .' In this attempt to give a certain 'style' or rule to this parasitical movement of greedy and violent men amidst the mountains and plains of Anatolia resides all his dignity: not tragic dignity, but rather a limited dignity, fundamentally a bourgeois dignity. We know that one can easily succeed in endowing the basest actions with style and dignity, even when they are not dictated as these were by a state of necessity. The Greek army, creeping through the mountain heights and fjords amidst constant ambushes and attacks, no longer able to distinguish just to what extent it is a victim or an oppressor, and surrounded even in the most chilling massacres of its men by the supreme hostility of indifference or fortune, inspires in the reader an almost symbolic anguish which perhaps only we today can understand.

[1978]

Ovid and Universal Contiguity

In the high heavens there is a roadway, which can be seen when the sky is clear. It is called the Milky Way, and it is famous for its whiteness. Here the gods pass by on their way to the palace of the great Thunderer. On the right and left sides of the road, with their doors open, stand the entrance halls of the nobler gods, always filled with crowds. The more plebeian deities live scattered about elsewhere. The more powerful and famous gods have settled their own household gods here, giving directly onto the road (. . . a fronte potentes / caelicolae clarique suos posuere penates). If the comparison did not seem irreverent, I would say that this place is the Palatine area of the mighty heavens.

This is Ovid at the beginning of the *Metamorphoses*, introducing us to the world of the celestial gods. He begins by bringing us so close to that world as to make it identical to the Rome of his day in terms of its urban topography, its class divisions, its local customs (the *clientes* calling in every day), and even in terms of religion: the gods themselves have their own Penates in the houses they inhabit, which means that the lords of the heavens and the earth in turn pay homage to their own little domestic gods.

Providing such a close-up does not necessarily mean diminishing or ironising: this is a universe in which space is densely packed with forms which constantly swap size and nature, while the flow of time is continually filled by a proliferation of tales and cycles of tales. Earthly forms and stories repeat heavenly ones, but both intertwine around each other in a double spiral. This contiguity between gods and humans – who are related to the gods and are the objects of their compulsive desires – is one of the dominant themes of the *Metamorphoses*, but this is simply a specific instance of the contiguity that exists between all the figures and forms of the existing world, whether anthropomorphic or otherwise. The fauna and flora, the mineral world and the firmament encompass within their common substance that collection of corporeal, psychological and moral qualities which we usually consider human.

The poetry of the *Metamorphoses* is rooted particularly in these blurred confines between different worlds, and as early as Book 2 offers an extraordinary example of this in the myth of Phaethon who dares to take over the reins of the Sun's chariot. In this episode the heavens appear both as unconfined space, abstract geometry, and at the same time as the scene of a human adventure recounted with such detailed precision that we never lose the thread even for a moment, as it carries our emotional involvement to fever pitch.

It is not just Ovid's precision in the most concrete particulars, such as the movement of the chariot which swerves and bounces because of its unusually light load, or the emotions of the young, unskilled charioteer, but also his exactness in the visualisation of unearthly forms such as the map of the heavens. It should be said straight away that this exactness is only an illusion: the contradictory details communicate their powerful spell both if taken one by one and as a general narrative effect, but they can never combine to form a totally consistent vision. The sky is a sphere criss-crossed by ascending and descending roads which are recognisable by their rutted wheeltracks, but at the same time this sphere is whirling vertiginously in the opposite direction to the Sun's chariot; it is suspended at a dizzying height above the lands and seas which can be seen down in the distance; at one point it appears as an overarching vault at whose highest point the stars are fixed; at another it is like a bridge supporting the chariot over the void causing Phaethon to be equally terrified of both continuing his journey and turning back ('Quid faciat? Multum caeli post terga relictum / ante oculos plus est. Animo metitur utrumque.' (What should he do? A huge tract of sky was already behind him, but in front of him lay even more. Mentally he measured up both.)); it is empty and deserted (it is not the city-like sky of Book 1, hence Apollo asks: 'Maybe you thought that here there were sacred woods and cities of gods and temples dripping with rich gifts?'), populated only by fierce beasts which are but *simulacra*, the shapes of the constellations, but no less menacing for that; in it an oblique track is just about visible, half-way up the ascent, which avoids both the southern and northern pole, but if you lose the track and stray amongst the steep precipices you end up going underneath the Moon, singeing the clouds and setting fire to the Earth.

After this ride through the heavens suspended over the void, which is the most evocative part of the tale, comes the awesome description of the Earth burning, the sea boiling with the bodies of seals floating belly-upwards on its surface – one of the classic pages of Ovid the poet of catastrophe – which acts as a sequel to the flood in Book 1. All the waters gather around *Alma Tellus*, Mother Earth. The dried-up springs try to return to hide in the dark womb of the mother ('fontes / qui se condiderant in opacae viscera matris . . .'). And the Earth, with her hair singed and her eyes shot through with cinders, pleads with Jupiter in a frail voice which sticks in her parched throat, warning him that if the poles catch fire, then the palaces of the gods will soon come crashing down. (But are these the Earth's poles or those of the heavens? There is also talk of the axis of the Earth which Atlas can no longer support because it is red hot. But the poles in Ovid's time were an astronomical notion, and in any case the next line is quite specific: 'regia caeli' (the palace of the heavens). So the palace of the gods was really up in the heavens? Why then did Apollo deny this, and why did Phaethon not encounter it on his journey? In any case these contradictions are not exclusive to Ovid; in Virgil too, as well as in the other canonical poets of antiquity, it is difficult for us to gain a proper idea of how the ancients really 'saw' the world.)

The episode culminates with the shattering of the Sun's chariot when it is struck by Jove's thunderbolt in an explosion of scattered fragments: 'Illic frena iacent, illic temone revulsus / axis, in hac radii fractarum parte rotarum . . .' (There lie the reins, there the axle ripped away from its pole, and further away lie the spokes of the shattered wheels). (This is not the only traffic accident in the *Metamorphoses*: another driver who goes off the road at full speed is Hippolytus in the last book of the poem, where the wealth of detail in recounting the accident is more anatomical than mechanical, providing gory particulars of his innards splitting open and his limbs scattering far and wide.)

The interpenetration between gods, humans and nature implies not a hierarchical order but an intricate system of interrelations in which every level may influence the other two, though to varying extents. In Ovid, myth is the field of tension where these forces clash and balance each other out. Everything depends on the tone in which the myth is narrated:

sometimes the gods themselves recount the myth in which they have played a key part, as moral examples to warn mortals; at other times humans use these same myths as an argument or challenge against the gods, as do the Pierides or Arachne. Or again there are myths which the gods love to hear recounted and others they would prefer were never mentioned. The daughters of Pierius know a version of the attack of the Titans on Olympus, a version from the Giants' side, full of the fear of the gods who are put to flight (Book 5). They recount it after challenging the Muses in the art of narration, and the Muses respond with another series of myths which re-establish the authority of the Olympians; they then punish the Pierides by turning them into magpies. The challenge to the gods implies an irreverent or blasphemous intention in the tale: Arachne the weaver challenges Minerva in the art of the loom and depicts in a tapestry the sins of the lustful gods (Book 6).

The technical precision with which Ovid describes the working of the looms in this contest might suggest a possible identification of the poet's work with the weaving of a tapestry of multicoloured threads. But with which tapestry does his text identify? Pallas-Minerva's, where four divine punishments exacted on mortals who have challenged the gods are portrayed in minute scenes in the four corners of the tapestry, framed by olive leaves, while the central scene depicts the great Olympian figures with their traditional attributes? Or with Arachne's, in which the insidious seductions of Jupiter, Neptune and Apollo, which Ovid had already recounted in some detail, reappear like sarcastic emblems amidst garlands of flowers and wreaths of ivy (each with the addition of some precious details: Europa, for instance, while being transported across the sea on the back of the bull, carefully lifts her feet so as not to get them wet: '. . . tactumque vereri / adsilientis aquae timidasque reducere plantas' (afraid of her feet being splashed by the surging waves and drawing up her fearful heels))?

The answer is with neither of them. In the great array of myths which constitute the whole poem, the myth of Pallas and Arachne seems to contain in turn two scaled-down selections in the tapestries, pointing in ideologically opposed directions: one to instil a sacred fear, the other inciting towards irreverence and moral relativity. But it would be a mistake for anyone to infer from this that the whole poem has to be read either in the first way – because Arachne's challenge is cruelly punished – or in the second – on the grounds that the poetry sides with the guilty victim. The *Metamorphoses* aim to portray the entirety of narratable tales that have been handed down by literature with all the force of imagery and meaning that tradition can convey, without privileging – as is only correct, according to the ambiguity typical of myth – any particular reading. Only by accepting into his poem all the tales and the intentions behind them which flow in every direction, pushing and shoving to squeeze them into the ordered ranks of the epic's hexameters, only in this way will the poet be sure of not serving a partial design but the living multiplicity that does not exclude any known or unknown god.

There is a case of a new, foreign god, not easily recognisable as such, a scandalous god at odds with all models of beauty and virtue, who is fully recorded in the *Metamorphoses*: Bacchus-Dionysus. It is his orgiastic cult which the devotees of Minerva (the daughters of Minyas) refuse to attend as they continue to weave and card wool on the days of the Bacchic festival, alleviating their long labours with story-telling. Here then is another use of stories, which is justified in secular terms as pure enjoyment ('quod tempora longa videri / non sinat' (to prevent time from seeming to drag)) and as an aid to productivity ('utile opus manuum vario sermone levemus' (we will lighten the useful labour of our hands with a variety of stories)), but which is still appropriately associated with Minerva, the 'melior dea' (superior goddess) for those hard-working girls who are revolted by the orgies and excesses of the cult of Dionysus which had swept into Greece after conquering the Orient.

It is clear that the art of narrating, so beloved by weavers, has a link with the cult of Pallas Athene. We saw it with Arachne, who was turned into a spider for having spurned the goddess; but we also see it in the opposite case, of an excessive cult of Pallas, which leads to a neglect of the other gods. So even the daughters of Minyas (Book 4), guilty inasmuch as they are overweening in their sense of virtue, and too exclusive in their devotion to 'intempestiva Minerva' (untimely Minerva), will also undergo a horrendous punishment, being turned into bats by the god who only recognises inebriation, not work, and who listens not to tales but to the obscure chant which overwhelms the mind. So as not to be turned into a bat as well, Ovid is careful to leave every door of his poem open to the gods of the past, present and future, indigenous and foreign gods, and gods of the Orient which in a world beyond Greece rubs shoulders with the world of fables, as well as to Augustus' restoration of Roman religion which is intimately bound up with the political and intellectual life of his own times. But the poet will not manage to convince the god of executive power closest to him, Augustus, who will turn a poet who wanted to make everything omnipresent and near to hand, into an exile for ever, an inhabitant of a remote world.

From the Orient ('in some ancestor of *The Arabian Nights*' says Wilkinson) comes the romantic tale of Pyramus and Thisbe (which one of the daughters of Minyas chooses from a list of others from the same mysterious source), with the hole providing access for whispered words but not kisses, with the night bathed in moonlight beneath the white mulberry tree, a tale which will transmit its echoes to a midsummer night in Elizabethan England.

From the Orient via an Alexandrian romance Ovid derives the technique for expanding the space inside the work, through tales contained within other tales, which here heightens the impression of a packed, teeming, tangled space. Such is the forest in which a boar hunt brings together the destinies of several illustrious heroes (Book 8), not far from the whirlpool of Achelous, which blocks the path home of those returning from the hunt. They are then offered hospitality in the river-god's dwelling, which thus is both their obstacle and refuge, a pause in the action, an opportunity for stories and reflection. Since one of the hunters there is Theseus, curious as always to find out the origin of everything he sees, as well as Pirithous the insolent unbeliever ('deorum / spretor erat mentisque ferox' (he was a spurner of the gods, and fiercely proud in spirit)), the river-god feels encouraged to tell tales of marvellous metamorphoses, and is then imitated by his guests. In this way new layers of stories continually join together in the *Metamorphoses*, like shells which eventually might produce a pearl: the pearl in this case being the humble idyll of Baucis and Philemon which contains a whole world of minute detail and a completely different rhythm.

It has to be said that Ovid only rarely avails himself of these structural complexities: the passion which dominates his compositional skills is not systematic organisation but accumulation, and this has to be combined with variations in point of view, and changes in rhythm. This is why when Mercury starts to recount the metamorphosis of the nymph Syrinx into a clump of reeds, to put Argus to sleep whose hundred eyelids never all close together, his narration is partly given in direct speech, and partly shortened into a single sentence, because the rest of the story is left in suspension; the god falls silent as soon as he sees that all the eyes of Argus have succumbed to sleep.

The *Metamorphoses* is the poem of rapidity: each episode has to follow another in a relentless rhythm, to strike our imagination, each image must overlay another one, and thus acquire density before disappearing. It is the same principle as cinematography: each line like each photogram must be full of visual stimuli in continuous movement. *Horror vacui* dominates both the poem's time and space. In page after page the verbs are all in the present; everything happening before our eyes; new events quickly follow on; all distance is abolished. And when Ovid feels the need to change rhythm, the first thing he does is not to change the tense but the person of the verb: he moves from third to second person, in other words he introduces the person of whom he is about to talk, by addressing him directly in the second person singular: 'Te quoque mutatum torvo, Neptune, iuvenco' (You too, Neptune, now changed into a fierce-looking ox). Not only is the present there in the verb tense, but the character's actual presence is evoked in this way. Even when the verbs are in the past, the vocative effects a sudden sense of immediacy. This procedure is often adopted when several subjects carry out parallel actions, to avoid the monotony of lists. If he has spoken of Tityus in the third person, Tantalus and Sisyphus are addressed directly with the vocative 'tu'. Even plants can be addressed in the second person ('Vos quoque, flexipedes hederae, venistis . . .' (You too came, tendril-trailing ivy), and no wonder, especially when these are plants which move like people and come running to the sound of Orpheus, now widowed, playing the lyre, clustering round him in a teeming array of Mediterranean flora (Book 10). There are also times – and the episode just mentioned is one of them – when the pace of narrative has to slow down, switch to a calmer rhythm, give the feeling of time being suspended, almost veiled in the distance. What does Ovid do at such times? To make it clear that the narrative is in no hurry, he stops to dwell on the smallest details. For instance: Baucis and Philemon welcome into their humble cottage the unknown visitors, the two gods. '. . . Mensae sed erat pes tertius impar: / testa parem fecit; quae postquam subdita clivum / sustulit, aequatam mentae tersere virentes . . .' (But one of the three legs of the table was too short. She put a piece of pottery under it to make it level. As soon as this had fixed the sloping surface, they cleaned the table surface with green mintleaves. On top they then put olives of both colours, sacred to the virgin Minerva, and autumnal cherries preserved in wine lees, and endives and radishes and a round of cheese, and eggs that had been cooked and turned gently in ashes that were not too hot; everything was served in terracotta dishes . . .) (Book 8).

It is by continuing to add to the detail of the picture that Ovid obtains an effect of rarefaction and pause. His instinct is always to add, never to take away; to go for greater and greater detail, never to shade off into vagueness – a procedure which produces differing effects depending on the tone, which is here restrained and in harmony with the humble ambience, but elsewhere is excited, impatient to saturate the marvellous elements of the tale with realistic observation of natural phenomena. For instance, that moment when Perseus is about to fight with the sea monster with its back encrusted with shells, and he rests Medusa's head, bristling with serpents, face-down on a rock, but only after spreading a layer of seaweed and underwater reeds so that the head should not suffer contact with the rough surface of the sand. Seeing the reeds turn to stone on contact with the Medusa, the Nymphs play at making other reeds suffer the same fate: this is how coral is born, which though soft underneath the water becomes petrified on contact with the air. So Ovid concludes the fabulous adventure on a note of etiological legend, dictated by his taste for nature's more bizarre forms.

A law of maximum internal economy dominates this poem which apparently seems devoted to unrestrained expansion. It is an economy particular to metamorphosis, which demands that the new forms recuperate as much as possible of the material of the old forms. After the flood, in the transformation of the stones into human beings (Book 1), 'if there was in the stones a part that was damp with moisture, or earthy, this became part of the body; whatever was solid and inflexible changed into bones; what had been veins in the rock stayed the same, including the name.' Here the economy extends even to the name (vein): 'quae modo vena fuit, sub eodem nomine mansit.' Daphne's most striking attribute (Book 1) is her hair dishevelled in the wind (so much so that Apollo's first thought on seeing her is 'What would that hair be like when properly combed' – 'Spectat inornatos collo pendere capillos / et "Quid si comantur?" ait . . .' (He gazes at her unadorned lock hanging down around her neck, and says to himself: 'What would that hair be like when properly combed?')), and she is already predisposed by the sinuous lines of her flight to a vegetable metamorphosis: 'in frondem crines, in ramos bracchia crescunt; / pes modo tam velox pigris radicibus haeret' (her hair turns into foliage, her arms into branches; her foot once so swift now sticks to the ground with immovable roots). Cyane (Book 5) merely carries to its logical conclusion her dissolving into tears ('lacrimisque absumitur omnis' (and she is completely consumed by her own tears)) until she evaporates into the pool whose nymph she once had been. And the Lycian peasants (Book 6), who hurl abuse and pollute the lake by stirring up its mud when wandering Latona wants to slake the thirst of her newborn twins, were already not too far from the frogs into which a just punishment changes them: all that has to happen is for the neck to disappear, the shoulders to join with the head, the back turn green and the belly assume an off-white colour.

This technique of metamorphosis has been studied by Sceglov in an extremely lucid and persuasive essay. 'All these transformations', says Sceglov, 'concern the distinctive physical and spatial characteristics which Ovid usually highlights even in elements not subject to metamorphosis ("hard rock", "long body", "curved back") . . . Thanks to his knowledge of the properties of things, the poet provides the shortest route for the metamorphosis, because he knows in advance what man has in common with dolphins, as well as what he lacks compared to them, and what they lack compared to him. The essential point is that since he portrays the whole world as a system made up of elementary components, the process of transformation – this most unlikely and fantastic phenomenon – is reduced to a sequence of quite simple processes. The event is no longer represented as a fairytale but rather as a collection of everyday, realistic facts (growing, diminishing, hardening, softening, curving, straightening, joining, separating etc.).'

Ovid's writing, as described by Sceglov, appears to contain within itself the model, or at least the programme, for Robbe-Grillet at his most cold and rigorous. Of course such a description does not exhaust everything we can find in Ovid. But the important point is that this way of portraying (animate and inanimate) objects *objectively*, 'as different combinations of a relatively small number of basic, very simple elements' sums up exactly the only incontrovertible philosophy in the poem, namely 'that of the unity and inter-connectedness of everything that exists in the world, both things and living creatures'.

Setting out his cosmogony in the first book and his profession of faith in Pythagoras in the last, Ovid clearly wanted to provide this natural philosophy with a theoretical basis, perhaps to rival the by now remote Lucretius. There has been considerable discussion as to the weight one should attach to these professions of faith, but probably the only thing that matters is the poetic consistency of the manner in which Ovid portrays and narrates his world: namely this swarming and intertwining of events that are often similar but are always different, in which the continuity and mobility of everything is celebrated.

Before he has even finished the chapter on the origins of the world and its early catastrophes, Ovid is already embarking on the series of love affairs that the gods have with nymphs or mortal girls. There are several constants in the love stories (which mostly occupy the liveliest part of the poem, the first eleven books): as Bernardini has shown they involve love at first sight, overwhelming desire, no psychological complications, and demand an immediate resolution. And since the desired creature usually refuses and flees, the motif of the chase through the woods constantly recurs; metamorphosis can occur at different times, either before (the seducer's disguise), during (the pursued maiden's escape), or afterwards (punishment inflicted by another jealous deity on the seduced girl).

Compared with the constant pressure of male desire, the instances of female initiative in love are rather rare; but to compensate, these are usually more complex desires, not sudden whims but real passions, which involve greater psychological richness (Venus in love with Adonis), often contain a more morbid erotic element (the nymph Salmacis who when she sexually embraces Hermaphroditus blends into a bisexual creature), and in some cases are totally illicit, incestuous passions (such as the tragic characters Myrrha and Byblis: the way in which the latter realises her desire for her brother, through a revelatory but upsetting dream, is one of the finest psychological passages in Ovid), or tales of homosexual love (Iphys), or of wicked jealousy (Medea). The stories of Jason and Medea open up right at the centre of the poem (Book 7) a space for a genuine romance tale, involving a mixture of adventure, brooding passion, and the 'black' grotesque scene of the magic philtres, which will resurface almost identically in *Macbeth*.

The move from one story to the next without any interval is underlined by the fact that – as Wilkinson points out – 'the end of a story rarely coincides with the end of a book. He will even begin a new one within the last few lines. This is partly the time-honoured device of the serial writer to whet the reader's appetite for the next instalment; but it is also an indication of the continuity of the work, which should not have been divided into books at all, were it not that its length necessitated a number of rolls. This then gives us the impression of a real and consistent world in which events which are usually considered in isolation interact with each other.'

The stories are often similar, never the same. It is not by chance that the most heart-rending tale is that of the unlucky love of Echo (Book 3), doomed to repeat sounds, for the young Narcissus, who in turn is condemned to contemplate his own repeated image in the reflecting waters. Ovid runs across this forest of love stories which are all the same and all different, pursued by the voice of Echo resounding from the rocks 'Coëamus!' 'Coëamus!' 'Coëamus!'

[1979]

The Sky, Man, the Elephant

For sheer pleasure of reading, I would advise anyone taking up Pliny the Elder's *Natural History* to focus mainly on three books: the two containing the fundamentals of his philosophy, that is to say Book 2 (on cosmography) and Book 7 (on man), and – for an example of his unique blend of erudition and fantasy – Book 8 (on land animals). Of course you can discover astonishing pages everywhere: in the books on geography (3–6), on aquatic animals, entomology and comparative anatomy (9–11), on botany, agronomy and pharmacology (12–32), or those on metals, precious stones and the fine arts (33–37).

It has always been the case, I believe, that people do not read Pliny, they go to Pliny to consult him, both to find out what the ancients knew or thought they knew about a certain topic, and to winkle out bizarre facts and curiosities. On this latter point one cannot ignore Book 1, an index of the whole work, whose charm derives from unpredictable juxtapositions: 'Fish which have a small stone in their head; Fish which hide in winter; Fish which are influenced by the stars; Fish which have fetched extraordinary prices'; or 'Roses: 12 varieties, 32 drugs; Lilies: 3 varieties, 21 drugs; Plants which grow from an exudation; Narcissus: 3 varieties; 16 drugs; The plant whose seed can be dyed to produce coloured flowers; Saffron: 20 drugs; Where the best flowers grow; What flowers were known at the time of the Trojan war; Floral patterns in clothes.' Or again, 'The nature of metals; Of gold; Of the amount of gold possessed by the ancients; Of the equestrian order and the right to wear gold rings; How many times the equestrian order has changed name'. But Pliny is also an author who deserves an extended read, for the measured movement of his prose, which is enlivened by his admiration for everything that exists and his respect for the infinite diversity of all phenomena.

We could distinguish Pliny the poet and philosopher, with his awareness for the universe, his sympathy for knowledge and mystery, from Pliny the neurotic collector of data, the compulsive compiler of facts, whose sole concern appears to be not to waste any note from his gigantic collection of index cards. (In his use of written sources he was both omnivorous and eclectic, but not uncritical: there were facts he recorded as true, others to which he gave the benefit of the doubt, others he rejected as obvious nonsense. The only problem is that his method of evaluation appears to be extremely inconsistent and unpredictable.) However, once one admits the existence of these two sides to him, one has to recognise that Pliny is just one writer, just as the world he wants to describe is just one world though it contains a great variety of forms. To achieve his objective, he is not afraid of trying to embrace the infinite number of existing forms in the world, which in turn is multiplied by the countless number of reports which exist about all these forms, since forms and reports both have the same right to be part of natural history and to be examined by someone who seeks in them that sign of a higher reason which he is convinced they must contain.

For Pliny the world is the eternal sky which was not created by anyone, and whose spherical, rotating vault covers all earthly things (2.2). But the world is difficult to distinguish from God, who for Pliny and the Stoic culture which he embraced is a single deity that cannot be identified with any single portion or aspect, nor with the crowd of Olympian gods (apart perhaps from the Sun, which is the soul, mind or spirit of the heavens (2.13)). But at the same time the sky is composed of stars as eternal as God (the stars weave the sky and at the same time they are interwoven into the heavenly fabric: 'aeterna caelestibus est natura intexentibus mundum intextuque concretis', 2.30), and is also the air (both above and below the moon) which seems empty and diffuses down here the vital spirit, generating clouds, hail, thunder, lightning and storms (2.102).

When we talk of Pliny we never know to what extent the ideas he advances can be attributed directly to him. He is scrupulous about putting down as little as possible of his own, and sticking closely to what his sources say: this conforms to his impersonal view of knowledge which excludes individual originality. To try to understand his real view of nature, what role is played in it by the arcane majesty of principles and what by the material existence of the elements, we have to restrict ourselves to what is definitely his own, to what the substance of his prose conveys. His discussion of the moon, for instance, blends together two elements: first a note of deep-felt gratitude for this 'ultimate star, the star most familiar to those who live on earth, their remedy against the dark' ('novissimum sidus, terris familiarissimum et in tenebrarum remedium') and for everything her changing phases and eclipses teach us; and second the nimble practicality of his phrasing, both of which combine to convey the moon's function with crystalline clarity. It is in this astronomical section of Book 2 that Pliny proves that he can be more than just the mere compiler of data with a taste for the bizarre that we usually think of. Here he shows that he possesses the main strength of great scientific writers of the future: the ability to communicate the most complex argument with limpid clarity, drawing from it a sense of harmony and beauty.

All this is done without ever veering towards abstract speculation. Pliny always sticks to the facts (to what he or his source considers facts): he does not accept an infinity of worlds because this world alone is already difficult enough to understand and an infinity would not simplify the problem (2.4). He does not believe the heavenly spheres produce sound, whether that sound be a roar too great to be heard or an ineffable harmony, because 'for us who are inside it, the world slips round day and night in silence' (2.6).

Having stripped God of the anthropomorphic trappings which myths attributed to the Olympian gods, Pliny is forced by this logic of his to bring God closer again to humans since this logical necessity has limited his powers (in fact in one respect God is less free than man since he could not kill himself even if he wanted to). God cannot resurrect the dead, nor make someone who has been alive never have lived; he has no power over the past, over the irreversibility of time (2.27). Like Kant's God, he cannot enter into conflict with the autonomy of reason (he cannot prevent ten plus ten making twenty), but to delimit him in this way would distance us from Pliny's pantheistic identification of him as immanent in nature ('per quae declaratur haut dubie naturae potentia idque esse quod deum vocamus' (these facts unquestionably prove the power of nature, which is what we call God), 2.27).

The lyricism, or rather the mixture of philosophy and lyricism which dominates the early chapters of Book 2 reflects a vision of universal harmony which is soon shattered: a substantial part of the book is devoted to heavenly portents. Pliny's scientific method hovers between a desire to find an order in nature and the recording of what is extraordinary and unique, and it is the latter tendency which always prevails in the end. Nature is eternal, sacred and harmonious, but it leaves a wide margin for the occurrence of miraculous, inexplicable phenomena. What general conclusion should we draw from all this? That in fact nature's order is a monstrous order, composed entirely of exceptions to rules? Or that her rules are so complex as to lie beyond our understanding? In either case, there must be an explanation for every occurrence, even though it may be unknown to us at present: 'All these are things of uncertain explanation and hidden in the majesty of nature' (2.101), or a little later on, 'Adeo causa non deest' (There must be some cause for this) (2.115): it is not that there is no cause, some explanation can always be found. Pliny's rationalism upholds the logic of cause and effect, but at the same time it minimalises it: even when you find an explanation for the facts, the facts do not thereby cease to be miraculous.

This last maxim acts as the conclusion to a chapter on the mysterious origin of the winds: perhaps folds in mountains, concave valleys in which gusts of wind rebound like echoes, a grotto in Dalmatia in which throwing even the lightest object is enough to unleash a storm at sea, a rock in Cyrenaica which you just have to touch with your hand to stir up a sandstorm. Pliny gives us plenty of these catalogues of strange, unconnected facts: catalogues of the effects of thunderbolts on man, causing cold wounds (the only plant not attacked by thunderbolts is the laurel, the only bird the eagle, 2.146), lists of strange things that rain from the sky (milk, blood, meat, iron or iron spunges, wool, bricks, 2.147).

Yet Pliny dismisses a large number of fanciful ideas, such as comets presaging the future: for instance, he rejects the belief that the appearance of a comet between the pudenda of a constellation – what did the ancients NOT see in the sky! – foretells a period of loose morals ('obscenis autem moribus in verendis partibus signorum', 2.93). Yet every strange event is for him a problem of nature, in that it represents a variation from the norm. Pliny rejects superstitions, yet he is not always able to recognise them himself, and this is particularly so in Book 7, where he discusses human nature: he quotes the most abstruse beliefs even regarding facts which are extremely easy to check. The chapter on menstruation is typical (7.63–66), but it has to be noted that Pliny's account is of a piece with the most ancient religious taboos regarding menstrual blood. There is a whole network of analogies and traditional values that does not clash with Pliny's rationality, almost as if the latter was founded on the same bedrock.

Consequently he is sometimes inclined to construct explanations based on poetic or psychological analogies: 'Men's corpses float on their back, women's on their front, as if nature wanted to respect the modesty of women even after death' (7.77).

It is only very rarely that Pliny quotes facts that he himself has witnessed directly: 'I have seen at night, while the sentries were on guard in front of the trenches, lights in the shape of a star shining on the soldiers' lances' (2.101); 'When Claudius was Emperor, we saw a centaur which he ordered to be sent from Egypt, conserved in honey' (7.35); 'I myself saw when in Africa a citizen of Thysdritum change from woman into man on the day of her wedding' (7.36).

But for a researcher like Pliny, who was in a sense the first martyr of empirical science, since he would die asphyxiated by the fumes of Vesuvius when it erupted, direct observation occupies a minimal place in his work, and counts neither more nor less than what he reads in books, which for him were all the more authoritative the older they were. At best he admits his uncertainty, saying: 'However, I would not give my word for the majority of these facts, preferring as I do to rely on the sources, to whom I refer you in all cases of doubt: I will never tire of citing the Greek sources, since they are not only the most ancient but also the most precise in observation' (7.8).

After this preamble Pliny feels he is now authorised to launch into the famous list of 'miraculous and incredible' characteristics of certain foreign races which was to be so popular in the Middle Ages and afterwards, and was to transform geography into a kind of living freak show. (Its echoes will continue even in the accounts of *true* journeys, such as those of Marco Polo.) That the unknown lands at the edge of the Earth harbour beings who border on the human, should not surprise us: the Arimaspians with one single eye in the middle of their forehead, who fight the griffins for possession of the gold mines; the inhabitants of the forests of Abarymon, who run at full speed with their feet turned backwards; the androgynous inhabitants of Nasamona who change sex when they couple; the Thybians who have two pupils in one eye, and the figure of a horse in the other. But this huge circus reserves its most spectacular stunts for India, where one can encounter a mountain tribe of hunters who have the head of a dog; and another of leaping dancers who have just one leg, and who when they want to rest in the shade, lie down raising their single foot up as a parasol; and another race still, this time nomads, whose legs are in the shape of serpents; while the Astomi who have no mouth, live by sniffing odours. In the midst of all this there are also accounts which we now know to be true, like the description of the Indian fakirs (Pliny calls them gymnosophist philosophers), or which continue to feed the mysterious reports which we read in our newspapers (Pliny's mention of enormous footprints could refer to the Himalayan Yeti), or legends which will be handed down for centuries to come, like that of the healing powers of kings (King Pyrrhus cured diseases of the spleen by the laying on of his big toe).

All this produces a dramatic view of human nature, as something precarious and unstable: man's shape and destiny hang by a very thin thread. Several pages are dedicated to the unpredictability of childbirth: its difficulties, perils and exceptional cases. This too is a frontier zone: whoever exists might also not exist, or exist in a different form, and childbirth is the moment when everything is decided:

> In pregnant women everything, for example even the way they walk, influences the child's birth: if they eat food that is too salty, the baby will be born without nails; if they do not know how to hold their breath, the birth is much more difficult; even a yawn during the birth can be fatal; similarly, a sneeze during intercourse can cause a miscarriage. Whoever considers how precarious is the birth of the proudest living being can only feel pity and shame: often even the smell of a lamp that has just been put out can cause a miscarriage. And to think that such fragile origins can produce a powerful tyrant or murderer. You who rely on your physical strength, who enjoy the benefits of Fortune, and consider yourself not her temporary ward but her son, who think you are a god the minute some success makes you puff out your chest, just think how little it would have taken to destroy you! (7.42–44)

It is easy to understand why Pliny was popular in the Christian Middle Ages, when he produced maxims like this: 'in order to weigh up life properly, one must always remind oneself of human fragility.'

Human beings form an area of the living world which must be defined by carefully drawing its boundaries: that is why Pliny records the extreme limits reached by man in every field, and Book 7 becomes something like today's Guinness Book of Records. Quantitative records above all, records of strength in lifting weights, of speed in running, of keen hearing, of memory, and even of the area of lands conquered. But there are also purely moral records, records of virtue, generosity and goodness. There are also extremely bizarre records: Antonina, Drusus' wife, who never spat; the poet Pomponius who never belched (7.80); or the highest price paid for a slave (the grammar tutor Daphnis cost 700,000 sesterces, 7.128).

Only in one aspect of human life does Pliny not feel like quoting records or attempting measurements or comparisons: in happiness. It is impossible to decide who is happy and who is not, since it depends on subjective and debatable criteria ('Felicitas cui praecipua fuerit homini, non est humani iudicii, cum prosperitatem ipsam alius alio modo et suopte ingenio quisque determinet', 7.130). If one wants to face the truth without illusions, no man can be said to be happy: and here Pliny's anthropological survey lists examples of illustrious destinies (mostly taken from Roman history), to prove that the men most favoured by fortune had to tolerate considerable unhappiness and misfortune.

It is impossible to force that variable which is destiny into the natural history of man: this is the sense of the pages that Pliny devotes to the vicissitudes of fortune, to the unpredictability of the length of any life, to the pointlessness of astrology, to disease and death. The separation between the two forms of knowledge which astrology held together – the objective nature of calculable and predictable phenomena and the feeling of the individual existence with its uncertain future – this separation which acts as a premiss for modern science could be said to be already present in these pages, but in the form of a question that has still not been definitively resolved, and for which one must collect exhaustive documentation. In adducing his examples in this area, Pliny seems to falter: every event that happens, every biography, every anecdote, can serve to prove that life, if considered from the point of view of the person living it, cannot be evaluated either in quantity or quality, cannot be measured or compared to other lives. Its value is intrinsic to itself; so much so that hopes and fears about an afterlife are illusory: Pliny shares the view that death is followed by another non-existence which is equivalent and symmetrical to the non-existence before birth.

That is why Pliny's attention concentrates on the things of this world, the heavenly bodies and the territories of the globe, as well as animals, plants and stones. The soul, which cannot survive death, if it turns in upon itself, can only enjoy being alive in the present. 'Etenim si dulce vivere est, cui potest esse vixisse? At quanto facilius certiusque sibi quemque credere, specimen securitas antegenitali sumere experimento!' (If it is sweet to live, who can find it sweet to have done living? Yet how much easier and safer it is just to rely on yourself, and to model your own peace of mind on your experience before birth) (7.190). 'Model your own peace of mind on your experience before birth': in other words, project yourself into contemplating your own absence, the only secure reality both before we came into the world and after we die. For the same reason we should also rejoice at recognising that infinite variety of what is different from us that Pliny's *Natural History* parades before our eyes.

But if man is defined by his limits, can he not also be defined by the peaks of his excellence? Pliny feels duty-bound to include in Book 7 the glorification of man's virtues, the celebration of his triumphs: he turns to Roman history as if it were the register of every virtue, and he is tempted to find a pompous conclusion by indulging in an imperial encomium which would allow him to signal the peak of human perfection in the figure of Caesar Augustus. But I would say that this tone is not typical of Pliny's treatment of his material: rather it is the tentative, limiting, almost bitter note that best suits his temperament.

We could recognise here some questions which accompanied the setting up of anthropology as a science. Must an anthropological science try to avoid a 'humanist' perspective in order to attain the objectivity of a natural science? Do the men in Book 7 count all the more, the more different, the more 'other' they are from us, the more they are no longer or not yet men? But is it possible for man to escape his own subjectivity to such an extent that he can make himself the object of a science? The moral which Pliny repeats invites caution and wariness: no science can enlighten us on *felicitas*, *fortuna*, on the mixture of good and evil in a life, on the values of existence; every individual dies and takes his secret with him to the grave.

Pliny could end this section on this disconsolate note, but he prefers to add a list of discoveries and inventions, both real and legendary. Anticipating those modern anthropologists who maintain that there is a continuity between biological evolution and technological development, from palaeolithic tools to electronics, Pliny implicitly admits that the additions made by man to nature become an integral part themselves of nature. This is but a step away from claiming that the true nature of man is culture. But Pliny does not know how to generalise, and seeks the specifics of human achievement in inventions and customs which can be considered universal. There are three cultural facts, according to Pliny (or his sources), upon which a tacit accord has been reached between peoples ('gentium consensus tacitus', 7.210): the adoption of the (Greek and Roman) alphabet; the shaving of men's faces by a barber; and the marking of the hours of the day on a sundial.

This triad could not be more bizarre nor debatable in its incongruous grouping of the three terms: alphabet, barber, sundial. In fact it is not true that all peoples have similar systems for writing, nor that they shave their beard, and as for the hours of the day, Pliny himself devotes some pages to a brief history of the various systems of dividing time. I am not trying here to underline a 'Eurocentric' perspective, which in fact is not typical of Pliny or his age, but rather the direction in which he moves: the intent to establish the elements which are constantly repeated in the most diverse cultures, in order to define what is specifically human, will become a principle of method in modern ethnology. And once he has established this point about the 'gentium consensus tacitus', Pliny can close his treatment of humanity and move on 'ad reliqua animalia', to the other animate beings.

Book 8, which reviews the living creatures of the earth, begins with the elephant, to which the longest chapter is devoted. Why is the elephant accorded this priority? Obviously because it is the biggest animal (and Pliny's treatment of living creatures continues according to an order of importance which largely coincides with that of physical size); but also and particularly because spiritually this is the animal 'closest to man'! 'Maximum est elephas proximumque humanis sensibus', is how Book 8 opens. In fact the elephant – as is explained immediately afterwards – recognises the language of its native land, obeys orders, memorises what he learns, can experience the passion of love and the ambition for glory, practises virtues which are 'rare even amongst men', such as probity, prudence, fairness, and even pays religious homage to the stars, the sun and the moon. Pliny does not waste a single word (except that superlative *maximum*) on describing this animal, but simply quotes the quaint legends he has found in books: the rites and customs of elephants are presented as though they were those of a people of a different culture to our own but were still worthy of respect and understanding.

In the *Natural History* man is lost in the middle of the multiform universe, a prisoner of his own imperfection, but on the one hand he has the solace of knowing that God too is limited in his powers ('Inperfectae vero in homine naturae praecipua solacia, ne deum quidem posse omnia', 2.27), and on the other he has as his immediate neighbour the elephant, which can be a spiritual model for him. Caught between these two imposing but benign eminences, man certainly appears to be diminished but not crushed.

The survey of land animals moves on – as in a child's visit to the zoo – from the elephant to the lions, panthers, tigers, camels, giraffes, rhinoceroses and crocodiles. Following a decreasing order of size, we then come to the hyenas, chameleons, porcupines, animals with lairs, and so on down to snails and lizards; pets are grouped together at the end of the book.

The main source here is Aristotle's *Historia Animalium* (*History of Animate Beings*), but Pliny gathers from more credulous or more imaginative authors the legends which Aristotle either rejected or cited merely to refute them. This is the case both for the account of more familiar animals and for the mention and description of fantastic creatures: the list of the latter is mixed up with that of the former. Thus while still discussing elephants, a digression informs us about their natural enemy, dragons; and talking of wolves, Pliny records the legends about werewolves, though he does criticise Greek credulity. This sort of zoology contains the amphisbaena, the basilisk, the catoblepas, the crocotas, corocottas, leucocrotas, leontophons, and mantichores which will migrate from these pages to populate medieval bestiaries

The natural history of man continues into that of animals for the whole of Book 8, and this is not only because the ideas quoted deal largely with the rearing of pets and the hunting of wild animals, as well as the practical utility which man derives from both kinds; but because the journey Pliny takes us on is also a journey into the human imagination. Animals, real or imaginary, have a privileged place in the realm of fantasy: the minute such an animal is named it is invested with the power of a phantasm, it becomes an allegory, a symbol, an emblem.

That is why I recommend the reader to browse and not to dwell just on the most philosophical Books, 2 and 7, but also on Book 8, since it is the most representative of an idea of nature which is articulated consistently throughout all 37 books of the work: nature as something external to humanity, but which is also indistinguishable from what is innermost in man's mind, his dictionary of dreams and catalogue of fantasies, without which we can have neither reason nor thought.

[1982]

Nezami's Seven Princesses

Belonging to a polygamous rather than a monogamous culture certainly makes things very different. At least in narrative structure (the only area in which I feel competent to give an opinion), it opens up countless possibilities which are unknown to the West.

For instance, one of the most common motifs in Western folktales – the hero sees a portrait of a beautiful woman and instantly falls in love with her – is found also in the Orient, but multiplied. In a twelfth-century Persian poem, King Bahram sees seven portraits of seven princesses and falls in love with all seven at one and the same time. Each princess is a daughter of a ruler of one of the seven continents; Bahram asks the hand of each of them in turn and marries them. He then orders seven pavilions to be built, each a different colour and 'built to reflect the nature of the seven planets'. Each one of the seven princesses has a corresponding pavilion, colour, planet and day of the week; the king will make a weekly visit to each of his brides and will hear her tell a tale. The king's clothes will be the colour of the planet of that day and the stories told by the brides will match the colour, and the specific power of the corresponding planet.

These seven stories are folktales full of marvellous happenings like *The Arabian Nights*, but each one has a moral conclusion (even though it is not always recognisable as such beneath its symbolic cloak), such that the weekly cycle of the newly-wed king rehearses the moral virtues which are the human equivalent of the properties of the cosmos. (The single male king practises carnal and spiritual polygamy on his many handmaid-brides; in this tradition the roles of the sexes are irreversible, so it is pointless to expect surprises here.) The seven tales in turn contain love stories which are presented in a multiplied form compared to Western models.

For example, the typical structure of an initiation-tale demands that the hero undergo several trials to win both the hand of the girl he loves and a royal throne. In the West this structure requires the wedding to be kept for the end, or if it does take place earlier, it is the prelude to further vicissitudes, persecutions or magic spells, where the bride (or groom) is first lost then found again. Instead here we have a tale where the hero wins a new bride with each trial he overcomes, each bride more royal than the previous one; and these successive brides do not cancel each other out, but are cumulative, like the store of wisdom and experience gathered in a lifetime.

The book I am discussing is a classic of medieval Persian literature, now available in a slim volume in Rizzoli's Biblioteca Universale Rizzoli series, and presented with commendable expertise: Nezami, *Le sette principesse* (*The Seven Princesses*), introduction and translation by Alessandro Bausani and Giovanna Calasso. Tackling masterpieces of Oriental literature is usually an unsatisfactory experience for those of us who are uninitiated, because it is so difficult to obtain even a distant glimmer of the original through the translations and adaptations; and it is always an arduous task situating a work in a context which we are not familiar with. This poem in particular is certainly an extremely complex text both as regards its stylistic make-up and its spiritual implications. But Bausani's translation – which seems to stick scrupulously close to the densely metaphorical text and does not hold back even when it comes to puns (the Persian words are given in parenthesis) – with its copious notes and introduction (along with its essential accompaniment of illustrations) gives us something more, I believe, than the illusion of understanding what this book is about and of savouring its poetic charm, at least as far as a prose translation can do so.

So then, we now have the rare good fortune to be able to add to our library of masterpieces of world literature a work that is both of some substance and highly enjoyable. I say rare good fortune because this privilege has been granted only to Italians amongst all other Western readers, if the bibliography in the volume is accurate. The only unabridged English version, made in 1924, is inaccurate, the German one is a partial and rather free adaptation, while no French version exists at all. (What the bibliography does not say, but it should be stated here, is that this same translation by Bausani came out some years ago, published in Bari by the 'Leonardo da Vinci' publishing house, though with far fewer notes.)

Nezami (1141–1204), a Sunnite Moslem (at that time the Shiites had not yet gained the upper hand in Iran), was born and died at Ganjè, in what is now Soviet Azerbaijan, so he lived in a territory in which Iranian, Kurdish and Turkish peoples mixed. In *The Seven Princesses* (*Haft Peikar* means literally 'the seven effigies', and was written around 1200 AD, one of five poems he wrote) he tells the tale of a ruler of the fifth century, Bahram the Fifth, of the Sassanid dynasty. Nezami thus conjures up Persia's Zoroastrian past in an atmosphere of Islamic mysticism. His poem celebrates both the divine will to which man must submit entirely and the various potentialities of the earthly world, with pagan and Gnostic resonances (and Christian ones too: there is a mention of the great miracle worker Isu, or Jesus).

Before and after the seven tales narrated in the seven pavilions, the poem illustrates the king's life, upbringing, love of hunting (he hunts lions, wild asses, dragons), wars against the Grand Khan's Chinese army, the building of his palace, his feasts and drinking bouts, even his minor love affairs. The poem is thus first and foremost a portrait of the ideal ruler, in which, as Bausani says, the ancient Iranian tradition of the Sacred King blends with the Islamic tradition of the Pious Sultan who submits entirely to divine law.

An ideal ruler – we think – ought to have a prosperous rule and happy subjects. Not at all! These are the prejudices of our rather basic ideas of kingship. That a king is a miraculous mixture of all perfections does not rule out the possibility that his rule should be marred by the most cruel injustices at the hands of treacherous and greedy ministers. But seeing that the king enjoys divine favour, there will come a time when the grim reality of his kingdom will be revealed to his eyes. Then he will punish the wicked Vizier and provide recompense for whoever comes to tell him of the injustices they have suffered: so we have the 'tales of the victims', again seven of them, but less attractive than the other seven.

Once he has re-established justice in his reign, Bahram can now reorganise the army and rout the Grand Khan of China. Having thus fulfilled his destiny, he has nothing left to do but disappear: in fact he does disappear, literally, riding into a cavern in pursuit of the wild ass he was hunting. The King in short is, in Bausani's words, 'Man par excellence': what counts is the cosmic harmony of which he is the incarnation, a harmony which is reflected to a certain extent in his rule and subjects, but which resides above all in his person. (In any case, even today there are regimes which claim to be praiseworthy in and of themselves, even though their subjects live abject existences.)

The Seven Princesses, then, blends two types of Oriental wonder-tale: the celebratory epic account in *The Book of the Kings* by Firdusi (the tenth-century poet whom Nezami follows) and the novelistic tradition which springs from ancient Indian collections and will eventually lead to *The Arabian Nights*. Of course our pleasure as readers is more gratified by this latter type of narration (so my advice would be to start with the seven tales and then turn to the frame story), but the frame is also rich in fantastic, magic and erotic refinement (foot-caressing, for example, is very much at a premium: 'the king's foot inserted itself between the stunning woman's silk and brocade garments, right through to her hip'). As in fairy tales, cosmic and religious sentiments reach new peaks. For example, in the story of the two men who go on a journey, one who resigns himself to the will of God, the other who wants to have a rational explanation for everything, the psychological characterisation of the two men is so persuasive that it is impossible not to empathise more with the first man: he never loses sight of the complexity of everything, while the second is a malevolent and mean-spirited know-all. The moral that we can derive from this is that what counts is not so much one's philosophical stance as how to live in harmony with the truth one believes in.

However, it is impossible to separate the various traditions which converge in *The Seven Princesses* because Nezami's heady figurative language blends them all together in his creative melting pot, and he spreads over every page a gilded patina studded with metaphors which are embedded inside each other like precious gems in a dazzling necklace. The result is that the stylistic unity of the book seems all-pervasive, extending even to the introductory sections on wisdom and mysticism. (In connection with the latter I will mention the vision of Mohammed, who rises to heaven upon a winged angel, upwards to the point where all three dimensions disappear and 'the Prophet saw God but no space, and heard words that came from no lips and carried no sounds'.)

The decorations of this verbal tapestry are so luxuriant that any parallels we might find in Western literature (beyond the analogies of medieval thematics and the wealth of fantasy in Renaissance works by Shakespeare and Ariosto) would naturally be with works of heaviest baroque; but even Marino's *Adonis* and Basile's *Pentameron* are works of laconic sobriety compared to the proliferation of metaphors which encrust Nezami's tale and germinate a hint of narrative in every single image.

This universe of metaphors has characteristics and constants all of its own. The onager, the wild ass of the Iranian highlands – which if you see it in encyclopedias and, if I remember correctly, in zoos, is no more than an average-sized donkey – in Nezami's verses acquires the dignity of more noble, heraldic creatures, and appears almost on every page. In Prince Bahram's hunts the onager is the most sought after and difficult quarry, often cited alongside the lion as the foe against which the hunter measures his strength and skill. When it comes to metaphors, the onager is an image of strength, and even virile sexual power, but also of amorous prey (the onager pursued by the lion), of female beauty and of youth in general. And since its flesh is extremely tasty, we find 'maidens with onagers' eyes, roasting onager thighs on the fire'.

Another polyvalent metaphor is that of the cypress tree: used to evoke virile strength as well as being a phallic symbol, we also find it used as a paragon of feminine beauty (height is always especially prized), and associated with female hair, but also with flowing waters and even with the morning sun. Almost all the metaphorical functions of the cypress tree are applied also at one point to a lit candle, as well as having several other functions. In fact the delirium of similes here is such that anything can mean anything else.

There are some bravura passages of strings of metaphors one after the other: for instance, a description of winter in which a series of frosty images ('the attack of cold had turned the swords into water and water into swords': the notes explain that the swords of the sun's rays turn into the water of rain and the rain becomes the sword-like flashes of lightning; and even if the explanation is not accurate, it is still a beautiful image) is followed by an apotheosis of fire, and a corresponding description of spring, full of plant personifications such as 'the breeze was then pawned for the basil's perfume'.

Another catalyst of metaphors is each of the seven colours which dominate each tale. How can one narrate a story all in the one colour? The simplest system is to have all the characters dressed in that colour, as in the black tale which tells of a woman who always dressed in black, because she had been the handmaid of a king who always dressed in black, because he had met a stranger dressed in black, who had told him of a place in China whose inhabitants all dressed in black . . .

Elsewhere the link is simply symbolic, based on the meaning attributed to each colour: yellow is the colour of the sun, therefore of kings; so the yellow tale will tell of a king and will end in a seduction, which is compared to the forcing of a casket which contains gold.

Surprisingly the white tale is the most erotic one, bathed as it is in a milky light in which we see girls moving 'with breasts like hyacinths and legs of silver'. But it is also the tale of chastity, as I shall try to explain, though everything is lost in a summary of it. A young man, who amongst his many claims to perfection has that of being chaste, sees his garden being invaded by beautiful young girls who dance there. Two of them, after whipping him when they take him for a thief (a certain masochistic element is not excluded here), recognise him as the owner, kiss his hands and his feet and invite him to choose for himself the girl that he likes best. He spies on the girls as they bathe, makes his choice and (still with the help of the two guardians or 'policewomen' who guide his every move in the story) meets up with his favourite girl on his own. But in this and in each successive encounter something always happens at the crucial moment which prevents them consummating their relationship: the floor of the room subsides, or a cat trying to catch a little bird lands on the two embracing lovers, or a mouse gnaws through the stalk of a pumpkin on a pergola and the thud of the pumpkin falling puts the young man off his stroke, and so on until the moralising conclusion: the young man realises that first he has to marry the girl because Allah does not want him to commit a sin.

This motif of constant coitus interruptus is one that is also common in popular tales in the West, where however it is always treated grotesquely: in one of Basile's *cunti* (tales) the unforeseen interruptions are remarkably similar to those in Nezami's tale, but out of it emerges a hellish picture of human squalor, scatology and sexual phobia. Nezami on the other hand paints a visionary world full of erotic tension and trepidation which is both sublimated and enriched with psychological chiaroscuro, where the polygamous dream of a paradise full of houris alternates with the reality of a couple's intimacy, while the unbridled licentiousness of the figurative language is an appropriate style for the upheavals of youthful inexperience.

[1982]

Tirant lo Blanc

The hero of the earliest Spanish chivalric romance, Tirant lo Blanc, makes his first appearance asleep on his horse. The horse stops to drink from a stream, Tirant wakes up and sees sitting by the stream a hermit with a white beard reading a book. Tirant tells the hermit of his intention to enter the chivalric order, and the hermit, a former knight, offers to instruct the young man in the rules of the order:

'Hijo mío,' dijo el ermitaño,
'toda la orden está escrita en ese
libro, que algunas veces leo para
recordar la gracia que Nuestro Señor
me ha hecho en este mundo, puesto
que honraba y mantenía la orden de
caballería con todo mi poder.'
('My son,' said the hermit, 'the entire rules of the order are written in that book, which I sometimes read in order to recall the favour which Our Lord has done me in this world, since I used to honour and maintain the order of chivalry with all my might.')

Right from its opening pages this first Spanish chivalric romance seems to want to warn us that every such text presupposes a preexisting chivalric book which the hero has to read in order to become a knight: 'Tot l'ordre és en aques llibre escrit.' From such a statement many conclusions can follow, including the one that perhaps chivalry never existed before chivalric books, or indeed that it only existed in books.

It is thus not hard to see how the last repository of chivalric virtues, Don Quixote, will be someone who has constructed his own being and his own world exclusively through books. As soon as the priest, the barber, the niece and housekeeper have consigned his library to the flames, chivalry is finished: Don Quixote will be the last exemplar of a species that has no successors.

The priest still manages to save from that provincial bonfire of vanities the major source texts, *Amadís de Gaula* and *Tirant lo Blanc*, along with the verse romances of Boiardo and Ariosto (in the original Italian and not in translation, in which they lose 'su natural valor'). As far as these books are concerned, unlike others which are spared because they are considered to conform to morality (such as *Palmerín de Inglaterra*), it appears as if their salvation is due largely to their aesthetic values: but which ones? We shall see that the qualities that count for Cervantes (but to what extent can we be sure that Cervantes' opinions coincide with those of the curate and the barber rather than with those of Don Quixote?) are literary originality (*Amadís* is defined as 'único en su arte') and human truth (*Tirant lo Blanc* is praised because 'aquí comen los caballeros, y duermen y mueren en sus camas, y hacen testamento antes de sua muerte, con otras cosas de que los demás libros deste género carecen' (here knights eat, sleep and die in their beds, and make a will before they die, along with other things which find no place in other books of this kind)). Thus Cervantes (or at least that part of Cervantes that coincides with etc.) respects chivalric works the more they contravene the rules of the genre: it is no longer the myth of chivalry that counts, but the worth of the book as a text. This is a criterion that is the opposite to Don Quixote's (and to that part of Cervantes that identifies with his hero), who refuses to distinguish between literature and life and wants to find the myth outside the books.

What will be the fate of the world of chivalric romance, once the analytical spirit intervenes and establishes clear boundaries between the realm of the marvellous, the realm of moral values, and that of reality and verisimilitude? The sudden but grandiose catastrophe, in which the myth of chivalry dissolves on the sun-scorched roads of La Mancha, is an event of universal relevance, but one which has no counterpart in other literatures. In Italy, or more precisely in the courts of northern Italy, the same process had taken place a century previously, though in less dramatic form, as a literary sublimation of that tradition. The waning of chivalry had been celebrated by Pulci, Boiardo and Ariosto in an atmosphere of Renaissance festival, with more or less marked parodistic tones, but also with nostalgia for the simple popular tales of the *cantastorie*: the empty remains of the chivalric imagination were now valued only as a repertoire of conventional motifs, but at least the heaven of poetry opened up to welcome its spirit.

It might be worth recalling that many years before Cervantes, in 1526, we already find a pyre for books of chivalry, or more precisely, a choice between which books to condemn to the flames and which to save. I refer to a very minor text which is hardly known at all: the *Orlandino*, a brief epic poem in Italian verse by Teofilo Folengo (who was more famous under the name of Merlin Cocai as the author of the *Baldus*, a poem in macaronic Latin mixed with Mantuan dialect). In the first canto of the *Orlandino*, Folengo recounts that he was taken by a witch flying on the back of a ram to a cavern in the Alps where the real chronicles of Bishop Turpin are preserved: Turpin was the legendary source of the entire Carolingian cycle. When he compares them with this source he discovers that the poems by Boiardo, Ariosto, Pulci and Cieco da Ferrara are all truthful, even though they contain rather arbitrary additions.

> *Ma* Trebisunda, Ancroja, Spagna *e* Bovo
> *coll'altro resto al foco sian donate;*
> *apocrife son tutte, e le riprovo*
> *come nemiche d'ogni veritate;*
> *Bojardo, l'Ariosto, Pulci e 'l Cieco*
> *autentici sono, ed io con seco.*
> *(But* Trebisunda, Ancroja, Spagna *and* Bovo *with all the others, should be consigned to the fire: they are all apocryphal, and I accuse them of being the enemies of all truthfulness; but Boiardo, Ariosto, Pulci and Cieco are authentic, and I along with them.)*

'El verdadero historiador Turpin', mentioned also by Cervantes, was a regular point of ludic reference in Renaissance Italian chivalric poems. Even Ariosto, when he feels he has been exaggerating too much, shields himself behind the authority of Turpin:

> *Il buon Turpin, che sa che dice il vero,*
> *e lascia creder poi quel ch'a l'uom piace,*
> *narra mirabil cose di Ruggiero,*
> *ch'udendolo, il direste voi mendace.* (O.F. *26.23*)

(But the good Turpin, who knows he is telling the truth, though he allows men then to believe what they like, tells incredible tales about Ruggiero, which if you heard them you would call him a liar.)

The legendary Turpin's role will be assigned by Cervantes in his work to the mysterious Cide Hamete Benengeli, whose Arabic manuscript he claims merely to be translating. But Cervantes is operating in a world that is by now radically different: truth for him has to be comparable with everyday experience, with common sense and also with the precepts of Counter-Reformation religion. For fifteenth- and sixteenth-century Italian poets (up to but not including Tasso, in whose case the question becomes really complicated) truth was still fidelity to a myth, as it was for the Knight of La Mancha.

We can see this even in a late sequel such as Folengo's, which is halfway between popular and erudite poetry: the spirit of myth, handed down from time immemorial, is symbolised by a book, Turpin's book, which lies at the origin of all books, a hypothetical book, accessible only through magic (Boiardo too, says Folengo, was a friend of witches), a book of magic as well as a book of magic tales.

The literary tradition of chivalry had died out first in its countries of origin, France and England: in England it received its definitive form in 1470 in Thomas Malory's romance, though it also revived again in the Elizabethan faery world of Spenser; while in France it slowly declined after its earliest consecration in poetry in the twelfth-century masterpieces of Chrétien de Troyes. The revival of chivalry in the sixteenth century largely concerns Italy and Spain. When Bernal Díaz del Castillo tries to convey the amazement of the conquistadors at the sight of a completely unimaginable world such as that of Montezuma's Mexico, he writes: 'Decíamos que parecía a las cosas de encantamiento que cuentan en el libro de Amadís' (We would say that it was like the enchanted things recounted in the book of Amadís). Here we feel that he can only compare this strange new reality to the traditions of ancient texts. But if we examine the dates, we shall see that Díaz del Castillo is recounting events which took place in 1519, when the *Amadís* could still be considered almost a publishing novelty . . . We can understand, then, that in the collective imagination the discovery of the New World and the Conquest went hand in hand with those stories of giants and magic spells which the contemporary book market offered in vast supply, in much the same way as the first European circulation of the

French cycle of tales a few centuries earlier had accompanied the propaganda that mobilised the Crusades.

The millennium which is about to end has been the millennium of the novel (the successor of the romance). In the eleventh, twelfth and thirteenth centuries the chivalric romances were the first secular books whose circulation had a profound impact on the life of ordinary people, not just on the learned. Dante himself provides evidence of this when he writes about Francesca da Rimini, the first character in world literature to find her life changed by the reading of romances, long before Don Quixote, long before Emma Bovary. In the French romance *Lancelot*, the knight Galahad persuades Guinevere to kiss Launcelot; in the *Divine Comedy* the book *Lancelot* takes on the role played by Galahad in the romance, persuading Francesca to let herself be kissed by Paolo. By seeing the identity between the character in the book who influences other characters and the book which influences its readers ('Galeotto fu il libro e chi lo scrisse' (the book and its author were Galahads to us)), Dante carries out the first ever, disorientating manoeuvre of metaliterature. In verses that are unsurpassed in density and sobriety, we follow Paolo and Francesca who, 'senza alcun sospetto' (completely unsuspecting), allow themselves to be carried away by the emotions aroused by their reading, looking into each other's eyes every now and then, turning pale, and when they reach the point where Launcelot kisses Guinevere on the mouth ('il desiato riso' (her desirable smile)), the desire described in the book makes obvious the desire felt in real life, and at that point life takes on the form narrated in the book: 'la bocca mi baciò tutto tremante' (trembling all over, he kissed me on the mouth).

[1985]

The Structure of the *Orlando Furioso*

The *Orlando Furioso* is an epic which refuses to begin and which refuses to end. It refuses to begin because it presents itself as the continuation of another poem, the *Orlando Innamorato* by Matteo Maria Boiardo, which had been left unfinished at the author's death. And it refuses to end because Ariosto never stopped working on the poem. Having published it in a first edition as a poem of forty canti in 1516, he constantly sought to expand it, first by trying to write a sequel, which also remained incomplete (the so-called *Cinque canti*, published posthumously), then by inserting new episodes into the central canti, so that in the third and definitive edition published in 1532 the number of canti rose to forty-six. In between there was a second edition, in 1521, which also bore the signs of the poem's unfinished nature in that it was simply a polished version of the first, consisting solely in a refinement of the language and metre to which Ariosto continued to devote great attention. An attention which lasted all his life, one could really say, since it had taken him twelve years' labour to produce the first edition of 1516, and another sixteen years' work before publishing the 1532 edition: one year later he was dead. This expansion from within, with episodes proliferating from other episodes, generating new symmetries and contrasts, seems to me to epitomise perfectly Ariosto's creative method: for him this was the only real way of continuing this poem with its polycentric, synchronic structure, whose episodes spiral off in every direction, continually intersecting with and bifurcating from each other.

In order to follow the vicissitudes of so many both principal and secondary characters, the poem requires a cinematic editing technique which allows the author to abandon one character or action-scene in order to turn to another. Such shifts sometimes occur without losing the continuity of the narrative, for instance when two characters meet and the story-line, which initially had been following the first character, pans away from him to follow the second. On other occasions, there is a clean break and the action is interrupted right in the middle of a canto. Usually it is the last couplet of the octave which intimates the interruption or delay in the plot, a rhymed couplet like the following:

> Segue Rinaldo, e d'ira si distrugge:
> ma seguitiamo Angelica che fugge.
> (Rinaldo is in pursuit, consumed with anger; but let us follow Angelica who is fleeing.)

or:

> Lasciànlo andar, che farà buon camino,
> e torniamo a Rinaldo paladino.
> (Let us leave him now, for he will make good progress, and instead go back to the paladin Rinaldo.)

or again:

> Ma tempo è ormai di ritrovar Ruggiero
> che scorre il ciel su l'animal leggiero.
> (But now is the time to go back and find Ruggiero, who is scurrying over the sky on the winged horse.)

While such shifts in the action take place in the middle of a canto, the close of every single canto promises that the story will continue in the following one. Here too the explanatory function is usually assigned to the final rhymed couplet which rounds off the last octave:

> Come a Parigi appropinquosse, e quanto
> Carlo aiutò, vi dirà l'altro canto.
> (How he came to Paris and how much help he gave Charlemagne will be told in the next canto.)

Often in order to conclude the canto Ariosto pretends once more that he is
a bard reciting his verses before a courtly audience:

Non più, Signor, non più di questo canto;
ch'io son già rauco, e vo' posarmi alquanto.
(No more, my lord, no more of this canto, for I am now hoarse, and want to
have some rest.)

Either that or – although this happens more rarely – he pretends that he is
in the physical act of writing:

Poi che da tutti i lati ho pieno il foglio,
finire il canto, e riposar mi voglio.
(Since I have filled the sheet of paper all over, I want to end the canto and go
and have some rest.)

So it is impossible to give a single definition of the structure of the *Orlando
Furioso*, because the poem possesses no rigid geometry. We could resort to
the image of an energy field which continually generates from within itself
other force fields. However we define it, the movement is always
centrifugal; right from the outset we are immediately in the middle of the
action, but this is true both for the poem as a whole as well as for each
canto and each episode.

The problem with every introduction to the *Furioso* is that if one starts
by saying 'This is a poem which is in fact a continuation of another poem,
which in turn continues a cycle of countless other poems . . .', the reader is
immediately turned off: if before starting this poem, the reader has to know
what happened in all the preceding poems, as well as in those that preceded
the preceding poems, when will it ever be possible to start Ariosto's poem?
But in fact every introduction turns out to be superfluous: the *Furioso* is a
book unique in its genre and can, or perhaps I should say must, be read
without reference to any other text that either precedes or follows it. It is a
self-contained universe, across whose length and breadth the reader can
roam, entering, exiting, getting lost.

The fact that Ariosto makes us believe that the construction of this
universe is nothing but a continuation of someone else's work, an
appendix, or as he himself terms it a 'gionta' or addition, can be interpreted
as a sign of Ariosto's extraordinary discretion, an instance of what the

English call 'understatement', that is to say that particular form of self-irony which leads us to downplay things that are actually enormously important. But it can also be seen as a sign of a conception of time and space which rejects the closed paradigm of the Ptolemaic universe, and opens itself towards the infinity of both past and future, as well as towards an endless plurality of worlds.

From its opening words the *Furioso* presents itself as the poem of movement, or rather it presents a particular type of movement which will inform the poem's entire length: a zig-zag. We could trace the general outline of the poem by following the constant intersections and divergences of these lines on a map of Europe and Africa, but the first canto alone is enough to give us its flavour: there three knights pursue Angelica through the wood, in a convoluted dance consisting of losing the way, chance encounters, mistaken paths, and changes of plan.

It is this zig-zag traced by the galloping horses and by the oscillations of the human heart that introduces us into the spirit of the poem. The pleasure deriving from the rapidity of the action instantly blends with a sense of breadth in the amount of time and space available. This aimless wandering is inherent not just in the knights but also in Ariosto himself: it is almost as if the poet when beginning the narration does not yet know at the start of the narration the direction the plot will take, though subsequently it will guide him as though perfectly planned. Yet he has one thing totally clear in his mind: his own mixture of narrative élan and informality, what we might define, to use an adjective loaded with meaning, as the 'errant' movement of Ariosto's poem.

These characteristics of Ariosto's 'space' in the poem can be perceived either on the scale of the whole poem, or in individual canti, or on an even more minute scale in each stanza or even each line. The ottava is the unit in which it is easiest to recognise what is distinctive about his poetry: Ariosto is relaxed in the ottava, he feels at home in it, and the miracle of his poetry resides above all in this nonchalance.

This is so for two reasons above all. One is intrinsic to the ottava itself, in that it is a stanza which can handle even lengthy speeches as well as an alternation of sublime, lyric tones with more prosaic, humorous notes. The other reason is inherent in Ariosto's method of writing poetry, which is not bounded by limits of any kind: unlike Dante, he has not set himself a rigid division of subject-matter, nor any rules of symmetry which would force him to write a set number of canti or set number of stanzas in each canto.

In the *Furioso* the shortest canto contains 72 stanzas, the longest 199. The poet can take things easy if he wants, using several stanzas to say something which others could say in a single line, or he can concentrate into a single verse something that could be the subject of a lengthy discourse.

The secret of Ariosto's ottava resides in his following the varied rhythm of the spoken language, in the profusion of what De Sanctis called the 'inessential accessories of language', as well as in the swiftness of his ironic asides. But the colloquial is only one of the many registers he deploys, which extend from the lyric to the tragic and sententious and which can all coexist in the same stanza. Ariosto can be of memorable concision, and many of his verses have become proverbial: 'Ecco il giudicio uman come spesso erra!' (This is how human judgment errs so often!) or 'Oh gran bontà de' cavallieri antiqui!' (Oh the wonderful goodness of the ancient knights!). But it is not only with such asides that he executes his changes of speed. It has to be said that the very structure of the ottava is based on a discontinuity of rhythm: the first six lines linked by just two alternating rhymes are then followed by a rhyming couplet, which produces an effect which today we would term *anticlimax*, a brusque shift not only in rhythm but also in the psychological and intellectual atmosphere, from the sophisticated to the popular, from the evocative to the comic.

Of course Ariosto plays with these contours of the ottava as the expert he is, but the play could become monotonous without the agility of the poet in giving movement to the stanza, introducing pauses and full stops in varying positions, adapting different syntactic structures to the metre, alternating long and short sentences, splitting the stanza in two or in some cases tagging another stanza on to the first, constantly changing the narrative tenses, switching from the remote past tense to the imperfect, the present, then the future, in short creating a whole array of narrative planes and perspectives.

This freedom and ease of movement which we have noted in his versification dominates even more at the level of narrative structure and composition of plot. There are, as we all remember, two main themes: the first tells how Orlando from being merely the hapless lover of Angelica went furiously mad, how the Christian armies without the presence of their hero risked losing France to the Saracens, and how the madman's wits were recovered by Astolfo on the Moon, and then forced back into the body of their rightful owner, thus allowing him to take his place again in the army ranks. Parallel to this runs the second plot, that of the predestined but constantly deferred love of Ruggiero, champion of the Saracen camp, for the Christian female warrior Bradamante, and of all the obstacles that come between them and their destined marriage, until Ruggiero manages to change sides, be baptised and win the hand of his warrior lover. The Ruggiero-Bradamante plot is no less important than the Orlando-Angelica one, because it is from them that Ariosto (like Boiardo before him) claims that the Este family descends, thus not only justifying the poem in the eyes of his patrons, but above all linking the mythical period of chivalry with the contemporary history of Ferrara and Italy. The two main plots and their countless ramifications thus proceed intertwined, but they also develop in turn around the more strictly epic trunk of the poem, namely the course of the war between the Emperor Charlemagne and Agramante, king of Africa. This epic contest is concentrated particularly in a block of canti which deal with the siege of Paris by the Moors, the Christian counter-offensive, and the discord in Agramante's camp. The siege of Paris is in a sense the poem's centre of gravity, just as the city of Paris presents itself as its geographical 'navel':

Siede Parigi in una gran pianura
ne l'ombelico a Francia, anzi nel cuore;
gli passa la riviera entro le mura
e corre et esce in altra parte fuore:
ma fa un'isola prima, e v'assecura
de la città una parte, e la migliore;
l'altre due (ch'in tre parti è la gran terra)
di fuor la fossa, e dentro il fiume serra.

Alla città che molte miglia gira
da molte parti si può dar battaglia;
ma perché sol da un canto assalir mira,
né volentier l'esercito sbarraglia,
oltre il fiume Agramante si ritira
verso ponente, acciò che quindi assaglia;
però che né cittade né campagna
ha dietro (se non sua) fino alla Spagna. (14.104–105)
(Paris stands in a huge plain, in the navel, or rather in the heart of France.
The river passes between its walls, flows and comes out the other side; but
before that it forms an island, and there makes safe one part, the best part, of

the city. As for the other two parts (for the great town is divided into three), they are locked in by the moat on the outside and the river within.

The city, which extends for many miles, can be attacked on many sides; but since Agramante wants to concentrate his assault on one side, and does not wish to expose his army to any danger, he retreats beyond the river towards the West in order to attack from there, for he has now neither city nor country behind him (except those on his side) all the way to Spain.)

From what I have said it might be thought that the journeys of all the main protagonists end up converging on Paris. But this does not happen: the majority of the most famous champions are absent from this collective epic episode. Only the giant mass of Rodomonte towers above the mêlée here. Where on earth are all the others?

It has to be said that the poem's space also contains another centre of gravity, a negative centre though, a trap, a kind of vortex which swallows up the principal characters one by one: the wizard Atlante's magic castle. Atlante's magic delights in architectural illusions: already in canto 4 it raises a castle entirely made out of steel in the hilltops of the Pyrenees, only to have it dissolve again into nothing; between canti 12 and 22 we see arise, not far from the Channel coast, a castle which is an empty vortex, in which all the images of the poem are refracted.

Orlando himself, while pursuing Angelica, happens to fall victim to its spell, a pattern which is repeated in almost identical terms for each of these gallant knights: he sees his beloved being carried off, pursues her captor, enters a mysterious palace, and wanders aimlessly through halls and deserted corridors. In other words, the palace is devoid of what they seek, and is populated only by those in pursuit.

Those wandering through loggias and passageways, rummaging beneath tapestries and canopies are the most famous of Christian and Moorish knights: they have all been lured into the castle by the vision of a beloved woman, or an enemy who is just out of reach, or a stolen horse, or a lost object. And now they can no longer leave those walls: if one of them tries to leave, he hears someone calling him back, turns round and the apparition he has sought in vain is there, the damsel in distress he has to save has appeared at a window, imploring his help. Atlante has created this kingdom of illusion; if life is always varied, unpredictable, and changing, illusion is monotonous, hammering away at the same obsession. Desire is a race towards the void, Atlante's spell concentrates all unsatisfied desires within the enclosure of a labyrinth, but does not alter the rules that govern men's movements in the open spaces of the poem and the world.

Astolfo also ends up in the palace pursuing – or thinking he is pursuing – a young peasant who has stolen his horse Rabicano. But there is no spell that will work on Astolfo. He possesses a magic book which explains everything about that kind of castle. He goes straight to the marble stone on the threshold: all he has to do is to lift it and the castle will go up in smoke. But just at that moment he is joined by a crowd of knights: nearly all of them are his friends, but instead of welcoming him, they stand in front of him as though wanting to run him through with their swords. What has happened? The wizard Atlante, defending himself in dire straits, has resorted to a last magic spell: he has made Astolfo appear to the various prisoners of the castle as the last person they had been pursuing when each of them entered the palace. But all Astolfo has to do is to sound his horn to dispel both the magician and his magic along with the victims of his spells. The castle, a cobweb of dreams, desires and jealousies, dissolves: that is to say, it ceases to be a space outside ourselves, with gates, stairways and walls, and recedes inside our minds, into the labyrinth of our thoughts. Atlante then restores to the characters that he had kidnapped free rein through the ways of the poem. Atlante or Ariosto? In fact the castle turns out to be a crafty structural device for the narrator, who because of the physical impossibility of developing simultaneously a large number of parallel plots, feels the need to remove characters from the action for the duration of a number of canti, setting aside a number of cards in order to continue his game and to bring them out at the appropriate moment. The magician who wants to delay the fulfilment of destiny and the poet-tactician who alternately multiplies and reduces the threads of the characters he deploys on the field, now grouping them together, now dispersing them, blend into one another until they are inseparable.

The forty-sixth and last canto opens with the list of a crowd of people who constitute the public for whom Ariosto thought he was writing his poem. This is the real dedication of the *Furioso*, much more so than the obligatory nod in the direction of his patron Cardinal Ippolito d'Este, the 'generosa erculea prole' (noble descendant of Hercules) to whom the poem is addressed, at the opening of the first canto. The boat of the poem is now coming into harbour, and waiting for him there on the pier are the most beautiful and noble women of the Italian cities along with their knights, poets and intellectuals. What Ariosto gives us here is nothing short of a roll-call of names and brief profiles of his friends and contemporaries: it is a definition of his ideal literary public, as well as an image of a model society. Through a kind of structural reversal, the poem steps out of itself and examines itself through the eyes of its readers, defining itself through this roll-call of those to whom it is addressed. And in turn it is the poem which acts as a definition or emblem for the society of present and future readers, for the entirety of people who will participate in its game and who will recognise themselves in it.

[1974]

Brief Anthology of
Octaves from Ariosto

On this, the 500th anniversary of Ariosto's birth, I have been asked what the *Orlando Furioso* has meant for me. But saying where, how and how much my predilection for this poem has left traces in my writings would force me to go back to work already done, whereas the Ariostan spirit for me has always meant thrusting forward, not turning back. In any case, I feel that such evidence of my predilection is so obvious that the reader will find it unaided. I prefer to use the opportunity to go through the poem again, and to attempt to select a personal anthology of octaves, guided both by memory and by chance reading.

The quintessence of Ariosto's spirit lies for me in the lines which introduce a new adventure. On several occasions, this situation is signalled by a boat approaching a riverbank on which the hero happens to be (9.9):

Con gli occhi cerca or questo lato or quello
lungo le ripe il paladin, se vede
(quando né pesce egli non è, né augello)
come abbia a por ne l'altra ripa il piede:
et ecco a sé venir vede un battello,
su le cui poppe una donzella siede,
che di voler a lui venir fa segno;
né lascia poi ch'arrivi a terra il legno.
(The knight was searching with his eyes the whole riverbank to find some way
(since he was neither fish nor bird) to cross to the opposite bank, when suddenly
he saw a boat coming towards him, with a woman sitting at its stern gesturing
that she wanted to come to him, but without letting the boat reach the bank.)

A study which I would like to have carried out, and which, if I do not manage it, someone else can do in my place, concerns this situation: a seashore or riverbank, a person on the bank, a boat a little way off, bringing news or an encounter which will initiate the new adventure. (Sometimes the situation is reversed: the hero is on the boat and the encounter is with someone on land.) A survey of the passages which contain similar situations would culminate with an ottava of purely verbal abstraction that amounts almost to a limerick (30.10):

> Quindi partito venne ad una terra
> Zizera detta, che siede allo stretto
> di Zibeltarro, o vuoi Zibelterra,
> che l'uno o l'altro nome le vien detto;
> ove una barca che sciogliea da terra
> vide piena di gente da diletto
> che solazzando all'aura mattutina,
> gía per la tranquillissima marina.
> (Leaving this place, he came to a land known as Algeçiras, which lies at the Straits of Gibraltar, or if you prefer Gibalterre, since both names are used of the place; there he saw a boat setting sail, full of people bent on relaxation, enjoying the morning breeze and cutting through the calmest of seas.)

This brings me to another research topic I would like to investigate, but which has already been studied: place-names in the *Furioso*, which always carry with them a hint of the nonsensical. It is above all English place-names that supply the verbal material with which Ariosto most enjoys playing, thus qualifying him for the title of the earliest Anglophile in Italian literature. In particular one could illustrate how names with exotic sounds set in motion a mechanism of exotic images. For instance, in the heraldic puzzles of canto 10 we find visions like those in the style of Raymond Roussel (10.81):

> Il falcon che sul nido i vanni inchina,
> porta Raimondo, il conte di Devonia.
> Il giallo e il negro ha quel di Vigorina;
> il can quel d'Erba; un orso quel d'Osonia.
> La croce che là vedi cristallina,
> è del ricco prelato di Battonia.
> Vedi nel bigio una spezzata sedia:
> è del duca Ariman di Sormosedia.

(The falcon lowering its wings over the nest is worn by Raymond, Count of Devon. The or and sable crest belongs to the Earl of Winchester; the dog to the Earl of Derby; the bear to the Earl of Oxford. The crystalline cross you see there is that of the rich Bishop of Bath. And that broken chair you see against the grey background belongs to Duke Hariman of Somerset.)

Talking of unusual rhymes, I cannot omit canto 32 stanza 63, in which Bradamante moves from the world of African place-names to the winter storms which envelop the Queen of Iceland's castle. In a poem which generally has a stable climate like the *Furioso*, this episode – which opens with the most dramatic drop in temperature found in the space of a single octave – stands out for its rainy atmosphere:

> *Leva al fin gli occhi, e vede il sol che 'l tergo*
> *avea mostrato alle città di Bocco,*
> *e poi s'era attuffato, come il mergo,*
> *in grembo alla nutrice oltr'a Marocco:*
> *e se disegna che la frasca albergo*
> *le dia ne' campi, fa pensier di sciocco;*
> *che soffia un vento freddo, e l'aria grieve*
> *pioggia la notte le minaccia o nieve.*
> *(Finally she looks up and sees that the sun has now gone behind King Bocchus' Mauritanian cities, and then plunged itself, like some diving bird, into the bosom of the all-nourishing sea beyond Morocco; but if she thinks that she will find shelter enough sleeping out in the open brushwood, this is a foolish thought: for a cold wind is blowing, and the air is heavy, threatening rain or snow by nightfall.)*

The most complicated metaphor belongs, I would say, to the register of Petrarchan love-lyric, but Ariosto injects into it all his need for dynamic motion, so that this ottava seems to me to hold the record for maximum spatial dislocation in describing a character's feelings:

> *Ma di che debbo lamentarmi, ahi lassa,*
> *fuor che del mio desire irrazionale?*
> *ch'alto mi leva, e sí nell'aria passa,*
> *ch'arriva in parte ove s'abbrucia l'ale;*

poi non potendo sostener, mi lassa
dal ciel cader: né qui finisce il male;
che le rimette, e di nuovo arde: ond'io
non ho mai fine al precipizio mio.
(But alas, what should I blame except my irrational desire? It lifts me so aloft,
and flies so high in the sky that it reaches the sphere of fire which scorches its
wings; then unable to bear me up, it drops me from the sky. But this is not the
end of my ordeal, for it sprouts wings anew, and is burned again, so there is
never any end to my rise and fall.)

I have not yet exemplified an erotic ottava, but the most outstanding
examples are all too well known; and if I wanted to choose something less
predictable, I would end up fixing on something rather heavy. The truth is
that in the most sexually charged moments Ariosto, a true inhabitant of the
Po valley, loses his touch and the tension goes. Even in the episode with
the most subtle erotic effects, the canto of Fiordispina and Ricciardetto
(canto 25), the finesse resides more in the story and its overall frisson than
in any isolated stanza. The best I can do is to cite a proliferation of limbs
intertwined like something in a Japanese print:

Non con più nodi i flessuosi acanti
le colonne circondano e le travi,
di quelli con che noi legammo stretti
e colli e fianchi e braccia e gambe e petti.
(Winding acanthus never surrounded columns and rafters with more knots
than those with which we tightly bound our necks and sides and arms and legs
and breasts.)

The truly erotic moment for Ariosto is not so much one of fulfilment as
one of anticipation, of initial trepidation, of foreplay. That is when he
reaches the heights. The undressing of Alcina is very famous but never fails
to leave the reader breathless (7.28):

ben che né gonna né faldiglia avesse;
che venne avvolta in un leggier zendado
che sopra una camicia ella si messe,
bianca e suttil nel più escellente grado.
Come Ruggier abbracciò lei, gli cesse

il manto; e restò il vel suttile e rado,
che non copria dinanzi né di dietro,
piú che le rose o i gigli un chiaro vetro.
(but she wore no skirt or petticoat; instead she came clothed in a light silk wrap
which she had put over a shift that was white and transparent and of the
highest quality. As soon as Ruggiero embraced her, her wrap came off, and she
was left in the thin, see-through shift which offered no more covering either in
front or behind than clear glass does to roses or lilies.)

The female nude preferred by Ariosto has none of the Renaissance fondness for exuberance: it could easily be part of the present taste for adolescent physiques, with their hint of cold whiteness. I would say that the movement of the octave approaches the nude like a lens going over a miniature but then departing, leaving everything rather vague. Staying with the most obvious examples, in that mixture of landscape and nude study that is the Olimpia episode, it is the landscape which wins out over the naked body (11.68):

Vinceano di candor le nievi intatte,
et eran piú ch'avorio a toccar molli:
le poppe ritondette parean latte
che fuor di giunchi allora allora tolli.
Spazio fra lor tal discendea, qual fatte
esser veggiàn fra piccolini colli
l'ombrose valli, in sua stagione amene,
che 'l verno abbia di nieve allora piene.
(Her skin outdid virgin snow in its whiteness and it was smoother to the touch
than ivory: her little round breasts were like fresh mozzarellas. The space
between them was like the shady valleys we see between gentle hills, in early
spring, which winter has filled with snow.)

These shifts towards vagueness cannot blind us to the fact that precision is one of the chief poetic values cultivated by Ariosto's narrative verse. In order to document how much richness of detail and technical precision an octave can contain, one has only to choose from the duel scenes. I shall limit myself to this stanza from the final canto (46.126):

Quel gli urta il destrier contra, ma Ruggiero
lo cansa accortamente, e si ritira,
e nel passare, al fren piglia il destriero
con la man manca, e intorno lo raggira;
e con la destra intanto il cavalliero
ferire al fianco o il ventre o il petto mira;
e di due punte fé sentirgli angoscia,
l'una nel fianco, e l'altra ne la coscia.
(Rodomonte charges his horse against him, but Ruggiero, on foot, cleverly
avoids it, and stepping aside grabs the horse's reins with his left hand, and
turns it round. At the same time, with his sword in his right hand, he aims
blows at his enemy's side, stomach or breast; and in fact makes him feel the
pain of two sharp jabs, one in the side and the other in the thigh.)

But there is another type of precision which one must not ignore: that of reasoning, the argumentation that unfolds within the enclosure of metrical form, which he articulates in the most detailed way, attentive to every implication. The maximum agility, of a type I would define as almost forensic, is to be found in the defence which Rinaldo, like a skilful lawyer, conducts against the crime passionnel of which Ginevra is accused, when he does not know whether she is guilty or innocent (4.65):

Non vo' già dir ch'ella non l'abbia fatto;
che nol sappendo, il falso dir potrei:
dirò ben che non de' per simil atto
punizión cader alcuna in lei;
e dirò che fu ingiusto o che fu matto
chi fece prima li statuti rei;
e come iniqui rivocar si denno,
e nuova legge far con miglior senno.
(Now I am not saying she did not commit this act, for since I do not know the
facts for sure, I might then be saying something false; but I will certainly say
that no punishment must fall on her for such an act, that he who first framed
these evil laws was either unjust or mad, and that as unjust laws they must be
revoked, and a new law passed with wiser counsel.)

The last thing I should exemplify is the violent ottava, one which contains maximum slaughter. Here there is an embarrassment of choice: sometimes it is the same formulae, indeed even the same verses, which are repeated or simply reordered. At a first, cursory glance, I would say that the record in the violence quotient for a single stanza is to be found in the *Cinque canti* (4.7):

> *Due ne partí fra la cintura e l'anche:*
> *restâr le gambe in sella e cadde il busto;*
> *da la cima del capo un divise anche*
> *fin su l'arcion, ch'andò in pezzi giusto;*
> *tre ferí su le spalle o destre o manche;*
> *e tre volte uscí il colpo acre e robusto*
> *sotto la poppa dal contrario lato:*
> *dieci passò da l'uno a l'altro lato.*
> *(He sliced two of them between the belt and the hips: their legs remained in the saddle while their upper half fell down; another one he split from the top of the head down to his seat, which then fell cleanly into two pieces; he struck three others in the back, either on the right or left shoulders, and in these three cases the strong, painful lance-blow emerged on the other side under their nipple; ten others he ran through from one side to another.)*

We note immediately that this homicidal fury has caused damage the author did not foresee: the repetition of the rhyme-word *lato* without it having a different meaning is clearly an oversight which the poet did not have time to correct. Actually, if one looks carefully, in the context of this catalogue of wounds which fills the stanza, the entire final line turns out to be a repetition, since being run through with a lance has already been exemplified. Unless this fine distinction is implied: while it is clear that the three preceding victims are run through back to front, the last ten victims could present a less usual case of lateral run-through, the lance going through from side to side not back to front. The use of *lato* (side) seems more appropriate in the last line if it is used in the sense of *fianco* (hip). Instead in the penultimate line *lato* could have been easily replaced by another word in '-ato' such as *costato* (ribcage): 'sotto la poppa al mezzo del costato' (under the nipple in the middle of the ribcage), a correction which Ariosto could not have failed to make had he continued to work on what are now known as the *Cinque canti*.

With this modest contribution towards Ariosto's work in progress, expressed in a spirit of friendliness, I close my homage to the poet.

[1975]

Gerolamo Cardano

What is Hamlet reading when he comes on stage in Act 2? To Polonius, who asks him this, he replies 'words, words, words', and our curiosity remains unsatisfied. However, if the 'To be or not to be' soliloquy, which opens the Prince of Denmark's next appearance on stage, offers any clue as to his recent readings, it ought to be a book which discusses death as though it were sleep, whether visited or not by dreams.

Now this theme is discussed in considerable detail in a passage of Gerolamo Cardano's *De Consolatione*, which was translated into English in 1573 and dedicated to the Earl of Oxford, therefore familiar in circles frequented by Shakespeare. Amongst other things, it says, 'Certainly the sweetest sleep is the deepest sleep, when we are almost like the dead, not dreaming anything; whereas the most irksome sleep is the one that is very light, restless, interrupted by constant waking, tormented by nightmares and visions, as happens to those who are ill'.

To conclude from this that the book read by Hamlet is definitely Cardano, as is held by some scholars of Shakespeare's sources, is perhaps unjustified. And certainly that little ethical treatise is not sufficiently representative of Cardano's genius to become evidence for Shakespeare ever having encountered his work. However, that passage does discuss dreams and this is no accident: Cardano returns insistently to dreams, especially his own, in several passages of his works, describing, interpreting and commenting on them. This is not only because in Cardano the factual observation of the scientist and the reasoning of the mathematician somehow derive from a life dominated by premonitions, signs of astrological destiny, magic influences, and diabolical interventions, but also because his mind refuses to exclude any phenomenon from objective enquiry, least of all those that surface from the deepest wells of subjectivity.

It is possible that some of the restlessness of Cardano the man comes across in the English translation of his rather awkward Latin. In that case it is highly significant that if it is Cardano's European reputation – Cardano was famous as a medical man, but his works embrace all branches of knowledge and enjoyed considerable posthumous popularity – which authorises the link between him and Shakespeare, it does so actually on the periphery of his scientific interests, in that vague territory which will be later thoroughly traversed by the pioneering experts in psychology, introspection and existential anguish. These were the areas into which Cardano probed in an epoch in which this branch of knowledge did not even have a name; nor did his enquiries have a clear objective, but were merely driven by an obscure but constant inner necessity.

This is what makes us feel close to Gerolamo Cardano, today on the fourth centenary of his death. But this is not to take anything away from the importance of his discoveries, inventions and intuitions which ensure that his name figures in the history of science as one of the founding fathers of various disciplines. Nor does it detract from his fame as a magus, a man endowed with mysterious powers, a reputation that followed him around but which he himself also broadly cultivated, and which was at times the object of his boasts, at times the source of his own apparent amazement.

His autobiography, De Propria Vita, which Cardano wrote in Rome shortly before his death, is the book which keeps his name alive for us both as a writer and as a personality. He was a writer manqué at least as far as Italian literature is concerned, because if he had tried to express himself in the vernacular (and it would certainly have been an Italian as rough and ungainly as Leonardo's), instead of doggedly composing all his works in Latin (he felt that only Latin could guarantee immortality), sixteenth-century Italian literature would have had not another classic writer, but another weird one, though one that was all the more representative of his age for being eccentric. Instead, adrift as he is on the high seas of Renaissance Latin, he is now read only by scholars: not that his Latin is as clumsy as his critics claimed (in fact the more elliptical and idiosyncratic his style, the more pleasant it is to read him), but because it forces us to read him through a glass darkly, as it were. (The most recent Italian translation is, I believe, the one published in 1945 in Einaudi's Universale series.)

Cardano wrote not just because he was a scientist who had to communicate the results of his research, or a polygraph bent on contributing to a universal encyclopedia, or a compulsive scribbler obsessed with filling page after page, but also because he was a genuine writer, who tried to capture with words something that appeared to elude them. Here is a passage about childhood memories which would merit a place in any future anthology of 'precursors of Proust': it is a description of visions or daydream rêveries or flights of fancy or psychedelic hallucinations to which he was subject – when he was aged between four and seven – when he stayed in bed in the morning. Cardano tries to provide the precisest possible record both of this inexplicable phenomenon and of the state of mind in which he watched this 'diverting spectacle'.

I saw aery images which seemed to be composed of tiny rings, like those in chain mail (lorica), even though I had never seen them at that age. They rose from the right-hand corner of the bed, ascending slowly from the bottom to form a semicircle and then descending to the left-hand corner where they disappeared: castles, houses, animals, knights on horseback, blades of grass, trees, musical instruments, theatres, men dressed in different guises, particularly trumpeters playing their trumpets, though no sound or voice could be heard, and then soldiers, crowds, fields, shapes I had never seen before, woods and forests, a whole range of things which flowed past without merging into each other but instead seeming to jostle each other. Diaphanous figures, but not like empty, non-existent forms: rather they were at once both transparent and opaque, shapes which lacked only colour to make them perfect, but which yet were not only made up of air. I used to enjoy gazing at these spectacles so much that once my aunt asked me: 'What are you looking at?' and I refused to answer, afraid that if I spoke, the source of these displays, whatever it was, might be annoyed and stop the entertainment.

This passage comes in the autobiography in a chapter dealing with the dreams and other unusual physical features he was heir to: being born with long hair, the cold of his legs at night, his hot sweats in the morning, the recurrent dream of a cockerel which seemed permanently on the verge of uttering some dire warning, the moon he saw shining in front of him every time he looked up from the page he was writing after solving a difficult problem, his emission of sulphurous or incense-filled odours, the fact that whenever he was in a fight he was never wounded, nor wounded other people or even saw others being wounded, so that once he realised he had this gift (which however did not work on several occasions) he would fling himself fearlessly into every quarrel and riot.

His autobiography is dominated by a constant preoccupation with himself, with the uniqueness of his own person and destiny, totally conforming to the astrological belief which held that the sum of disparate particulars which make up the individual finds its origin and raison d'être in the configuration of the sky at the moment of birth.

Thin and unhealthy, Cardano was triply concerned with his own health: as a doctor, as an astrologer, and as a hypochondriac, or as we would say now, as someone with a psychosomatic condition. As a result the clinical chart he has left us is extremely detailed, ranging from lengthy life-threatening illnesses to the tiniest spots on his face.

This is the subject matter of one of the first chapters of *De Propria Vita*, which is a biography constructed around themes: there are chapters on his parents ('mater fuit iracunda, memoria et ingenio pollens, parvae staturae, pinguis, pia' (my mother was an irascible woman with a powerful memory and intellect, small in stature, fat and pious)), his birth and star sign, a physical self-portrait (which is meticulous, ruthless and complacent in a kind of inverted narcissism), his diet and physical routine, his virtues and vices, his favourite things, his consuming passion for gaming (dice, cards, chess), his manner of dress, his gait, his religion and other devout practices, houses he lived in, poverty and losses to the family patrimony, risks taken and accidents, books written, the most successful diagnoses and therapies of his medical career, and so on.

The chronological account of his life occupies just one chapter, not very much for such an incident-packed existence. But many episodes are recounted at greater length in various chapters of the book, from his adventures as a gambler both in his youth (including how he managed to escape with the help of his sword from the house of a Venetian patrician card-sharp) and when a grown man (at that time chess was played for money and he was such an invincible chessplayer that he was tempted to abandon medicine to earn a living from gaming), to his amazing journey across Europe as far as Scotland where an archbishop who suffered from asthma was waiting for him to cure him (after several unsuccessful attempts, Cardano managed to improve the archbishop's condition by forbidding him the use of his feather pillow and mattress), to the tragedy of his son who was beheaded for killing his wife.

Cardano wrote over 200 works of medicine, mathematics, physics, philosophy, religion and music. (It was only the figurative arts that he steered clear of, almost as if the shade of Leonardo da Vinci, a spirit who resembled his own in so many other ways, was enough for that area.) He also wrote a eulogy of the Emperor Nero, and an encomium of gout, as well as a treatise on spelling and one on gambling (*De Ludo Aleae*). This last work is also important as the first text on probability theory: hence the attention devoted to it in an American book which, leaving aside its more technical chapters, is extremely informative and enjoyable, and is, I think, still the most recent monograph on Cardano to this day (Oystein Ore, *Cardano, The Gambling Scholar*, Princeton, 1953).

'The gambling scholar': was that Cardano's secret? Certainly his life and works seem to be a succession of games involving risk, and the possibility of losing as much as winning. Renaissance science no longer seems to be for Cardano a harmonious unity of macrocosm and microcosm, but rather a constant interaction of 'chance and necessity' which is refracted in the infinite variety of things, and in the irreducible uniqueness of individuals and phenomena. The new direction of human knowledge had by now begun, aimed as it was at deconstructing the world bit by bit rather than at holding it together.

'This goodly frame, the earth,' says Hamlet, with this book in his hand, 'seems to me a sterile promontory; this most excellent canopy, the air, look you, this brave o'erhanging firmament, this majestical roof fretted with golden fire, why it appears no other thing to me than a foul and pestilent congregation of vapours . . .'

[1976]

The Book of Nature in Galileo

The most famous metaphor in Galileo – and one which contains within itself the kernel of the new philosophy – is that of the book of Nature written in mathematical language.

> *Philosophy is written in this enormous book which is continually open before our eyes (I mean the universe), but it cannot be understood unless one first understands the language and recognises the characters with which it is written. It is written in a mathematical language, and its characters are triangles, circles, and other geometric figures. Without knowledge of this medium it is impossible to understand a single word of it; without this knowledge it is like wandering hopelessly through a dark labyrinth. (Il saggiatore (The Assayer), 6)*

This image of the book of the world already had a long history before Galileo, from the medieval philosophers to Nicholas Cusanus and Montaigne, and it was used by contemporaries of Galileo such as Francis Bacon and Tommaso Campanella. Amongst Campanella's poems, published the year before Galileo's *Il saggiatore*, there is a sonnet that begins with these words: 'Il mondo è il libro dove senno eterno, scrive i propri concetti' (The world is the book in which eternal wisdom writes its own ideas).

Already in his *Istoria e dimostrazioni intorno alle macchie solari* (*The History and Proof of the Spots on the Sun*) (1613), that is to say ten years before *Il saggiatore*, Galileo had contrasted direct reading (of the book of the world) with indirect reading (of the books of Aristotle). This passage is extremely interesting because in it Galileo describes Arcimboldo's paintings, offering critical judgements which remain valid for painting in general (and which provide evidence of his links with Florentine artists such as Ludovico Cigoli), and in particular providing reflections on combinatory systems which can be put alongside those which will be cited later on.

The only people who oppose this point of view are a few rigid defenders of philosophical minutiae. These people, as far as I can see, have been brought up and nourished from the very start of their education in this opinion, namely that philosophy is and can be nothing other than continuous study of such texts of Aristotle as can be immediately collected in great numbers from different sources and stuck together to resolve whatever problem is posed. They never want to raise their eyes from these pages as though this great book of the world was not written by nature to be read by others apart from Aristotle, and as though his eyes could see for the whole of posterity after him. Those who impose such strict laws on themselves remind me of those whimsical painters who as a game set themselves constraints such as that of deciding to depict a human face or some other figure by simply juxtaposing agricultural implements or fruits or flowers of different seasons. All of this bizarre art is fine and gives pleasure as long as it is done for amusement, and it proves that one artist is more perceptive than another, depending on whether he has been able to choose more suitably and use a particular fruit for the part of the body to be depicted. But if someone who had spent all his training in this kind of painting should then decide that in general any other form of painting is inferior and defective, certainly Cigoli and all other illustrious painters would laugh him to scorn.

The most original contribution made by Galileo to this metaphor of the book of the world is his emphasis on its special alphabet, on 'the characters with which it is written'. To be more precise, one could actually say that the real metaphorical link is not so much between world and book as between world and alphabet. In this passage from the second day of his *Dialogue Concerning the Two Chief World Systems*, it is the alphabet which is the world:

I have a little book which is considerably shorter than Aristotle and Ovid, which contains all sciences, and which with just a little study can allow others to form a perfect idea of it. This book is the alphabet, and there is no doubt that the person who knows how to put together and juxtapose this or that vowel with those or other consonants, will get the most accurate responses to all doubts and he will derive lessons pertaining to all the sciences and the arts. In exactly the same way the painter can choose from different primary colours set separately on his palette and by juxtaposing a little of one colour with a little of another can depict men, plants, buildings, birds, fishes; in short, he can represent all visible objects even though there are no eyes, feathers, scales, leaves or stones on the palette. In fact it is essential that none of the things to be represented, or even any part of them, should actually be there amongst the colours, if one wants to use them to depict all manner of things, because if there were on the palette, say, feathers, these could only be used to depict birds or plumage.

Thus when Galileo speaks of the alphabet, he means a combinatory system capable of representing everything in the universe. Here too we see him introducing the comparison with painting: the combination of the letters of the alphabet is the equivalent of the mixing of colours on the palette. It is clear that this is a combinatory system of a different order from that used in the paintings of Arcimboldo in the preceding quotation: a combination of objects which are already endowed with meaning (a painting by Arcimboldo, a *collage* or collection of feathers, a pastiche of quotations from Aristotle) cannot represent all of reality; in order to achieve this one needs to turn to a combinatory system of minimal elements such as primary colours or the letters of the alphabet.

In another passage in the *Dialogue* (at the end of the first day) in which there is a eulogy of the great inventions of the human spirit, the highest place is reserved for the alphabet:

But above all other wondrous inventions, what eminence of mind was his who first devised the way of communicating his innermost thoughts to any other person however distant in time or space? the way of communing with those in the Indies, with those who have not yet been born or with those who will come into being a thousand or ten thousand years hence? and consider how simple it is: merely the different combinations of twenty small characters on a page. This must be the most wonderful of all human inventions.

If we reread the passage from *Il saggiatore* which I quoted at the beginning in the light of this passage, we will understand more clearly how for Galileo mathematics, and in particular geometry, performs the function of an alphabet. This point is made very clearly in a letter to Fortunio Liceti written in January 1641 (a year before his death):

But I truthfully believe that the book of philosophy is the one which is permanently open before our eyes; but because it is written in different characters from those of our alphabet it cannot be read by everyone: and the characters of this book are triangles, squares, circles, spheres, cones, pyramids and other mathematical figures which are highly suited for just such a reading.

We notice that Galileo in his list of figures does not mention ellipses despite having read Kepler. Is it because in his combinatory system he has to start from the simplest forms? or because his battle against the Ptolemaic model is still being conducted within a classical idea of proportion and perfection where the circle and the sphere are the supreme images?

The problem of the alphabet of the book of nature is connected with that of the 'nobility' of forms, as can be seen in this passage from the dedication of the *Dialogue Concerning the Two Chief World Systems* to the Grand Duke of Tuscany:

Whoever aims higher stands out more eminently; and to turn to the great book of nature, which is the proper object of philosophy, is the way to raise your eyes. Although everything we read in this book, having been created by an omnipotent Demiurge, is therefore most proportionate, those things are even more perfect and worthy in which the labour and artifice appear greater to us. Amongst those physical objects that can be perceived, the setting up of the universe, in my view, can be given the first place: since it contains all things, it surpasses everything in size, and since it governs and maintains everything else, it must outstrip all other things in nobility. Consequently if anyone was destined to stand out in intellect far above all other men, it is Ptolemy and Copernicus since they read, and observed and philosophised on the constitution of the world.

A question that Galileo asks himself several times, to poke ironic fun at the old way of thinking, is this: regular, geometric forms must be considered more 'noble', more 'perfect' than natural, empirical, irregular forms, etc. It is particularly with regard to the irregularities of the moon that this question is discussed. There is a letter by Galileo to Gallanzone Gallanzoni which is entirely devoted to this subject, but the passage from *Il saggiatore* conveys the idea just as well:

As for me, I have never read the chronicles and particular genealogies of the forms, so I do not know which of them is more or less noble, or more or less perfect. But I believe that they are all ancient and noble in one way, or to be more precise, that they are neither noble and perfect nor ignoble and imperfect except in the sense that for building walls square shapes, I believe, are better than spherical ones, and for rolling or driving carts, round shapes are superior to triangular ones. But to return to Sarsi, he says that I supply him with ample arguments to prove the roughness of the concave surface of the sky, because I myself claim that the Moon and the other planets (they are also bodies, albeit heavenly ones, and even more noble than the sky itself) have a surface that is mountainous, rough and irregular; and if this is true, why can one not say that such irregularity can also be found in the body of the heavens? Here Sarsi himself can take as a reply what he would answer to someone who wanted to prove to him that the sea was full of bones and scales because whales, tuna and other fish are full of those things.

As a passionate geometer one would expect Galileo to champion the cause of geometric shapes, but as an observer of nature he rejects the idea of an abstract perfection and contrasts the image of the 'mountainous, rough and irregular' Moon with the purity of the heavens in Aristotelian and Ptolemaic cosmology.

Why should a sphere (or a pyramid) be more perfect than a natural shape, say that of a horse or a locust? This question recurs throughout the *Dialogue Concerning the Two Chief World Systems*. In this passage from the second day we find a comparison with the artist, in this case a sculptor:

That is the reason why I would like to know if it is equally difficult to represent the solid of some other shape, that is to say whether it is harder to try to shape a block of marble into a perfect sphere or perfect pyramid or into a perfect horse or perfect locust.

One of the finest and most important passages in the *Dialogue* comes in the first day, where we find the eulogy of the Earth as something subject to alteration, mutation and generation. Galileo evokes with terror the image of an Earth made of solid jasper or crystal, an incorruptible Earth, as though it had been petrified by Medusa:

I cannot hear without marvelling greatly, indeed without my intellect revolting at the concept, people attributing great nobility and perfection to the natural bodies that make up the universe just because they claim they are impassive, immutable, inalterable and so on, whereas they consider it to be a major imperfection if anything can change, grow, mutate and the like. As far as I am concerned, I consider that the Earth is most noble and admirable precisely because of the many different ways it endlessly changes, mutates and evolves. For if the Earth were not subject to any change and consisted entirely of a vast desert of sand or a mass of jasper, or if during the time of the flood the waters covering her surface had frozen and she had simply remained an immense crystal sphere, where nothing was ever born, changed or developed, I would consider the Earth a big but useless body in the universe, paralysed by inertia, and in short superfluous and unnatural: for me there would be the same difference as there is between a living and a dead creature. I feel exactly the same as regards the Moon, Jupiter and the other spheres in the cosmos. . . . Those who so exalt incorruptibility, unchangeability and the like, are, I think, reduced to saying such things both because of the inordinate desire they have to live for a long time and because of the terror they have of death; and they do not realise that if men were immortal, they would never have come into the world. Such people deserve to be exposed to the stare of a Gorgon's head which would turn them into statues of jasper or diamond, so they can become even more perfect than they are.

If one puts Galileo's passage about the alphabet of the book of Nature alongside this eulogy of the small changes and mutations of the Earth, one can see that the real opposition is between mobility and immobility, and it is against that image of the inalterability of Nature that Galileo campaigns, conjuring up the nightmare of the Gorgon. (This image and this topic were already present in Galileo's first astronomical work, *Istoria e dimostrazioni intorno alle macchie solari* (*The History and Proof of the Spots on the Sun*).) The geometric or mathematical alphabet of the book of Nature will be the weapon which – because of its capacity to be broken down into minimal elements and to represent all forms of movement and change – will abolish the opposition between the unchanging heavens and the elements of the Earth.

The philosophical thrust of this operation is well illustrated by this exchange in the *Dialogue* between the Ptolemaic supporter Simplicio and the author's spokesman Salviati, where the theme of 'nobility' surfaces once more:

SIMP. *This way of philosophising tends to subvert the whole of natural philosophy, as well as undermining the order of the heavens, the Earth and the whole universe. But I believe that the fundamental principles of the Peripatetics are such that there is no danger that by destroying their principles one can construct new sciences.*

SALV. *Don't worry about the heavens, the Earth, or their possible undermining, or even about philosophy itself, because as far as the heavens are concerned it is pointless for you to fear for something that you believe to be inalterable and impassive; and as for the Earth, we are seeking to raise her to even greater nobility and perfection by trying to regard her as similar to the heavenly bodies and in a certain sense to place her in the heavens, the place from whence your Aristotelian philosophers banished her.*

[1985]

Cyrano on the Moon

Just at the time when Galileo was clashing with the Papacy, a Parisian follower of his put forward an intriguing version of a heliocentric system: for him the universe was like an onion which 'protected by the hundreds of thin skins that surround it, conserves the precious bud from which tens of millions of other onions must draw their own essence ... The embryo inside this onion is the little Sun of this little world, which heats and nourishes the vegetative salt of the whole mass.'

With those millions of onions we move from the solar system to the system of infinite worlds put forward by Giordano Bruno: in fact all these heavenly bodies 'both visible and invisible, which are suspended in the blue of the universe, are nothing but the scum of the various suns as they purify themselves. For how could all these great fireballs exist unless they were fed by some substance which nourishes them?' This 'scumogenous' theory is not really so different from the explanation given by today's experts of how the planets formed together from the primordial nebula and how the stellar masses expand and contract: 'Every day the Sun discharges and purges itself of the remains of the matter which feeds its fire. But when it eventually consumes all the matter of which it consists, it will expand in all directions in search of other nourishment, spreading to all the worlds which it constructed in the past, particularly to those nearest it. Then that great ball of fire will melt all the spheres together and relaunch them all over the place as before, and having gradually purged itself of all imperfections will start to act once more as a Sun to those other planets which it will form by spouting them forth from within its own sphere.'

As for the Earth's movement, this is caused by the Sun's rays which 'when they strike the Earth make it spin with their circular motion, just as we get a top to spin by striking it with our hand'; or else it is caused by the Earth's own vapours which, having been first heated by the Sun, 'then struck by the cold of the polar regions fall back to Earth and being able only to strike it obliquely, thus make it go round'.

The imaginative cosmographer behind these theories is Savinien de Cyrano (1619–1655) – better known to us as Cyrano de Bergerac – and the work quoted from here is his *L'autre Monde, ou les États et Empires de la Lune* (*The Other World, or the States and Empires of the Moon*).

A forerunner of science fiction, Cyrano feeds his imaginings on the scientific knowledge of his time, as well as on Renaissance traditions of magic. In this way he comes up with prophetic ideas which only we three centuries later can appreciate as such: the movements of an astronaut free of the pull of gravity (he reaches space in the first place thanks to jars of dew which are attracted upwards by the Sun), rockets involving several stages, 'sound books' (the mechanism is wound up, a needle is placed on the required chapter, and then one can listen to the sound that emerges from a kind of mouth).

But his poetic imagination stems from a true cosmic sense which leads him to reproduce the emotional affirmations of Lucretius' atomist philosophy. Thus he celebrates the unity of all things, living or inanimate, and even Empedocles' four elements are but one single element, with atoms that are sometimes more rarefied and at other times more dense. 'You are amazed how this matter which is a purely haphazard mixture, and governed only by chance, can have produced a human being, since there were so many things essential to the construction of man's being, but you are not aware that hundreds of millions of times this same matter, when it was on the brink of producing a man, stopped and formed a stone, lead, coral, a flower, or a comet, all because of the fact that too few or too many patterns were necessary to plan a human.' This system of combinations of basic patterns which determines the variety of living forms links Epicurean science with DNA genetics.

The various methods for going up to the Moon already offer a wide sample of Cyrano's inventiveness: the Old Testament patriarch Enoch tied underneath his armpits two vases full of the smoke of a sacrifice, since it has to rise to heaven; the prophet Elijah made the same journey by settling himself into a little iron boat and throwing up into the air a magnetic ball; as for Cyrano himself, he spread an unguent based on bull's marrow over the bruises he had sustained in previous attempts, and felt himself being raised towards the Earth's satellite, because the Moon usually sucks up animals' marrow.

The Moon contains amongst other things the so-called Earthly (but it should be Lunar) Paradise, and Cyrano lands right on the Tree of Life itself, his face plastered with one of its famous apples. As for the serpent, after original sin God confined him inside the body of man in the shape of the intestine, a serpent coiled round itself, an insatiable animal which dominates man and binds him to his wishes, tormenting him with his invisible teeth.

This last is the explanation given by the prophet Elijah to Cyrano who cannot resist a salacious variation on this theme: the serpent is also the one that sticks out of a man's belly and extends towards the woman in order to spit out its venom at her, thus causing her to swell for nine months. But Elijah does not appreciate these jokes of Cyrano at all, and at one of his most outrageous impertinences chases him from Eden. This only proves that in this totally jocular work, there are jokes which must be taken as truths as well as others which are only there for fun, even though it is not easy to tell one from the other.

Once he has been banished from Eden, Cyrano visits the cities of the Moon: some are completely mobile, with houses on wheels so they can have a change of air each season; others are more sedentary, and are screwed into the ground, so they can delve deep into it during winter to escape the harsh climate. His guide will be someone who has been on Earth on several occasions in different centuries, namely Socrates' 'daimon' about whom Plutarch wrote a short work. This wise spirit explains why the Lunar people not only abstain from eating meat but also are very particular about their vegetables: they only eat cabbages which have died a natural death, because for them to decapitate a cabbage is murder. For the fact is that there is nothing to say that after Adam's sin men are more precious to God than are cabbages, nor that the latter are not endowed with greater sensitivity and beauty and made more in God's likeness than men. 'Consequently if our soul is no longer in God's image, we are no more like Him in our hands, feet, mouth, forehead and ears than the cabbage is in its leaves, flower, stalk, root and outer covering.' And as for intelligence, although they may not have an immortal soul, they are perhaps part of a universal intellect; and if we have never gleaned anything regarding their secret knowledge, this may be only because we are not capable of receiving the messages they send us.

Intellectual and poetic qualities converge in Cyrano to make him an extraordinary writer not just for seventeenth-century France but for all times. Intellectually he belongs to the 'libertine' tradition, a polemicist involved in the upheavals which are in the process of undermining the old conception of the world. He is in favour of Gassendi's sensism and Copernicus' astronomy, but he is fired most of all by the sixteenth-century Italian 'natural philosophers': Cardano, Bruno, Campanella. (As for Descartes, Cyrano will meet him in the *Voyage aux États du Soleil* (*Journey to the States of the Sun*), the sequel to *The States and Empires of the Moon*, and have him welcomed into that empyrean by Tommaso Campanella who goes over to embrace him.)

In literary terms he is a baroque writer – his 'letters' contain bravura pieces, such as the *Descrizione di un cipresso* (*Description of a Cypress Tree*) in which it is as if the style and the object described become one and the same thing. But above all he is a writer to his very core, who does not want so much to illustrate a theory or defend a thesis as to set in motion a merry-go-round of inventions which are the equivalent in imagination and language of what the new science and new philosophy were setting in motion in terms of thought. In *The Other World*, it is not the coherence of his ideas that counts, but the fun and freedom with which he takes hold of all the intellectual stimuli which appeal to his mind. This is the beginning of the *conte philosophique*: and this does not mean a story with a thesis to prove, but one in which ideas are taken up and dismissed and mock each other in turn for the fun of someone who is at home enough with them to be able to play with such ideas even when he takes them seriously.

One could say that Cyrano's journey to the Moon anticipates in some episodes Gulliver's travels: on the Moon as in Brobdignag, the visitor finds himself surrounded by human beings much bigger than himself who keep him on display like a pet animal. Similarly the sequence of disastrous adventures and meetings with characters who possess paradoxical wisdom is a forerunner of the ups and downs of Voltaire's Candide. But Cyrano's fame as a writer came much later: this book of his was published posthumously and was ruthlessly censored by friends who feared for his reputation and was only published in its entirety in this century. The rediscovery of Cyrano took place in the Romantic period: Charles Nodier was the first, and then notably Théophile Gautier, on the basis of one or two anecdotes, fashioned a portrait of the jocular, sword-fighting poet, which the brilliant dramatist Rostand transformed into the hero of the popular play in verse.

However, Savinien Cyrano was in actual fact neither noble nor a Guascon, but a Parisian bourgeois. (He himself added the Bergerac element, drawing on the name of a farm owned by his father who was a lawyer.) He probably did have the famous nose, especially as we find in this book an 'encomium of important noses', a eulogy which although belonging to a very widespread genre in baroque literature is unlikely to have been written by someone with a small, snub or pug-like nose. (The inhabitants of the Moon, when they want to tell the time, use their natural sun–dial, their nose, which projects its shadow over their teeth which then function as the dial.)

But it is not only noses that are flaunted: the Lunar nobility go around naked and as if this was not enough they carry round their waist a bronze pendant in the shape of the male member. ' "This custom seems so extraordinary to me," I said to my young guide, "because in our world the sign of nobility is to carry a sword." But he was not astonished at this and simply exclaimed: "My little man, how fanatical are the grandees of your world, wanting to display a weapon which symbolises the executioner and is only designed to destroy us, in short the sworn enemy of all that lives, whereas they want to hide the member without which we would not be alive at all, the Prometheus of all living beings, the indefatigable healer of all of nature's weaknesses! What an unfortunate land yours is, in which the symbols of procreation are the object of shame while those of destruction are held in honour! And yet you call that member 'the shameful parts', as though there were something more glorious than giving life and something more infamous than taking it away!" '

This extract proves that Rostand's quarrelsome swordsman was in reality an expert at 'making love not war', although still inclined to indulge in a procreatory rhetoric that our contraceptive age can only consider obsolete.

[1982]

Robinson Crusoe, Journal of Mercantile Virtues

The life and strange surprising adventures of Robinson Crusoe, of York, mariner: who liv'd eight and twenty years all alone in an uninhabited island on the coast of America, near the mouth of the great river Oroonoque; having been cast on shore by shipwreck, wherein all the men perish'd but himself. With an account how he was at last as strangely deliver'd by pyrates. Written by himself.

Thus the frontispiece of the first edition of *Robinson Crusoe*, printed in London in 1719 by a publisher of popular books, W. Taylor, 'at the Ship (in Pater Noster Row)'. No author's name was given, for it purported to be the genuine memoir of a shipwrecked sailor.

This was a time when tales of the sea and pirates were all the rage. The theme of shipwreck on a desert island had already caught the public's attention because of an episode that had genuinely taken place ten years previously, when a Captain Woodes Rogers had discovered on the island of Juan Fernandez a man who had lived on it all alone for four years, a Scottish sailor, Alexander Selkirk. This inspired a writer of pamphlets who was down on his luck and short of money to tell a similar tale in the form of an unknown sailor's memoir.

This man who had suddenly turned novelist despite being nearly sixty was Daniel Defoe (1660–1731), well known to political columns of the time particularly for having been in the pillory, and the author of a plethora of works of every kind, either written in his own name or anonymously, as was more often the case. (The most complete bibliographies of his works list almost 400 titles ranging from pamphlets of religious and political controversy, to short satirical poems, books on the occult, and works on history, geography and economics, in addition to the novels.)

This forerunner of the modern novel, then, first comes to the fore far from the cultivated terrain of high literature (whose supreme model in England at the time was the classicist Pope): instead it emerges amidst the rank undergrowth of commercial book production which was aimed at a reading public composed of serving girls, backstreet traders, innkeepers, waiters, sailors, and soldiers. Though intended to conform to the tastes of this public, such literature was always careful to inculcate some moral lesson (and not always in a hypocritical way), and Defoe is anything but indifferent to this requirement. But it is not the edifying sermons, punctuating the pages of *Crusoe* at regular intervals, that make it a book of sound moral backbone: these are in any case rather generic and perfunctory; rather it is the natural and direct way in which a kind of morality and an idea of life, a particular relationship of man with the objects and possibilities in his hands, are expressed in images.

Nor can it be said that the 'practical' origin of the book, which the author drafted as part of a 'deal', undermines the prestige of what would come to be thought of as the bible of mercantile and industrial virtues, the epic in praise of individual initiative. That mixture of adventure, practical spirit and moralistic compunction, which would in fact become the staple ingredients of Anglo-Saxon capitalism on both sides of the Atlantic, is not inconsistent with Defoe's own life, given his paradoxical role as both preacher and adventurer. Starting out as a merchant, Defoe soon became a trusted wholesaler in hosiery and a brick-manufacturer before going bankrupt; he became a supporter and adviser to the Whig party which backed William of Orange, a pamphleteer for the 'Dissenters', then he was imprisoned and saved by a moderate Tory minister, Robert Harley, for whom he acted as spokesman and secret agent, before going on to become the founder and sole editor of the newspaper *The Review*, for which he is known as 'the inventor of modern journalism'. After Harley's fall he moved first of all closer to the Whigs, then back to the Tories until the financial crisis which turned him into a novelist.

Sure evidence of his story-telling gifts had already surfaced on many occasions in Defoe's previous writings, especially when narrating contemporary or historical events, which he embellished with imaginative detail, or when recounting the biographies of famous men which were based on apocryphal evidence.

With these experiences behind him, Defoe set about writing his novel. Given the autobiographical thrust of the work, it not only deals with the adventures of the shipwreck and the desert island, but actually starts from the beginning of the protagonist's life and continues until his old age. In this respect Defoe was paying homage to a moralistic pretext, a kind of didacticism which, it must be said, is too narrow and elementary to be taken seriously: obedience to one's father, the superiority of middle-class life, and of the modest bourgeois existence over all the blandishments of outrageous fortune. It is for contravening these lessons that Robinson meets such disaster.

Avoiding both seventeenth-century bombast and the sentimentality typical of eighteenth-century English narrative, Defoe's language has a sobriety and an economy which, like Stendhal's 'dry as the Napoleonic code style', one might compare to that of a 'business report': here the device of the first-person sailor-merchant, who is capable of entering in columns as in an accounts book both the 'evil' and the 'good' of his situation, and of maintaining an arithmetical calculation of the number of cannibals killed, turns out to be as much an appropriate stylistic expedient as a practical one. Like a business report or a catalogue of goods and utensils, Defoe's prose is unadorned but at the same time scrupulously detailed. The accumulation of detail is aimed at convincing the reader of the veracity of his account, but also expresses better than any other style could the sense of the value of every object, every action, every gesture in the shipwreck's condition (just as in *Moll Flanders* and *Colonel Jack* the anxiety and joy of material possession is conveyed by the lists of stolen objects).

The descriptions of Robinson's manual operations are given in painstaking detail: how he digs his house out of the rock, surrounds it with a palisade, builds himself a boat which he is then unable to carry as far as the sea, and learns how to shape and heat vases and bricks. Because of this interest and delight in reporting Robinson's technical progress, Defoe is famous even today as the writer who celebrates man's patient struggle with matter, and exalts the lowliness and difficulty but also the greatness of all activity, as well as the joy of seeing things being created by our hands. From Rousseau to Hemingway, all those writers who have shown us that testing ourselves, and succeeding or failing in 'doing something' however great or small, are real measures of human worth, can recognise Defoe as their first model.

Robinson Crusoe is without doubt a book to be reread line by line, and we will continually make new discoveries. His capacity for avoiding, at crucial moments, any excessive self-congratulation or exultation by using just a few words before moving on to practical questions may seem to contrast with the sermonising tone of certain pages later on, once a bout of illness has led the protagonist back to the thought of religion: for instance, that moment when he realises that he is the sole survivor of all the crew – 'as for them, I never saw them afterwards, or any sign of them, except three of their hats, one cap, and two shoes that were not fellows' – and after the briefest of thanks to God he immediately starts to look round and consider his plight.

But Defoe's approach in both *Crusoe* and in the later novels is very similar to that of the business man who obeys the rules, who when it is time for the service goes into church and beats his breast, but then hurries back out so as not to waste time away from his work. Hypocrisy? His behaviour is too open and urgent to deserve such a charge; Defoe maintains even in his brusque alternations of tone a basic, healthy sincerity which is his unmistakable hallmark.

Then again, sometimes his humorous vein broaches even the battlefields of the political and religious controversies of his age: as when we hear the arguments between the savage who cannot comprehend the idea of the devil and the sailor who cannot explain it to him. Or as in that situation when Robinson is lord of 'but three subjects, and they were of three different religions. My man Friday was a Protestant, his father was a Pagan and a cannibal, and the Spaniard was a Papist. However, I allowed liberty of conscience throughout my dominions.' But not even this subtle and ironic emphasis is present when we read one of the most paradoxical and significant moments in the book: after longing for years to reestablish contact with the rest of the world, now every time he sees a human presence appear around the island Robinson feels the threats to his life increase; and when he learns of the existence of a group of shipwrecked Spanish sailors on a nearby island he is afraid of joining them in case they want to hand him over to the Inquisition.

Even on the shores of the desert island, then, 'near the great river Oroonoque', the ebb and flow of the ideas, passions and culture of an epoch are still felt. Certainly, although in his determination to play the role of adventure-story writer he dwells on the horror in his descriptions of the cannibals, he was not unaware of Montaigne's reflections on the anthropophagi (these same ideas had left their mark on Shakespeare in his story of another mysterious island in *The Tempest*): without such ideas Robinson would never have reached the conclusion that 'these people were not murderers', but men from a different civilisation, obeying their own laws: 'They do not know it to be an offence any more than those Christians were murderers who often put to death the prisoners taken in battle.'

[1955]

Candide, or Concerning Narrative Rapidity

Geometric characters, animated by a flickering mobility, stretch and twist in a saraband of precision and lightness: that was how Paul Klee illustrated Voltaire's *Candide* in 1911, giving visual – and almost musical – form to the energetic brio which this book continues to communicate to today's readers, above and beyond its thick network of references to its own epoch and culture.

What most delights us today in *Candide* is not the 'conte philosophique', nor its satire, nor the gradual emergence of a morality and vision of the world: instead it is its rhythm. With rapidity and lightness, a succession of mishaps, punishments and massacres races over the page, leaps from chapter to chapter, and ramifies and multiplies without evoking in the reader's emotions anything other than a feeling of an exhilarating and primitive vitality. In the bare three pages of Chapter 8 Cunégonde recounts how having had her father, mother and brother hacked to pieces by invaders, she is then raped and disembowelled, then cured and reduced to living as a washerwoman, bartered and sold in Holland and Portugal, torn between two different protectors of different faiths on alternate days, and in this condition happens to witness the *auto da fé* whose victims are Pangloss and Candide himself whom she then rejoins. Even less than two pages of Chapter 9 are enough for Candide to find himself with two corpses at his feet and for Cunégonde to be able to exclaim: 'How did you who were born so mild ever manage to kill in the space of two minutes a Jew and a prelate?' And when the old woman has to explain why she has only one buttock, she starts by telling the story of her life from the moment when as the thirteen-year-old daughter of a Pope, she had experienced in the space of three months poverty, enslavement, and almost daily rape, before having to endure famine and war and nearly dying of the plague in Algiers: and all this before she can get to her tale of the siege of Azov and of the unusual nutrition that the starving Janissaries discover in female buttocks . . . well, here things are rather more leisurely, two whole chapters are required, something like six and a half pages.

The great discovery of Voltaire the humorist is a technique that will become one of the most reliable gags in comic films: the piling up of disaster on disaster at relentless speed. There are also the sudden increases in rhythm which carry the sense of the absurd almost to the point of paroxysm: as when the series of misfortunes already swiftly narrated in the detailed account is then repeated in a breakneck-speed summary. What Voltaire projects in his lightning-speed photograms is really a worldwide cinema, a kind of 'around the world in eighty pages', which takes Candide from his native Westphalia to Holland, Portugal, South America, France, England, Venice and Turkey, and this tour then splits in turn into supplementary whirlwind world tours by fellow protagonists, male and especially female, who are easy prey for pirates and slavers operating between Gibraltar and the Bosphorus. A huge cinema of contemporary world events most of all: villages wiped out in the Seven Years' War between the Prussians and the French (the 'Bulgars' and the 'Abars'), the Lisbon earthquake of 1755, the *auto da fés* organised by the Inquisition, the Jesuits of Paraguay who reject Spanish and Portuguese rule, the legendary gold of the Incas, and the odd snapshot of Protestantism in Holland, of the spread of syphilis, Mediterranean and Atlantic piracy, internecine wars in Morocco, the exploitation of black slaves in Guyana, but always leaving a certain space for literary news, allusions to Parisian high life, interviews with the many dethroned kings of the time, who all gather at the Venice carnival.

A world in total disarray; nobody anywhere is saved except in the only country that is wise and happy, El Dorado. The link between happiness and wealth ought not to exist since the Incas are unaware that the gold dust of their streets and their diamond cobbles is so precious to the men from the Old World; and yet, strange as it may seem, Candide does find a wise and happy society in that exact spot, amidst the deposits of precious metals. It is there that Pangloss might finally be right, that the best of all possible worlds might become reality: except that El Dorado is hidden amidst the most inaccessible mountain ranges of the Andes, perhaps in a piece of the map that has been torn away, a non-place, a utopia.

But if this land of Cockaigne possesses vague and unconvincing touches typical of all utopias, the rest of the world, with its constant tribulations, despite the rapidity with which these are recounted, is not at all a mannered representation. 'That is the price that must be paid for you to eat sugar in Europe!', says the Dutch Guyana negro, after telling the protagonists about his punishments in just a few lines; similarly the courtesan in Venice says, 'Oh, sir, if you could only imagine what it is like to be forced to caress, whether you like it or not, an old merchant, a lawyer, a friar, a gondolier, an abbot; to be exposed to all manner of insults and affronts; often to be reduced to having to beg the loan of a skirt just in order to have it removed by a repulsive old man; to be robbed by one man of what one has just earned from another; to have a price on one's head set by those who administer justice, and to have nothing else to look forward to but a horrendous old age, in a hospital or a dungheap . . .'

It is true that the characters in *Candide* appear to be made of rubber: Pangloss is wasted by syphilis, then they hang him, they tie him to the oar of a galley, and then he pops up again alive and kicking. But it would be wrong to say that Voltaire glosses over the cost of suffering: what other novel has the courage to present the heroine who at the beginning had been 'comely in complexion, fresh, plump, attractive', later as a Cuné-gonde who is 'turned dark in complexion, gummy-eyed, flat-chested, with wrinkled cheeks, and the skin of her arms red and chapped'?

By this stage we realise that our reading of *Candide*, which was intended to be totally external, a surface reading, has taken us back to the core of its 'philosophy', of Voltaire's vision of the world. Which is not solely the polemical attack on Pangloss's providential optimism: if we look closely, we see that the mentor who accompanies Candide longest is not the unfortunate Leibnitzian pedagogue, but the 'Manichean' Martin, who is inclined to see in the world only the victories of the devil; and if Martin does embody the role of anti-Pangloss, we cannot definitely say that he is the one who triumphs. It is pointless, says Voltaire, to seek a metaphysical explanation for evil, as the optimist Pangloss and the pessimist Martin do, because this evil is subjective, indefinable, and unmeasurable; no design of the universe exists, or if one does exist, it is God who knows it not man. Voltaire's 'rationalism' is an ethical, voluntaristic attitude, which stands out against a theological background which is as incommensurate with man as Pascal's was.

If this carousel-round of disasters can be contemplated with a smile playing around our lips it is because human life is brief and limited; there is always someone who can call himself worse off than ourselves; and if there was someone who by chance had nothing to complain about and had every good thing that life can give, he would end up like Signor Pococurante, the Venetian Senator, who turns up his nose at everything, finding fault where he ought only to find reason for satisfaction and admiration. The really negative character in the book is the bored Pococurante; deep down Pangloss and Martin, though they give hopeless, nonsensical replies to questions, fight back against the torments and risks which are the stuff of life.

The subdued vein of wisdom which emerges in the book through marginal spokesmen such as the Anabaptist Jacques, the old Inca, and that Parisian *savant* who so much resembles the author himself, is articulated in the end by the mouth of the dervish in the famous maxim to 'cultivate our garden'. This of course is a very reductive moral; one which ought to be understood in its intellectual significance of being anti-metaphysical: you should not give yourself problems other than those that you can resolve with your own direct practical application. And in its social significance: this is the first enunciation of work as the substance of all worth. Nowadays the affirmation '*il faut cultiver notre jardin*' sounds to our ears heavy with egotistical, bourgeois connotations: as inappropriate as could be, given our present worries and anxieties. It is no accident that it is enunciated in the final page, almost after the end of this book in which work appears only as a curse and in which gardens are regularly devastated. This too is a utopia, no less than the realm of the Incas: the voice of reason in *Candide* is nothing but utopian. But it is also no accident that it is the sentence from the book that has become most famous, so much so that it has become proverbial. We must not forget the radical epistemological and ethical change which this phrase signalled (we are in 1759, exactly 30 years before the Bastille fell): man judged no longer by his relation to a transcendent Good or Evil but in the little or much that he can actually achieve. And this is the source both of a work ethic that is strictly 'productive' in the capitalist sense of the word, and of a moral of practical, responsible and concrete commitment without which there are no general problems which can be resolved. In short, man's real choices in life today stem from this book.

[1974]

Denis Diderot, *Jacques le Fataliste*

Diderot's status amongst the founding fathers of contemporary literature is continually rising, and mostly because of his antinovel, or metanovel, or hypernovel, *Jacques the Fatalist and his Master*: the text's richness and innovative thrust will never be fully exhausted.

The first thing to note is that Diderot reverses what was the principal intention of all authors of the time, that of making the reader forget that he is reading a book, and of then having him abandon himself to the story being narrated as though he were experiencing the events for himself. Instead Diderot foregrounds the conflict between the author who is telling his story and the reader who is waiting only to hear it: the curiosity, expectations, disappointments and protests of the reader, which are pitted against the intentions, polemics and whims of the author in deciding how the plot will develop, constitute a dialogue which frames the dialogue between the two protagonists, which in turn acts as a frame for other dialogues . . .

Diderot transforms the reader's relationship to the book from one of passive acceptance to that of continuous debate or rather one of constant surprise which keeps his critical spirit alive. In doing so he anticipates by two centuries Brecht's aims in the theatre. The only difference is that Brecht will do so on the basis of very precise didactic aims, whereas Diderot gives the impression of wanting only to abandon any deliberate authorial intention.

It must be said that Diderot plays a kind of cat and mouse game with the reader, opening up a range of different possibilities at every turning in the plot, almost leaving him to select the development which he prefers, only then to delude him by rejecting all of them but one, and that one is always the least 'novelistic' development. In this respect Diderot is a forerunner of the idea of 'potential literature' which would be so dear to Raymond Queneau, yet he also rejects it to a certain extent: for Queneau will set up a model for his *Un Conte à votre façon* (*Yours for the Telling*) in which we seem to hear Diderot inviting the reader to choose a sequel, whereas in fact Diderot wanted to prove that there could only be one sequel to the plot. (And this corresponds to a precise philosophical option, as we shall see.)

Jacques the Fatalist is a work that eludes rules and classification, and acts as a kind of touchstone against which to test several definitions coined by literary theorists. The structure is one of 'deferred narrative': Jacques starts telling the story of his love affairs but, after interruptions, digressions, and other stories inserted into the middle of his own, only concludes them at the end of the book. This structure, articulated in a Chinese-box pattern of stories inside other stories, is not only dictated by a taste for what Bakhtin will term 'polyphonic', 'Menippean', or 'Rabelaisian' narrative: it is for Diderot the only authentic image of the living world, which is never linear nor stylistically homogeneous, though its linkages, while discontinuous, always reveal an inner logic.

In all of this one cannot ignore the influence of Sterne's *Tristram Shandy*, an explosive novelty of the time in terms of literary form and of attitude towards the things of this world: Sterne's novel is an example of a freewheeling, digressive narrative which lies at the opposite extreme from eighteenth-century French taste. Anglophilia in literature has always been a vital stimulus for the literatures of continental Europe: Diderot made it his emblem in his crusade for expressive 'truth'. Critics have pointed out phrases and episodes which have migrated from Sterne's novel to *Jacques*; and Diderot, in order to prove how little he cared about charges of plagiarism, actually declares before one of the final scenes in the book that he has copied it from *Tristram Shandy*. In truth whether he lifted the odd page either word for word or paraphrased does not matter very much; in its broad outlines *Jacques*, a picaresque story about the wanderings of two characters on horseback who narrate, listen to and live through various adventures, is as different as could be from *Tristram Shandy*, which embroiders on largely domestic episodes involving a group of family members or people from the same parish, dealing in particular with the grotesque particulars of a birth and the early misfortunes of the infant. The similarity between the two works should be sought at a deeper level: the real theme of both books is the concatenation of causes, the inextricable linkage of circumstances which determines every event, even the most insignificant, and which has taken the place of Fate for modern writers and readers.

What counted in Diderot's poetics was not so much the originality of a book as the fact that it answered, argued with or completed other books in turn: it is in the cultural context as a whole that a writer's every endeavour acquires significance. The great gift bequeathed by Sterne not just to Diderot but to world literature as a whole, which would subsequently affect a fashion for romantic irony, was his unbuttoned attitude, his giving vent to his humours, the acrobatics of his writing.

Nor should it be forgotten that a major model openly admitted by both Sterne and Diderot was Cervantes' masterpiece, even though they both inherited different elements from it: one combining it with his felicitous English mastery in creating fully realised characters by underlining the peculiarity of a few almost caricature traits, the other drawing on the repertoire of picaresque adventures that take place in inns or on the highways in the tradition of the *roman comique.*

Jacques the servant, the squire, comes first – even in the title – before his master, the knight (whose name we are never told, almost as if he existed only as a function of Jacques, as his maître; and even as a character he remains more shadowy than his servant). That their relationship is one of servant to master is certain, but it is also that of two friends: hierarchical relationships have not yet been questioned (the French Revolution is at least ten years away), but they have lost some of their significance. (On all these aspects there is an excellent introduction by Michele Rago to the Italian translation, *Jacques il fatalista e il suo padrone,* in Einaudi's 'Centopagine' series: it provides a complete and accurate account of the historical, literary and philosophical context of the book.) It is Jacques who takes all the important decisions; and when his master becomes imperious, he can occasionally refuse to obey, though only up to a certain point and no further. Diderot describes a world of human relationships which are based on the reciprocal influences of individual qualities, which do not cancel out social roles but at the same time are not crushed by them: it is a world which is neither a utopia nor one which denounces social mechanisms, but one which is observed almost transparently in a period of huge change.

(The same could be said about relations between the sexes: Diderot is 'feminist' through his own innate mentality not because he wants to deliver a particular message. For him women are on the same moral and intellectual plane as men, and are equally entitled to the pursuit of emotional and sensual happiness. And in this respect there is an unbridgeable gulf between this work and the cheerful, indefatigable misogyny of *Tristram Shandy*.)

As for the 'fatalism' which Jacques purports to represent (everything that happens has already been 'written up above'), we see that far from justifying resignation or passivity, it leads Jacques always to display initiative and never to give up, while his master, who seems to incline more towards free will and individual choice, tends to become discouraged and to let himself be swept away by events. As philosophical dialogues, their discussions are somewhat rudimentary, but scattered allusions refer to the idea of necessity in Spinoza and Leibniz. Against Voltaire, who in *Candide or Concerning Optimism* takes Leibniz to task, Diderot in *Jacques le Fataliste* seems to side with Leibniz and even more with Spinoza, who had upheld the objective rationality of a single, ineluctable world, proved by his geometrical method. If for Leibniz this world was only one of many possible worlds, for Diderot the only possible world is this one, whether it is good or bad (or rather, always a mixture of good and bad), and man's behaviour, whether good or bad (or rather, it too is always a mixture), is valid only insofar as it is capable of responding to the set of circumstances in which he finds himself. (This includes cunning, deceit, and ingenious fictions – see for instance the 'novels within the novel', the intrigues involving Madame de La Pommeraye and Father Hudson who devise in real life calculated, theatrical fictions. This is very far from Rousseau, who exalted the goodness and sincerity in nature and in the 'natural' man.)

Diderot had worked out that actually the most rigidly deterministic conceptions of the world are the ones which generate in the individual will an urge to move forward, as though will and free choice can only be effective if they carve out their openings against the hard rock of necessity. This had been true of the religions which had exalted the will of God to the maximum over man's will, and it will also be true in the two centuries after Diderot which will see new theories of a determinist kind assert themselves in biology, economics and society, and psychology. We can say today that these theories have opened the way to genuine freedoms even as they established an awareness of necessity, whereas cults of will and activism have only led to disasters.

Nevertheless, one cannot say outright that *Jacques the Fatalist* 'teaches' or 'proves' this or that. There is no fixed theoretical point which is compatible with the constant movement and cavortings of Diderot's heroes. His horse twice goes its own way and leads Jacques to a hill where the gallows stand, but the third time explains all, for it takes him to the house of its former owner, who was the hangman. This is certainly an Enlightenment parable against belief in premonitory signs, but it is also a forerunner of the darker vein of Romanticism with its images of ghostly hanged men on barren hillsides (even though we are still a long way from the special effects of a writer like Potocki). And if the finale descends into a succession of adventures condensed into a few sentences, with his master killing a man in a duel, and Jacques turning into a brigand with Mandrin and then rediscovering his master and saving his castle from being sacked, we recognise here that eighteenth-century concision which clashes with the Romantic pathos of the unexpected and of destiny, such as we find in Kleist.

Life's accidents in their uniqueness and variety cannot be reduced to laws and classification, even though each one follows a logic of its own. The story of the two inseparable officers, who are unable to live apart but who nevertheless regularly feel the urge to duel with each other, is told by Diderot with a laconic objectivity which however does not conceal the ambivalence of a passionate element in their relationship.

If *Jacques* is an anti-*Candide*, it is because it was conceived as an anti-*conte-philosophique*: Diderot is convinced that truth cannot be constrained into one form, or into one didactic fable. He wants his literary creativity to match the inexhaustible details of life, not to prove a theory that can be enunciated in abstract terms.

Diderot's wide-ranging way of writing is opposed as much to 'literature' as it is to 'philosophy', but today what we recognise as genuinely literary writing is actually Diderot's. It is no accident that *Jacques the Fatalist* has been recently given a modern, theatrical form by a writer of the calibre of Milan Kundera, and that Kundera's novel, *The Unbearable Lightness of Being*, shows him to be the most Diderotian of contemporary writers for his skill in blending together the novel about emotions with the existential novel, philosophy and irony.

[1984]

Giammaria Ortes

Once upon a time there was a man who wanted to calculate everything: pleasures, pains, virtues, vices, truths, errors. This man was convinced that he could establish an algebraic formula and a system of numerical quantification for every aspect of human feeling and action. He fought against the chaos of existence and the indeterminacy of thought with the weapon of 'geometrical precision', a weapon, in other words, derived from an intellectual style which was all clear oppositions and irrefutable logical consequences. The desire for pleasure and the fear of force were for him the only certain premises from which to embark on a journey towards knowledge of the human condition: only by this route could he succeed in establishing that even qualities such as justice and self-denial had some solid foundation.

The world was a mechanism containing ruthless forces: 'The true worth of opinions is wealth since it is wealth that changes hands and buys up opinions'; 'Man is basically a trunk of bones held together by tendons, muscles and other membranes.' Predictably, the author of these maxims lived in the eighteenth century. From the machine-man of La Mettrie to the triumph of the cruel pleasures of Nature in de Sade, the spirit of that century knew no half-measures in its rejection of any providential vision of man and the world. It is also predictable that he lived in Venice: in its slow decline the Serenissima felt itself more and more caught up in the crushing contest between the great powers, and obsessed by profits and increasing losses in its trade; and more and more immersed in its hedonism, its gaming halls, its theatres and carnivals. What other place could have provided greater stimulus to a man who wanted to calculate everything? He felt a vocation to devise a system to win at the card-game 'faraone', to calculate the right quantity of passion in a melodrama, and even to discourse on the interference of government in the economy of the private individual and on the wealth and poverty of nations.

But the man in question was not a libertine in learning like Helvétius, nor a libertine in practice like Casanova: he was not even a reformer battling on behalf of Enlightenment values, like his Milanese contemporaries who worked on *Il Caffè*. (Pietro Verri's *Discourse on the Nature of Pleasure and Pain* was published in that journal in 1773, some time after our Venetian author had published in 1757 his *Calcolo de' piaceri e de' dolori della vita umana* (*A Calculation of the Pleasures and Pains of Human Life*)). Giammaria Ortes, for that was his name, was a dry, irritable priest, who wielded the spiky carapace of his logic against the premonitions of the upheaval pervading Europe and rumbling even amongst the foundations of his native Venice. He was a pessimist like Hobbes, loved paradoxes as much as Mandeville, was peremptory in his argumentation, and dry and acerbic in style. Reading him, we are left without a shadow of doubt about his position as one of the most unmisty-eyed champions of Reason with a capital R. Indeed we have to make a real effort to accept the other details supplied by biographers and experts of his entire *oeuvre*, particularly as regards his intransigence on matters religious and his substantial conservatism. (See, for instance, Gianfranco Torcellan's 1961 Einaudi edition of *Riflessioni di un filosofo americano* (*Reflections of an American Philosopher*), one of Ortes' most significant 'operette morali'.) And this should be a lesson to us never to trust received notions and clichés, such as the traditional view that the eighteenth century was dominated by the clash between a religious spirit heavy with sentiment and a cold, unbelieving rationality: reality is always much more nuanced, the same elements continually combining in a whole range of different assortments. Behind the most mechanical and mathematical vision of human nature can easily lie a Catholic pessimism about earthly matters: precise, crystalline forms emerge from the dust and take shape before returning to dust again.

At that time Venice was more than ever the ideal backdrop for eccentrics, for a whole kaleidoscope of characters straight out of Goldoni. Ortes, this misanthropic priest obsessed by arithmetical calculations, whom a contemporary drawing portrays as composed and bewigged, with a sharp chin and a slightly malicious little smile, can easily be imagined entering on stage with the look of someone who is used to finding himself amidst people who have no wish to understand what to him is so straightforward, but despite this he insists on having his say and commiserating with others on their errors, until finally we see him disappear from the little piazza shaking his head.

It is no accident that Ortes belongs to a theatrical century, and to the theatrical city par excellence. The motto with which he usually ended his works, 'Who can say if I am inventing?', sows the seed of doubt in us that his mathematical proofs are nothing but satirical paradoxes, and that the rigorous logician who appears as their author is nothing but the mask of a caricature underneath which hides another science, another truth. Was it simply a formula dictated by a perfectly understandable prudence, in order to preempt condemnation by Church authorities? Not for nothing did Ortes admire above all others Galileo: Galileo had placed at the centre of his *Dialogue* a character, Salviati, who was his spokesman, who declared that he was only playing the part of a Copernican even though he was an agnostic, and that he was participating in the debate only in the way he would participate in a masque . . . This sort of system can turn out to be more or less efficient as a precaution (it was not for Galileo, but it worked for Ortes, as far as we know), but in any case it demonstrates the pleasure the author takes in such literary games. 'Who can say if I am inventing?': in this question, the play of light and shadow typical of the theatre is established at the heart of the discourse, of this and perhaps every other human discourse. Who decides whether what is being said is upheld as truth or fiction? Not the author, since he submits to the verdict of his audience ('Who can say . . . ?'); but not the public either, since the question is addressed to a hypothetical 'Who', who might not even exist. Perhaps all philosophers harbour within themselves an actor who plays his part without the philosopher being able to intervene; perhaps every philosophy, every dogma contains an element of theatrical sketch, though it is impossible to tell where the sketch begins or ends.

(Just over half a century later Fourier would cut an equally contradictory figure in the literary world, but again typical of the eighteenth century: he too was an arithmomaniac, a radical rationalist and yet also an enemy of the *philosophes*, he too was a hedonist and sensationalist and a Eudaimonist in dogma, he too was austere, solitary and stern in life, but also a theatre enthusiast, constantly forcing us to ask ourselves 'Who can say if I am inventing?' . . .)

'All men by nature are led to the pleasure of the senses', so runs the opening of *A Calculation of the Pleasures and Pains of Human Life*; and it continues, 'for this reason all external objects become at the same time the particular object of desire of each man.' In order to possess these objects of his desire man is led to use force and enters into conflict with the power of others; hence the necessity of calculating forces which can cancel each other out. For Ortes nature does not have a maternal image as it does for Rousseau, and the social contract which emerges from his idea is more like a parallelogram of forces in a physics manual. If men in the pursuit of pleasure do not destroy each other in turn, this is because of opinion, which is the foundation of all aspects of what today we call culture in the broad sense. Opinion is the 'reason why the combined force of all men works more or less on behalf of each individual'. This is not virtue, which is a heavenly gift and as such allows us to sacrifice ourselves for the good of others; but here we are on earth, and what counts is opinion in as much as its objective is 'one's own interests'. Ortes provides proofs of how sublime examples of heroism and patriotism from Roman history can be explained as calculated acts in the interests of the individual, and Ortes' proofs could be backed up by the behaviourism of B. F. Skinner or the sociobiology of E. O. Wilson.

'Opinions' are those forms of thought on the basis of which we accept that certain categories of people possess, each in its own way, certain levels of wealth or privilege. Ortes cites four in particular: nobles, merchants, soldiers and men of letters. He tries to define the formula to establish the 'value' of each of these 'opinions', and by 'value' he means nothing more nor less than revenue.

In short, 'opinion' in his view amounts to what in more recent times we used to term 'ideology', and in particular, 'class ideology'; but Ortes, more brutally than any historical materialist, loses no time in observing its superstructural specificity, and quickly translates everything into economic terms, or rather into income and expenditure.

His conclusion, that in a more numerous society one enjoys more pleasures and suffers fewer fears (in which, in short, men are free), than one does living outside any society or within a very limited one, is an axiom which could be developed in a sociological treatise, and subsequently confirmed, modified or corrected in the light of our experience today. In the same way an entire typology and categorisation of conformisms and rebellions, judged according to their relative levels of sociability or unsociability, could be elaborated from the final sentence of the work where there is a contrast between he who is 'susceptible' to a greater number of 'opinions' and he who is 'susceptible to fewer opinions': the former becomes 'more and more reserved, civil and dissimulating', the latter 'more sincere, more free and more savage'.

As a constructor of systems and mechanisms, Ortes could never have had a special penchant for history; on the contrary, one could say that he understood very little about what history is. He who had proved how society is based solely on opinion, considered historical truth only as something to which one can be an eye-witness, hence history, as something only heard from others, was on a level immediately below the living voice of those who witnessed the events. But in his conclusions to *A Calculation of the Truth of History*, Ortes reveals a desire for cosmic knowledge that focuses on infinitesimal and irrepeatable details: he who always tends to subsume humanity into an algebraic formula of abstract elements, here condemns any pretence at an overall knowledge that is not based on an unfathomable sum of all individual experiences.

Certainly, his methods pushed him towards generalisations, abetted by his talent for conceptual syntheses. For example, he provided characterisations of the Italians, French, English and Germans, by analysing the respective theatres of the four nations: French theatre is based on change, the English on 'fixation', the Italian on 'first impression', and the German on 'final impression'. 'First impression', I believe, means immediacy, and 'final impression' means reflection; the most difficult term to decode is 'fixation', but presuming that it was almost certainly Shakespeare that he had in mind for the English theatre, I think he meant carrying passions and actions to their ultimate consequences, as well as a certain excess in characterisation and theatrical effects. From all this Ortes postulated an affinity between the Italians and the English whose qualities are based on 'imagination', and between the French and the Germans for whom 'reason' counts for more.

This is the discourse that opens the liveliest and richest of Ortes' texts, his *Reflections on the Musical Theatre*, where the 'geometrical precision' of his method is applied to the symmetries and reversals of the situations in melodrama. Here Ortes' programmatic hedonism focuses on a good that is less uncertain than so many others: that 'divertimento' which Venetian civilisation skilfully placed at the centre of social life. And here we can see how it is much more empirical experience than mathematical reasoning that is the basis for the author's reflections. 'Every "divertimento" consists in a different movement being experienced by one of the sense organs. Pleasure derives from that diversity of movement, just as boredom stems from the continuation of it. Therefore he who aims to provide pleasure for more than three hours should be certain that he will only produce boredom.'

Perhaps the pleasure of music and theatre, and the emotions and hopes aroused in gaming, are the only pleasures that are not illusory. As for the rest, behind all his certainties lurks a feeling of melancholy relativism. *A Calculation of the Pleasures and Pains of Human Life* ends on these words: 'If such doctrines as mine are thought to betray a contempt for the human species, I myself belong to this species without feeling aggrieved; and if I conclude that all the pleasures and pains of this life are but illusions, I can add that all human ratiocination is but folly. And when I say all ratiocination, I do not exclude my own "calculations".'

[1984]

Knowledge as Dust-cloud in Stendhal

It was during his Milanese period that Henri Beyle – who up until then had been a man of the world, more or less a genius, a dilettante without a precise vocation and a miscellaneous writer of uneven success – elaborated something that cannot be called his philosophy, since he proposed to go in directly the opposite direction to philosophy, nor his poetics as a novelist since he defined his poetics as an antithesis to the novel, perhaps without realising that he himself would shortly become a novelist, but something which can only be called his epistemological method.

This Stendhalian method, based on the individual's lived experience in all its unique irrepeatability, is opposed to philosophy which tends towards generalisation, universality, abstraction and geometric pattern. But it is also in opposition to the world of the novel, which is seen as a world of physical, one-dimensional energies, of continuous lines, of vectorial arrows pointing towards an end, whereas his method aims to purvey knowledge of a reality that manifests itself in the shape of small events, localised in place and time. I have been trying to define this epistemological method of Stendhal's as something independent of its object; but the object of Beyle's epistemological quest is something psychological, the nature of passions, or rather of the passion par excellence, love. And the treatise the as yet unknown author wrote in Milan was *De l'Amour* (*On Love*), the fruits of his longest and most unhappy Milanese love affair, that with Matilde Dembowski. But we can try to extract from *On Love* what is now called in the philosophy of science a 'paradigm', and see whether this paradigm is valid not just for his psychology of love but for all aspects of Stendhal's vision of the world.

In one of the prefaces to *On Love* we read:

Love is like what is called the Milky Way in the heavens, a shining mass formed by minute stars, each one of which is often itself a nebula. Books on the subject have noted four or five hundred small subsequent emotions which are hard to identify and which make up this passion, but these are only the grossest of them, often making errors and mistaking what is merely accessory for what is its substance.

The text goes on to take issue with eighteenth-century novels, including *La Nouvelle Héloïse* and *Manon Lescaut*, just as in the page before this he had refuted the philosophers' claim to be able to describe love as a complicated but geometrical figure.

We can say, therefore, that the reality whose essence Stendhal wants to explore is punctiform, discontinuous, unstable, a pulviscular cloud of heterogeneous phenomena, each one isolated from the other, and in turn subdivisible into even more minute phenomena.

At the start of the treatise one might think that the author confronts his subject with the classificatory, cataloguing spirit that in those same years led Charles Fourier to draw up his minute synoptic tables of the passions based on their harmonious, combinatory satisfactions. But Stendhal's spirit is at the opposite extreme from a systematising order, which it continually avoids even in what he wanted to be his most ordered book. His rigour is of a different type: his discourse is organised around one basic idea, which he terms crystallisation, and from there it branches out to explore the range of meanings which extends beneath the nomenclature of love, as well as the adjacent semantic areas of *happiness* and *beauty*.

Happiness too, the more one tries to confine it within a definition of substance, the more it dissolves into a galaxy of different moments each separated from the other, just like love. Because (as Stendhal says in chapter 2) 'the soul becomes sated with everything that is uniform, even with perfect happiness'; and the relevant note explains: 'One single moment in existence provides only one instant of perfect happiness, but the way a passionate man lives changes ten times a day.'

Nevertheless this powdery *happiness* is a quantifiable entity, it can be counted using precise units of measurement. In chapter 17 we read:

Albéric meets in a theatre box a woman more beautiful than his mistress: if you will allow me to use a mathematical evaluation, let us say she is a woman whose features promise three units of happiness instead of two (and let us suppose that perfect beauty gives a quotient of happiness which can be expressed by the number four). Is it any wonder that he still prefers the features of his mistress which promise him one hundred units of happiness?

We can instantly see that Stendhal's mathematics immediately become extremely complicated: on the one hand the quantity of happiness has an objective size, proportionate to the quantity of beauty, but on the other it has a totally subjective size in its projection on the hypermetrical scale of amorous passion. Not by chance is this chapter 17, one of the most important chapters in the book, entitled 'Beauty Dethroned by Love'.

But then the invisible line which divides every sign also passes through *beauty*, and we can distinguish an objective aspect – though this is difficult to define – and the subjective aspect of what is beautiful for us, which is made up of 'every new beauty that we discover in the object of our love'. The first definition of beauty which the treatise provides (in chapter 11) is 'a new capacity for giving you pleasure'. This is followed by a page on the relativity of beauty, exemplified by two fictitious characters in the book: Del Rosso's ideal of beauty is a woman who at every moment suggests physical pleasure, while for Lisio Visconti it is a woman who at every turn must incite him to love as passion.

If we realise that Del Rosso and Lisio are both personifications of two aspects of the author's psyche, then things become even more complicated, because the process of fragmentation pervades even the subject. But here we become involved in the theme of the multiplication of the Stendhalian self through pseudonyms. Even the ego can become a galaxy of egos: 'the mask must become a succession of masks, and the use of pseudonyms a systematic use of multiple names', says Jean Starobinski in his important article, 'Stendhal pseudonyme'.

But let us not go any further down this road; instead let us consider the person in love as a single, indivisible soul, particularly as just at this point there is a note which is more precise about the definition of beauty as *my* beauty, namely what beauty is for me: 'it is the promise of a character useful to my soul . . . and is more important than the attraction to my senses.' Note that here we find the term 'promise' which in a note to chapter 17 forms part of his most famous definition: '*la beauté est la promesse du bonheur*' (beauty is the promise of happiness).

On this phrase, and its predecessors, premisses and later echoes, right down to Baudelaire, there is a very interesting essay by Giansiro Ferrata ('Il valore e la forma', *Questo e altro*, VIII (June 1964), pp. 11–23), which highlights the central point of the theory of *cristallisation*, namely the transformation of a negative feature of the loved one into a pole of attraction. It is worth recalling that the metaphor of crystallisation derives from the Salzburg mines into which branches without leaves were thrown: when they were recovered some months later they were covered with crystals of rock salt, dazzling like diamonds. The branch as it had been was still visible, but every knot, twig and thorn now possessed a transfigured beauty; in the same way the mind of the lover fixes on every detail of the beloved in a sublime transfiguration. And here Stendhal pauses on a very striking example, which seems to hold for him the highest importance both on a general theoretical level and on the level of lived experience: the '*marque de petite vérole*' on the loved woman's face.

> *Even the little defects of her face, for example a smallpox scar, make the man who loves her feel tender towards her, throwing him into a deep reverie when he sees them in another woman. This is because faced with that smallpox scar he has felt a thousand emotions, mostly delicious, but all of them of great interest, feelings which in any case are stirred up again with incredible force at the sight of that mark, even if he sees it on the face of another woman.*

It could almost be said that the whole of Stendhal's discourse on beauty revolves around the *marque de petite vérole*, almost as though only by confronting the symbol of absolute ugliness, a scar, can he arrive at the contemplation of absolute beauty. In the same way it could almost be said that his entire typology of passions revolves around the most negative situation, that of the fiasco of male impotence, almost as if the whole treatise *On Love* has its centre of gravity in the chapter 'Des fiasco' (On fiascos), and that this famous chapter was the sole reason for writing the book which the author subsequently did not dare publish and which only appeared posthumously.

Stendhal broaches his subject by quoting Montaigne's essay on the same topic, but while for the latter this is just one example in a general meditation on the physical effects of the imagination, and inversely on the *indocile liberté* of the parts of the body which obey the will – a discourse that predates Groddeck and modern treatments of the problematics of the body – for Stendhal, who always proceeds by subdivisions and never by generalisations, it is a question of unravelling a knot of psychological processes, including *amour propre*, sublimation, imagination and loss of spontaneity. The most desirable moment for Stendhal, the eternal lover, the first moment of intimacy with a new conquest, can become the most anguished moment; but it is precisely upon such a consciousness of this glimpse of total negativity, of this vortex of darkness and void, that one can build up a system of knowledge.

It is by starting at this point that we could imagine a dialogue between Stendhal and Leopardi, a Leopardian dialogue in which the latter would exhort the former to draw from his lived experiences the bitterest conclusions. This would not be without historical foundation since the two men actually did meet, in Florence in 1832. But we can also imagine Stendhal's reactions on the basis of, say, those parts of *Rome, Naples et Florence* which deal with the intellectual conversations he had in Milan sixteen years earlier (1816), in which he manifests the sceptical detachment of the man of the world, concluding that in the company of philosophers he always manages to make himself unpopular, something which never happens to him with beautiful women. In this way Stendhal would have quickly abandoned the Leopardian dialogue and followed the path of the man who does not want to miss out on any pleasure or pain, because the inexhaustible variety of situations which derives from this approach is what makes life interesting.

Consequently, if we wish to read *On Love* as a 'Discourse on Method', it is hard for us to square this method with those that operated in Stendhal's times. But perhaps we could see a correspondence between it and that 'evidential paradigm' that the historian Carlo Ginzburg has recently tried to discern in the human sciences in the last twenty years of the last century ('Spie. Radici di un paradigma indiziario' (Clues: roots of an evidential paradigm), in *Crisi della ragione*, ed. A. Gargani (Turin: Einaudi, 1979), pp. 59–106). One can trace a long history of this evidential knowledge, based on semiotics, on awareness of traces, symptoms, involuntary coincidences, which privileges the marginal detail, the rejected elements, everything that our consciousness habitually refuses to pick up. It is not inappropriate to see as part of this line Stendhal and his punctiform knowledge which connects the sublime with the infinitesimal, *amour-passion* with the *marque de petite vérole*, without ruling out the possibility that the most obscure trace may be the sign of the most dazzling destiny.

Can we say that this programmatic method articulated by the anonymous author of the treatise *On Love* will be one which will be faithfully observed by the Stendhal of the novels and the Henry Brulard of the autobiographical works? For the latter we can certainly reply in the affirmative, inasmuch as his aim is defined in precise opposition to that of the novelist. The Stendhalian novel (at least in its most obvious and popular guise) tells stories that have cleanly delineated outlines, in which clearly drawn characters follow their dominant passions with consistency and determination, whereas the autobiographical Stendhal tries to catch the essence of his own life, of his own individual uniqueness in the shapeless, directionless welter of inessential facts. Carrying out this kind of exploration of a life ends up by becoming quite the opposite of what is intended by 'narrative'. *La Vie de Henri Brulard* opens like this:

> *Will I have the courage to write these confessions in an intelligible manner? I have to narrate, and I write 'considerations' on minimal happenings, but ones which because of their microscopic nature need to be told clearly. What patience you will need, reader!*

It is memory itself which is fragmentary by its very nature, and several times in *La Vie de Henri Brulard* it is compared to a crumbling fresco.

> *It is always just like the frescoes in the Camposanto in Pisa, where one can discern an arm very clearly but the bit next to it representing the head has fallen away. I see a sequence of very precise images but they have no other appearance except that which they had in relation to me; or rather I see their appearance only through the memory of the effect that they produced on me.*

Because of this, Stendhal claims, 'there is no originality or truth except in the details'. Here are Giovanni Macchia's words in an essay dedicated to this very obsession with detail (in his 'Stendhal tra romanzo e autobiografia', in *Il mito di Parigi*):

> *The whole course of our existence is wrapped in an array of small, seemingly unimportant events but which mark and reveal the rhythm of life, like the banal secrets of one day, which we pay no attention to and which in fact we try to destroy. . . . From Stendhal's ability to look at everything with a human gaze, from his refusal to select, correct, or falsify, came the most striking*

*psychological intuitions and social insights. (*Il mito di Parigi *(Turin: Einaudi, 1965), pp. 94–95)*

But fragmentariness concerns not only the past: even in the present something that is only glimpsed involuntarily can have an even more powerful effect, like the half-open door through which, in one page of his *Journal*, he spies a young woman undressing and hopes to catch a glimpse of a breast or a thigh. 'A woman who, spread out on a bed, would have no effect on me, glimpsed secretly gives me the most enchanting sensations, for in this situation she is natural and I am not preoccupied with my own role and can abandon myself to the sensation.'

And it is often by starting from the most obscure and private moments that the epistemological process develops, rather than from the moment of full realisation. Here there is a link with the title chosen by Roland Barthes for his paper: '*On échoue toujours à parler de ce qu'on aime*' (Any attempt to talk about the object of our love is always doomed to failure). The *Journal* ends on his moment of greatest happiness: his arrival in Milan in 1811. But Henry Brulard had begun by acknowledging his happiness on the Janiculine hill on the eve of his fiftieth birthday, and immediately felt the need to start narrating his unhappy childhood in Grenoble.

Now is the point when I wonder whether this type of knowledge also holds any relevance for the novels, that is to say I wonder how this squares with the canonical image of Stendhal as the novelist of vital energies, of the will to assert oneself. Another way of asking the same question: does the Stendhal who fascinated me in my youth still exist or was it an illusion? To this latter question I can reply immediately: yes, he exists, he is there just the same as always, Julien is still contemplating from his rock the sparrowhawk in the sky, identifying with its strength and isolation. I notice, however, that now this concentration of energy interests me less, and I am much more intrigued to discover what lies underneath it, all the rest of the picture, which I cannot call the hidden mass of the iceberg because it is not in fact hidden but it does somehow support and keep together everything else.

Of course the Stendhalian hero typically possesses a linearity of character, a continuity of will, and a compactness of ego as he lives through his internal conflicts. All of this seems to take us to the opposite extreme from a notion of existential reality which I have tried to define as punctiform, discontinuous and pulviscular. Julien is entirely defined by the conflict in him between shyness and will which commands him, as though by some categoric imperative, to take Madame de Rênal's hand in the darkness of the garden, in that extraordinary passage describing his internal struggle in which the reality of his passionate attraction finally triumphs over his presumed hardness and her presumed innocence. Fabrizio is so cheerily allergic to any form of anguish that even when imprisoned in the tower he is never once affected by the depression of incarceration, and his prison transforms itself into an incredibly versatile means of communication, and becomes almost the very condition under which his love will be fulfilled. Lucien is so caught up in his own self-esteem that his desire to recover from the mortification of falling from his horse or from the misunderstanding of a careless phrase by Madame de Chasteller, or from the *gaucherie* of having kissed her hand, conditions all his future actions. Naturally the course of Stendhal's heroes is never a linear one: since the scene of their actions is so far from the Napoleonic battlefields that they dream about, in order to express their potential energies they have to don the mask that is at the opposite extreme from their inner image of themselves. Julien and Fabrizio don priestly vestments and undertake an ecclesiastical career whose credibility from the point of view of historical verisimilitude is at least debatable; Lucien simply buys a missal, but he has a double mask, that of an Orléanist officer and that of a nostalgic Bourbon sympathiser.

This bodily self-consciousness in living out their passions is even more marked in the female characters. Madame de Rênal, Gina Sanseverina, Madame de Chasteller, are all above their young lovers either in age or in social standing, and more clear-minded, decisive and experienced than them, as well as being willing to tolerate them in their hesitations before becoming their victims. Perhaps they are projections of the image of the mother that the writer never had and that in *Henri Brulard* he immortalised in the snapshot of the resolute young woman who leaps over the baby's bed; or perhaps projections of an archetype whose traces he constantly sought in the ancient chronicles he read as sources: like that young stepmother with whom a Farnese prince fell in love, the prince who is evoked as the first prisoner in the tower, almost as though Stendhal wanted to establish them emblematically as the mythical core behind the relationship between Sanseverina and Fabrizio.

In addition to this tussle between the wills of the female and male characters, there is also the will of the author and his plan for the work: but each will is autonomous and can only present opportunities which the other wills can either exploit or reject. There is a marginal note in the manuscript of *Lucien Leuwen* which reads: 'The best hunting dog can only get the quarry to pass within the range of the hunter's rifle. If he does not fire, the dog can do nothing about it. The novelist is like the hero's hunting dog.'

Amidst these trails followed by the dog and the hunters, we can see taking shape in Stendhal's most mature work, *Lucien Leuwen*, a representation of love which is genuinely like a Milky Way, dense with emotions and sensations and situations which follow, supersede and cancel out one another, following the programme outlined in *On Love*. This happens particularly during the ball at which Lucien and Madame de Chasteller have the chance to talk for the first time and get to know each other. The ball, which begins in chapter 15 and ends in chapter 19, chronicles a succession of minimal incidents, bursts of unremarkable dialogue, gradations of shyness, hauteur, hesitation, love, suspicion, shame and contempt on the part both of the young officer and of the woman.

What strikes us in these pages is the profusion of psychological detail, the variety of fluctuating emotions and of *intermittences du coeur* – and the echo of Proust, who will be the inevitable destination along this road, only serves to emphasise how much is achieved here by an extremely economical use of description and a linearity of procedure which ensures that our attention is always concentrated on the knot of essential relationships in the plot.

Stendhal's portrait of aristocratic society in the legitimist provinces during the July monarchy is like the objective observation of the zoologist, sensitive to the morphological specifics of the tiniest of fauna, as is openly declared in these very pages in a sentence attributed to Lucien: 'I should study them as one studies natural history. Cuvier used to tell us, in the Jardin des Plantes, that a methodical study of worms, insects and the most repellent sea crabs, carefully noting their differences and similarities, is the best way to cure oneself of the disgust they inspire.'

In Stendhal's novels the settings – or at least certain settings, such as receptions and salons – are used not just to establish atmosphere but to chart positions. Scenes are defined by the movements of characters, by their position at the moment when certain emotions or conflicts are aroused, and in turn each conflict is defined by its happening in that particular place and time. In the same way Stendhal the autobiographer feels the strange necessity to fix places not by describing them but by sketching rough maps of them, where as well as giving a summary account of *décor* he marks the points where the various characters were, so that the pages of *La Vie de Henri Brulard* come before us as detailed as an atlas. What does this topographical obsession derive from? From that haste of his which makes him omit initial descriptions only to develop them subsequently on the basis of those notes which merely served to jog his memory? Not only from this, I think. Since it is the uniqueness of every event that interests him, the map serves to fix that point in space in which the event happens, just as the story helps to fix it in time.

The settings described in the novels are more often exterior than interior: the Alpine landscapes of Franche-Comté in *The Red and the Black*, or those of Brianza gazed upon by the abbé Blanès from the belltower in *The Charterhouse of Parma*, but the prize Stendhalian landscape for me would be the plain, unpoetic one of Nancy, as it appears in chapter 4 of *Lucien Leuwen*, in all its utilitarian squalor typical of the start of the industrial revolution. This is a landscape which betokens a conflict in the protagonist's conscience, caught as he is between his prosaic bourgeois existence, and his aspirations towards an aristocracy that is now a mere ghost of itself. It represents an objectively negative element but one which is ready to crystallise for the young lancer into buds of beauty if only it can be invested with an existential and amorous ecstasy. The poetic power of Stendhal's gaze lies not merely in its enthusiasm and euphoria, it lies also in the cold repulsion for a completely unattractive world which he feels himself forced to accept as the only reality possible, such as the outskirts of Nancy where Lucien is sent to quell one of the first workers' uprisings, as the soldiers on horseback file past through those grim streets in the grey morning.

Stendhal registers these social transformations through the minute vibrations in the behaviour of individuals. Why does Italy occupy this unique place in his heart? We continually hear him repeat that Paris is the realm of vanity: in opposition to Italy, which is for him the country of sincere and objective passions. But we must not forget that in his spiritual geography there is another pole, England, a civilisation with which he is continually tempted to identify himself.

In his *Souvenirs d'égotisme* (*Memoirs of an Egotist*) there is a passage in which he makes a decisive choice for Italy over England, and precisely because of what we today would call its underdevelopment, whereas the English way of life which obliges its workers to labour for eighteen hours per day seems to him 'ridiculous':

The exaggerated and oppressive workload of the English labourer is our revenge for Waterloo. . . . The poor Italian, dressed only in rags, is much closer to happiness. He has time to make love, and for eighty to a hundred days per year he gives himself over to a religion which is so much more interesting because it actually makes him a little bit afraid.

Stendhal's idea is a certain rhythm of life in which there should be room for many things, especially wasting a bit of time. His starting point is his rejection of provincial squalor, his anger against his father and Grenoble. He heads for the big city: Milan for him is a great city where both the discreet charms of the Ancien Régime and the passions of his own Napoleonic youth live on, even although many aspects of that country of religion and poverty are not to his liking.

London too is an ideal city, but there the aspects which satisfy his snobbish tastes have to be paid for with the harshness of advanced industrialism. In this internal geography of his, Paris is equidistant between London and Milan: both the priests and the law of profit rule there, hence Stendhal's continual centrifugal urge. (His is a geography of escape, and I should also include Germany in it, since it was there that he found the name with which he signed his novels: this name was thus a more serious identity than so many other masks that he used. But I would have to say that for him Germany represents only his nostalgia for Napoleon's epic struggle, a memory that tends to disappear in Stendhal.)

His *Souvenirs d'égotisme*, an autobiographical fragment about his time in Paris in between Milan and London, is the text which contains the essential map of Stendhal's world. It could be defined as his best novel manqué: manqué perhaps because he lacked a literary model that could convince him that it could become a novel, but also because only in this manqué form could a story about absences and missed opportunities develop. In *Souvenirs d'égotisme* the dominant theme is his absence from Milan, which he abandons after the famous, disastrous love affair. In a Paris that is seen as a place of absence, every adventure turns into a fiasco: physiological fiascos in his affairs with prostitutes, mental fiascos in his relations with society and in intellectual exchanges (for instance, in his meetings with the philosopher he most admired, Destutt de Tracy). Then comes the journey to London, in which his chronicle of failure culminates in the extraordinary tale of the duel that never happens, his search for the arrogant English captain whom he had failed to challenge at the right moment and for whom he continues to hunt in vain through the dockland taverns.

There is but one oasis of unexpected happiness in this tale of disasters: the house of three prostitutes in one of the poorest London suburbs, which instead of turning out to be a sinister trap as he had feared, is instead a space that is tiny but elegant like a doll's house. The inhabitants are poor young girls who welcome the three noisy French tourists with grace and dignity and discretion. Here at last is an image of *bonheur*, a poor and fragile *bonheur*, as far as could be from the aspirations of our 'egotist'!

Must we therefore conclude that the real Stendhal is Stendhal in negative, a writer who must be sought out only in his disappointments, adversities and defeats? No, the value championed by Stendhal is one of existential tension which stems from measuring one's own specific nature (and limits) with the specific nature and limits of one's environment. Precisely because existence is dominated by entropy, by the dissolution of everything into instants and impulses like corpuscles devoid of shape or connection, he wants the individual to fulfil himself according to a principle of energy conservation, or rather of constant reproduction of energy charges. This is an imperative that becomes so much more rigorous the closer he comes to realising that entropy will in any case triumph in the end, and that all that will remain of the universe with all its galaxies will be a vortex of atoms floating in the void.

[1980]

Guide for New Readers of Stendhal's *Charterhouse*

How many new readers will be attracted to Stendhal's *The Charterhouse of Parma* by the new film version of the novel, shortly to be broadcast on television? Perhaps very few when compared to the total number of the TV audience, or perhaps very many when compared to the statistics for the number of books Italians read. But no data can ever supply us with the most important figure, and that is how many young people will be smitten right from the opening pages, and will be instantly convinced that this has to be the best novel ever written, recognising it as the novel they had always wanted to read and which will act as the benchmark for all the other novels they will read in later life. (I'm talking particularly about the opening chapters; as you get into it, you will find that it is a different novel, or several novels each different from the other, all of which will require you to modify your involvement in the plot; whatever happens, the brilliance of the opening will continue to influence you.)

This is what happened to me and to so many others in the various generations that have read the work in the last hundred years. (*The Charterhouse* came out in 1839, but you have to exclude the forty years that it had to wait before Stendhal was understood, a period he himself had foreseen with extraordinary precision; even although of all his works this was the most instantly successful, and could count for its launch on a lengthy and enthusiastic essay by Balzac, a good 72 pages long!)

Whether this miracle will happen again and for how long, we cannot be sure: the reasons why a book fascinates us (that it is to say, its powers of seduction, which is something very distinct from its absolute worth) are composed of so many imponderable elements. (As is a book's absolute worth, presuming that that phrase means anything at all.) Certainly, if I open *The Charterhouse* again even today, as on every occasion I have reread the book in different periods and throughout all the changes in tastes and expectations, what I find is that the charge of its music, that Allegro Con Brio, immediately recaptures me: those opening chapters in Napoleonic Milan in which history with the rumble of its cannons marches side by side with and at the same pace as the rhythm of the individual life. And the atmosphere of pure adventure which you enter, as the sixteen-year-old Fabrizio wanders around the damp battlefield of Waterloo amidst the victuallers' carts and fleeing horses, is the archetypal novelistic adventure, full of a deliberately calibrated amount of danger and safety and not without a strong dose of youthful candour. And the open-eyed corpses with outstretched arms are the first real corpses exploited by literature to try to explain what a war really is. And that amorous female atmosphere which starts to circulate from the very first pages, full of protective trepidation and jealous intrigue, already reveals the novel's real theme, which will accompany Fabrizio right to the end (an atmosphere which cannot but become oppressive in the long run).

Perhaps it was because I belonged to a generation which in its youth lived through wars and huge political upheavals that I have become a life-long reader of *The Charterhouse*. Yet in my personal memories, which are so much less free and serene, what dominates are discords and stridency, not that seductive music. Perhaps the exact opposite is true: we consider ourselves children of a particular epoch because we project Stendhalian adventures onto our own experiences in order to transform them, just as Don Quixote did.

I said that *The Charterhouse* contains many different novels and I concentrated on the opening: it starts as a chronicle about history and society, and a picaresque adventure. Then we enter into the heart of the novel, in other words into the world of the small court of Prince Ranuccio Ernesto IV (this apocryphal Parma is historically identifiable with Modena, as is passionately claimed by the Modenese, such as Antonio Delfini, but even Parma people like Gino Magnani remain happy with this account, as though it were a sublimated version of their own history).

At this point the novel becomes a kind of theatre, a closed space, a chessboard for a game involving a finite number of players, a grey, fixed place in which a whole chain of mismatched passions develops: Count Mosca, a powerful man who is the love slave of Gina Sanseverina;

Sanseverina who obtains what she wants but who only has eyes for her nephew Fabrizio; Fabrizio who loves himself first and foremost, enjoys a few, quick adventures as sideshows, and finally concentrates all these energies gravitating around him into his hopeless passion for the angelic and pensive Clelia.

All this in the petty world of court and society intrigue, between a prince haunted by fear for having hanged two patriots and the 'fiscal général' (justice minister) Rassi who is the incarnation (perhaps for the first time in a character in a novel) of a bureaucratic mediocrity which also has something terrifying in it. And here the conflict is, in line with Stendhal's intentions, between this image of the backward Europe of Metternich and the absolute nature of those passions which brook no bounds and which were the last refuge for the noble ideals of an age that had been overcome.

The dramatic centre of the book is like an opera (and opera had been the first medium which had helped the music-mad Stendhal to understand Italy) but in *The Charterhouse* the atmosphere (luckily) is not that of tragic opera but rather (as Paul Valéry discovered) of operetta. The tyrannical rule is squalid but hesitant and clumsy (much worse had really taken place at Modena) and the passions are powerful but work by a rather basic mechanism. (Just one character, Count Mosca, possesses any psychological complexity, a calculating character but one who is also desperate, possessive and nihilistic.)

But the element of 'court novel' does not end here. On top of the novelistic transformation of Italy into a nation espousing the Bourbon Restoration there is the Renaissance chronicle plot, from one of those historical sagas which Stendhal had hunted out in the libraries to draw on for his own *Chroniques italiennes* (*Italian Chronicles*). This one dealt with the life of Alessandro Farnese. Being very much loved and protected by one of his aunts, a gallant and scheming noblewoman, Alessandro enjoyed a glorious ecclesiastical career despite having spent his youth in libertine adventures (he had also killed a rival and had been imprisoned for it in Castel Sant'Angelo) before becoming Pope Paul III. What has this violent tale of Rome in the fifteenth and sixteenth centuries got to do with that of Fabrizio in a society riddled with hypocrisy and scruples of conscience? Nothing at all, and yet Stendhal's projected novel had begun as just that, a transposition of Farnese's life into the contemporary age, demonstrating an Italian continuity of vital energy and passionate spontaneity in which he never tired of believing (though he was also able to discern less obvious things in Italians: their lack of confidence, their anxiety, their caution).

Whatever the original source of inspiration, the opening of the novel contains such autonomous drive that it could easily continue under its own steam, ignoring the Renaissance chronicle. Instead, Stendhal goes back to it every so often and resorts to Farnese again as his model. The most incongruous result of following this source is that as soon as Fabrizio removes his Napoleonic soldier's uniform, he enters a seminary and takes his vows. For the rest of the novel we have to imagine him dressed as a monsignor, a rather uncomfortable notion both for him and for us, because we need to make a considerable effort to reconcile the two images, and his ecclesiastical condition impinges only on his external behaviour and not at all on his spirit.

Already some years previously another Stendhalian hero, he too a young man thirsty for Napoleonic glory, had decided to don the cassock, seeing that the Restoration had blocked a military career to all except the scions of the nobility. But in *The Red and the Black*, Julien Sorel's alternative vocation is the novel's central theme, a situation with much more serious and dramatic consequences for Julien than for Fabrizio del Dongo. Fabrizio is not Julien inasmuch as he lacks his psychological complexity, but nor is he Alessandro Farnese who was destined to end up as Pope, and as such is the emblematic hero of a tale which can be interpreted as much as a scandalous anticlerical revelation as an edifying legend about a sinner's redemption. Well then, who is Fabrizio? Leaving aside the clothes he wears and the events in which he lets himself become embroiled, Fabrizio is someone who tries to read the signs of his destiny, guided by the science that he has been taught by the abbé-astrologer Blanès, his real teacher. He asks himself about the future and the past (was Waterloo *his* battle or not?), but his whole reality is in the present, moment by moment.

Like Fabrizio, the whole of *The Charterhouse* overcomes the contradictions of its composite nature thanks to constant motion. When Fabrizio ends up in prison, a new novel opens up within the novel: the novel about the prison, the tower and his love for Clelia, which is something completely different from the rest of the book, and even more difficult to define.

There is no human condition more anguished than that of the prisoner, but Stendhal is so refractory to anguish that even when he has to represent isolation in a cell inside a tower (after an arrest in mysterious and distressing circumstances) the mental attitudes he conveys are always extrovert and full of hope: '*Comment! moi qui avait tant de peur de la prison, j'y suis, et je ne me souviens pas d'être triste!*' ('What? I who was so afraid of it, am now in prison and I have forgotten that I should be sad!') I have forgotten that I should be sad! Never was a refutation of romantic self-pity uttered so blithely and lustily.

This Farnese Tower, which never existed either in Parma or Modena, has a very precise shape: actually composed of two towers, a thinner one built on top of the thicker one (in addition there is a house built on the terrace which sticks out, with an aviary on top, where the young girl Clelia appears). This is one of the magic spaces in the novel (in some respects it reminded Trompeo of Ariosto, in others of Tasso), a symbol, clearly: so much so that, as happens with all true symbols, one can never decide what on earth it symbolises. Isolation within one's own self, obviously; but also, and perhaps even more, coming out of oneself, and amorous communication; for never has Fabrizio been so expansive and loquacious as when using the improbable, highly complicated wireless-telegraph systems with which he manages to correspond from his cell both with Clelia and with his ever resourceful aunt Gina.

The tower is the place where Fabrizio's first romantic love flowers, his passion for the unattainable Clelia, daughter of his gaoler, but it is also the gilded cage of Sanseverina's love which has held Fabrizio prisoner from the outset. So much so that the origin of the tower (chapter 18) goes back to the story of a young Farnese imprisoned in it because he had become his step-mother's lover: this is the mythical core behind Stendhal's novels, the 'hypergamy' or love for women of superior age or social standing (Julien and Madame Rênal, Lucien and Madame de Chasteller, Fabrizio and Gina Sanseverina).

The tower is also height, the ability to see into the distance: the incredible view on which Fabrizio gazes from up there embraces the whole range of the Alps from Nice to Treviso, and the whole course of the river Po from Monviso to Ferrara. But that is not all; he can also see his own life, and that of others, as well as the network of intricate relations which make up a human destiny.

Just as the outlook from the tower covers the whole of Northern Italy, so from the height of this novel written in 1839 the future of Italian history is already in view: Prince Ranuccio Ernesto IV is an absolutist petty tyrant, but at the same time he is also a Carlo Alberto able to foresee the future developments of the Risorgimento, and in his heart he cultivates the hope of one day becoming a constitutional king of Italy.

An historical and political reading of *The Charterhouse* has always been a predictable and even obligatory approach, starting with Balzac (who defined this novel as the new Machiavelli's *Prince*!). Similarly it has always been both easy and essential to show that Stendhal's claim to exalt the ideals of liberty and progress which were suffocated by the Restoration is extremely superficial. But this very lightness of Stendhal can teach us a historical and political lesson not to be underestimated, when he shows us with what ease the ex-Jacobins or ex-Bonapartists become (and remain) authoritative and zealous members of the legitimist establishment. That such risky stances and actions, which appeared dictated by the most powerful convictions, could show that what lay behind them was very little indeed, is something that we have seen time and time again, in the Milan of those days and elsewhere, but the beauty of *The Charterhouse* is that this is stated without crying scandal, and accepted like something that is taken for granted.

What makes *The Charterhouse of Parma* a great 'Italian' novel is that sense of politics as a calculated readjustment and redistribution of roles: there is the prince who while he persecutes the Jacobins worries about establishing future balances of power with them, which will allow him to put himself at the head of the imminent movement of national unity; and there is Count Mosca, who having been a Napoleonic officer becomes a hard-line minister and head of a reactionary party (but only ready to encourage a faction of reactionary extremists in order to show himself up as a moderate by distancing himself from them), and all this without becoming in the least way involved in his inner essence.

As we read further into the novel, the other Stendhalian image of Italy recedes further into the distance, that of the country of generous sentiments and spontaneity, that locus of happiness which opened up to the young French officer on his arrival in Milan. In *La Vie de Henri Brulard*, once he reaches this moment and is about to describe his happiness, he interrupts his account with the words: '*On échoue toujours à parler de ce qu'on aime*' (Any attempt to talk about the object of our love is always doomed to failure).

This sentence provided both the subject and the title of Roland Barthes' last paper, which he was to have read at the Stendhal conference in Milan in 1980 (but it was while he was writing it that he was involved in the road accident that cost him his life). In the pages that he completed, Barthes observes that in his autobiographical works Stendhal emphasises on several occasions the happiness of his time in Italy as a young man, but he never manages to describe it.

> *And yet twenty years later, in a kind of* après–coup *which also forms part of the contorted logic of love, Stendhal writes magisterial pages on Italy: yes, those pages enkindle in the reader like me (but I am sure I am not the only one) that ecstasy, that radiance that his intimate diary mentioned but could not communicate. There is a sort of miraculous empathy between the mass of happiness and pleasure which broke out in Milan with the arrival of the French and our joy in reading: at last the effect narrated coincides with the effect produced.*

[1982]

The City as Novel in Balzac

The enterprise which Balzac feels impelled to undertake when he starts to write *Ferragus* is a vast one: to turn a city into a novel; to represent its districts and streets as characters, each endowed with a personality totally different from the others; to summon up human figures and situations like spontaneous vegetation burgeoning from the pavements of this or that street, or as elements that provoke such a dramatic contrast with those streets that they cause a series of cataclysms; to ensure that in every changing minute the real protagonist is the living city, its biological continuity, the monster that is Paris.

And yet he had set out with a totally different idea in his head, namely the power exercised by mysterious characters through an invisible network of secret societies. To put it another way, his favourite sources of inspiration, which he wanted to blend to write a single novel-cycle, were two: secret societies, and the hidden omnipotence of an individual on the fringes of society. The myths that will inform both popular and highbrow fiction for over a century all surface in Balzac. The Superman who takes his revenge on the society that has outlawed him by turning into an elusive demiurge will pervade the various volumes of the *Comédie humaine* in the ever-changing guise of Vautrin and will be reincarnated in all the Counts of Montecristo, Phantoms of the Opera and perhaps even the Godfathers that the most successful novelists would later put into circulation. The murky conspiracy that spreads its tentacles everywhere will become a half-serious, half-playful obsession for the most sophisticated English novelists of the turn of the nineteenth century and will reemerge in the serial production of violent spy thrillers in our own times.

With *Ferragus* we are still in the middle of a romantic, Byronic vogue. In an issue of the *Revue de Paris* for 1833 (a weekly for which Balzac had a contract to write forty pages a month, amidst the constant complaints of the publisher for his delay in delivering manuscripts and for the excessive number of corrections made at proof stage) we find the preface to the *Histoire des treize* (*History of the Thirteen*) in which the author promises to reveal the secrets of thirteen determined outlaws bound by a secret pact of mutual help which makes them invincible, and announces the first instalment as *Ferragus, chef des Dévorants*. (The term *Dévorants* or *Devoirants* traditionally signified the members of a guild, 'The Companions of Duty', but Balzac certainly played on its false etymology from the much more sinister 'dévorer' (to devour), and wants us to think of Devourers.)

The preface is dated 1831, but Balzac only started work on the project in February 1833, and did not manage to deliver the first chapter in time for the issue following the one that contained the preface, hence it was only two weeks later that the *Revue de Paris* published the first two chapters together; the third chapter caused the following week's issue to be delayed, while the fourth and the conclusion came out in a special supplement in April.

But the novel as published was very different from what the preface had promised: the author was no longer interested in the original project, he was much more concerned with something else which made him agonise over his manuscripts instead of turning out pages to comply with the rhythm demanded by the journal, something which forced him to cover his proofs with corrections and additions, completely altering the typographers' layout. The plot he followed was still enough to make readers hold their breath at its astonishing mysteries and reversals, and the dark character with the Ariostesque nickname of Ferragus plays a central role, but the adventures to which he owes both his secret power and his public notoriety are in the past and Balzac allows us only to witness his decline. And as for the Thirteen, or rather the other twelve members, the author apparently forgot about them, having them appear only in the distance, in an almost decorative role, at a ceremonial requiem mass.

What now obsessed Balzac was a topographical epic about Paris, following the intuition that he had been the first to have of the city as language, as ideology, as something that conditions every thought, word and deed, where the streets '*impriment par leur physionomie certaines idées contre lesquelles nous sommes sans défense*' (by virtue of their appearance impress upon us certain notions which we are powerless to resist), the city as monstrous as a giant crustacean whose inhabitants are merely the limbs which propel it. Already for some years now Balzac had been publishing in journals sketches of city life and portraits of typical characters: but now he had the idea of organising this material into a kind of encyclopedia of Paris in which there was space for a mini-treatise on following women in the streets, a genre sketch (worthy of Daumier) of passers-by caught in the rain, a survey of street vagabonds, an account of the *grisette*, and a register of the various kinds of language spoken (when Balzac's dialogues lose their usual rhetorical emphasis they are able to imitate the most fashionable phrases and neologisms, even down to reproducing the intonation of people's voices – for instance, when a streetseller claims that marabou feathers give to women's coiffure '*quelque chose de vague, d'ossianique et de très comme il faut*' (something airy, almost Ossianic and very much up to date)). To these exterior scenes he adds a similar range of interiors, from the squalid to the luxurious (with studied pictorial effects such as the vase of wallflowers in the widow Gruget's hovel). The description of the Père-Lachaise cemetery and the labyrinthine bureaucracy connected with funerals rounds off the picture, so that the novel which had opened with the vision of Paris as a living organism closes on the horizon of the Parisian dead.

Balzac's *History of the Thirteen* turned into an atlas of the continent that is Paris. After *Ferragus*, he went on to write (his obstinacy never permitted him to leave a project half-finished) for different publishers (he had already quarrelled with *La Revue de Paris*) two further stories in order to complete a trilogy. These are two novels which are very different from the first and from each other, but which have in common, apart from the fact that their protagonists turn out to be members of the mysterious club (a detail which is in reality quite marginal to the aim of the plot), the presence of long digressions adding other entries to his encyclopedia of Paris: *La Duchesse de Langeais* (a novel of passions written on an autobiographical impulse) offers in its second chapter a sociological study of the aristocracy of the Faubourg Saint-Germain; *La Fille aux yeux d'or* (which is much more important: one of the key texts in that line in French literature which starts with Sade and still continues today, down to, say, Bataille and Klossowski) opens with a kind of anthropological museum devoted to Parisians divided into their various social classes.

If the richness of such digressions is greater in *Ferragus* than in the other two novels of the trilogy, that is not to say that it is only in these digressions that Balzac invests the full power of his writing, for even the intimate psychological drama of the relationship between M. and Mme. Desmarets absorbs him totally. Of course we find this drama of a couple who are too perfect much less interesting, given our reading habits which at a certain height of the sublime allow us only to see dazzling clouds and prevent us from discerning movement and contrast. Nevertheless, the way in which the shadow of suspicion that refuses to go away is unable to scratch the exterior of their amorous trust but rather corrodes it from within, is a process narrated in anything but banal terms. Nor must we forget that passages which might only seem to us exercises in conventional eloquence, like the last letter from Clémence to her husband, were the virtuoso passages of which Balzac was proudest, as he himself confessed to Madame Hanska.

The other psychological drama, concerning a father's excessive love for his daughter, is less convincing, even though it can be seen as a first draft of *Père Goriot* (though here the egoism is all on the side of the father, and the sacrifice entirely the daughter's). Dickens was able to develop a quite different plot from the return of an ex-convict father in his masterpiece *Great Expectations*.

But once we accept the fact that the importance given to these psychological dramas also helps to relegate the adventure plot to a secondary level, we must recognise how much the latter still contributes to our pleasure as readers: the suspense works, even though the emotional centre of the story shifts constantly from character to character; the rhythm of events is exhilarating even though many sequences in the plot limp somewhat through illogicality or inaccuracy; the mystery of the visits by Madame Jules to the street of ill repute is one of the first criminal mysteries to confront an amateur detective at the opening of a novel, even though the solution is discovered too quickly and is disappointingly simple.

The work's whole strength as a novel is supported and enhanced by being founded on the myth of the metropolis, a metropolis in which every character still appears to have a distinctive face, as in portraits by Ingres. The age of the anonymous crowd has not yet begun: and it really is a short period, those twenty years that separate Balzac and the apotheosis of the city in the novel from Baudelaire and the apotheosis of the city in poetry. In order to offer a definition of that transition, two quotations will suffice, by readers from a century later, both arriving at an interest in such problems by different routes.

Balzac discovered the big city as something bristling with mystery, and the sense which he always keeps alert is that of curiosity. This is his Muse. He is never either comic or tragic, simply curious. He immerses himself in a tangle of things but is always capable of sniffing out and promising us a mystery, and he sets about dismantling the whole machine bit by bit with keen, lively and in the end triumphant enthusiasm. Look at how he approaches new characters: he examines them up and down as though they were rare specimens, describing, sculpting, defining and commenting on them until he conveys all their individuality and guarantees us marvels. His conclusions, observations, tirades, and bon mots, do not contain psychological truths, but the hunches and tricks of a presiding magistrate flailing away at the mystery which dammit must be cleared up. For this reason, when the quest to solve the mystery is at an end and – at the beginning or in the course of the book (never at the end because by then all is revealed, along with the mystery) – Balzac discourses on his own mystery complex with an enthusiasm that is at once sociological, psychological and lyrical, he is wonderful. See the opening of Ferragus *or the beginning of the second part of* Splendeurs et misères des courtisanes: *here he is sublime. His work is the overture to Baudelaire.*

The author of this passage was the young Cesare Pavese, writing in his diary on 13 October 1936.

Almost at the same time Walter Benjamin, in his essay on Baudelaire, writes a passage in which all one has to do is to substitute for Victor Hugo's name the even more appropriate one of Balzac, for Benjamin to develop and complete Pavese's point:

One looks in vain, in Les Fleurs du mal *or in* Spleen de Paris *for something analogous to those large frescoes of the city at which Victor Hugo excelled. Baudelaire describes neither the people nor the city. And this very refusal allowed him to conjure up the one in the image of the other. His crowds are always those of the metropolis; his Paris is always overpopulated . . . In* Tableaux parisiens *one can, almost always, sense the secret presence of the masses. When Baudelaire takes as his subject the morning dawning, there is in the deserted streets something of the 'swarming silence' which Hugo senses in Paris at night . . . The masses were really the fluttering veil through which Baudelaire saw Paris.*

[1973]

Charles Dickens, *Our Mutual Friend*

The Thames at nightfall, dark and muddy, with the tide rising up the piers of the bridges: against this backdrop, which this year's news stories have brought to our attention in the most lugubrious light, a boat approaches, almost touching the floating logs, barges and rubbish. At its prow stands a man staring with vulture-like eyes at the current as though looking for something; at the oars, half-hidden by the hood of her cheap cloak, is a girl with an angelic face. What are they looking for? We soon learn that the man recovers the corpses of suicides or murder victims who have been flung into the river: the waters of the Thames seem to contain every day a rich catch for this particular fisherman. As soon as he sees a corpse floating on the water's surface, the man removes the gold coins from his pockets, and then drags him with a rope to a riverside police station, where he will receive a reward. The angelic girl, the daughter of the boatman, tries not to look at this macabre booty: she is terrified, but continues to row.

The openings of Dickens' novels are often memorable, but none is better than the first chapter of *Our Mutual Friend*, the second last novel he wrote, and the last one he completed. Carried along on the corpse-fisher's boat, we seem to enter the dark side of the world.

In the second chapter everything changes. We are now surrounded by characters out of a comedy of manners, attending a dinner-party at the house of parvenus where everyone pretends to be old friends but in fact they barely know each other. However, before the chapter ends the guests' conversation suddenly turns to the mystery of a man who drowned just as he was about to inherit a vast fortune, and this takes us back to the suspense of the opening chapter.

The huge inheritance is that of the late king of rubbish, an extremely greedy old man whose house still stands in the London suburbs next to a field dotted with huge piles of rubbish. We continue to move in that sinister world of detritus to which the opening chapter had introduced us by way of the river. All the other scenes in the novel, tables set out sparkling with silver, sleeked ambitions, tangles of interest and speculation, are nothing but thin screens covering the desolate substance of this apocalyptic world.

The custodian of the Golden Dustman's fortune is his former labourer, Boffin, one of Dickens' great comic characters, particularly for the pompous air with which he preens himself, whereas the only experience he has ever had has been one of abject poverty and limitless ignorance. (He is a likeable character, all the same: he and his wife possess both human warmth and kind intentions. Subsequently, in the course of the novel, he becomes greedy and selfish, but in the end he is once more shown to have a heart of gold.) Suddenly finding himself rich, the illiterate Boffin can give free rein to his repressed enthusiasm for culture, buying the eight volumes of Gibbon's *Decline and Fall of the Roman Empire* (a title which he can barely make out, so that instead of *Roman* he reads *Rooshan* and thinks it is about the Russian Empire). Accordingly he employs a beggar with a wooden leg, Silas Wegg, as his 'man of letters', to read to him in the evening. After Gibbon, Boffin, who is now obsessed by the fear of losing his riches, searches the bookshops for lives of famous misers, and has these read to him by his trusted 'man of letters'.

The irrepressible Boffin and the shady Silas Wegg form an extraordinary twosome, and they are joined by Mr Venus, by trade an embalmer and someone who makes human skeletons using bones which he has found lying around: Wegg asks him to make him a leg out of real bones to replace his wooden one. In this wasteland milieu, inhabited by clown-like and ghostly characters, Dickens' world becomes before our eyes the world of Samuel Beckett: in the black humour of Dickens' late works we can discern a definite foretaste of Beckett.

Of course the darkness in Dickens always contrasts with the light, even though nowadays it is the 'darker' aspects that stand out more in our reading of him. The light usually radiates from young girls who are all the more virtuous and kind-hearted the more steeped they are in a kind of black hell. This emphasis on virtue is the hardest thing to take for modern readers of Dickens. Of course, Dickens as a man had no more direct access to virtue than we have, but the Victorian mentality found in his novels not only the faithful exemplification of its ideals but almost the founding images of its own mythology. And even though we maintain that for us the real Dickens is to be found only in his personifications of evil and in his grotesque caricatures, it would still be impossible to ignore his angelic victims and consoling presences: without the one kind of character the other would not exist. We have to regard both as structural elements which relate to each other, like supporting walls and beams of the same solid building.

Even amongst the 'goodies' Dickens can create unusual, unconventional figures, like the bizarre trio in this novel comprising a dwarf girl, full of sarcasm and wisdom, Lizzie who is angelic both in her face and in her heart, and a Jew with his beard and gaberdine. Wise little Jenny Wren, who makes dolls' clothes, who can only move on crutches, and who transforms all the negative elements in her life into flights of fancy which are never cloying, is one of Dickens' most captivating and humorous characters. And Riah the Jew, employed by a sordid racketeer, Lammle (who terrorises and insults him and at the same time uses his name to act as money-lender, while continuing to pretend to be a respectable and fairminded person), tries to counteract the evil which he is forced to carry out by secretly lavishing his gifts on one and all, like the charitable spirit he is. This provides a perfect illustration of anti-Semitism, the mechanism through which a hypocritical society feels the need to create an image of the Jew on which to offload its own vices. This Riah is such a mild-mannered man that he could almost be thought a coward except that when he is at the nadir of his misfortunes he manages to create a space in which he can be free and seek revenge, along with the other two outcasts, especially following the active advice of the dolls' dressmaker (she too is angelic, but capable of inflicting on the odious Lammle a diabolical punishment).

This space for good is represented in physical terms by a terrace on the roof of a seedy pawnshop, in the middle of the squalor of the City, where Riah provides the two girls with material for dolls' dresses, beads, books, flowers and fruit, whilst 'the encompassing wilderness of dowager old chimneys twirled their cowls and fluttered their smoke, rather as if they were bridling, and fanning themselves, and looking on in a state of airy surprise'.

In *Our Mutual Friend* there is room for an urban romance and a comedy of manners, but also for complex and even tragic characters such as Bradley

Headstone, a former labourer who as soon as he becomes a schoolmaster is overtaken by an obsession for social climbing and status which becomes a form of diabolical possession. We follow him first as he falls in love with Lizzie, then as his jealousy becomes a fanatical obsession, and we watch his meticulous planning and execution of a crime, before subsequently seeing him condemned to go over all its details in his mind, even when he is teaching his pupils: 'As he paused with his piece of chalk at the blackboard before writing on it, he was thinking of the spot, and whether the water was not deeper and the fall straighter, a little higher up, or a little lower down. He had half a mind to draw a line or two upon the board, and show himself what he meant.'

Our Mutual Friend was written in 1864–65, *Crime and Punishment* in 1865–66. Dostoevsky was an admirer of Dickens, but could not have read this novel. Pietro Citati says, in his excellent essay on Dickens (in his *Il Migliore dei Mondi Impossibili*, Rizzoli): 'The strange providence which governs literature decreed that in the very years when Dostoevsky was writing *Crime and Punishment*, Dickens was unconsciously trying to rival his distant pupil, in writing the episode of Bradley Headstone's crime. . . . If Dostoevsky had read this part, he would surely have found sublime this last passage about the drawing on the blackboard.'

Citati's title *The Best of All Impossible Worlds* was taken from the twentieth-century writer who most admired Dickens, G. K. Chesterton. He wrote a whole book on Dickens as well as the introductions to many of his novels for the 'Everyman's Library' series. In the introduction to *Our Mutual Friend* Chesterton starts by quibbling about the title: 'Our common friend' means something in English (as does 'il nostro comune amico' in Italian); but 'our mutual friend', 'our reciprocal friend', what on earth can that mean? One could answer Chesterton by pointing out that the expression appears for the first time in the mouth of Boffin, whose English is always faulty, and that, even though the title's connection with the substance of the novel is not very obvious, nevertheless the theme of friendship, true or false, vaunted or concealed, twisted or tried and tested, is there on every page. But after condemning the title's linguistic impropriety, Chesterton announces that he likes the title precisely because of it. Dickens had never had a regular education and had never been a sophisticated man of letters; but it is for this very reason that Chesterton likes him, or rather likes him when he is himself, not when he tries to be something different. Chesterton's predilection for *Our Mutual Friend* is also for a Dickens who has returned to his origins, after various efforts to improve himself and to display his aristocratic tastes.

Although Chesterton has been the strongest champion of Dickens' literary stature in the twentieth century, I feel that his essay on *Our Mutual Friend* betrays an element of condescension, as the refined writer looks down on the popular novelist.

As far as I am concerned, *Our Mutual Friend* is an unqualified masterpiece, both in its plot and in the way it is written. As examples of writing, I will mention not only the rapid similes which crisply define a character or situation ('with an immense obtuse drab oblong face, like a face in a tablespoon'), but also the descriptive cityscapes which are worthy of a place in any anthology of urban landscapes: 'A grey, dusty, withered evening in London city has not a hopeful aspect. The closed warehouses and offices have an air of death about them, and the national dread of colour has an air of mourning. The towers and steeples of the many house-encompassed churches, dark and dingy as the sky that seems descending on them, are no relief to the general gloom; a sundial on a church wall has the look, in its useless black shade, of having failed in its business enterprise, and stopped payment for ever; melancholy waifs and strays of housekeepers and porters sweep melancholy waifs and strays of papers and pins into the kennels, and other more melancholy waifs and strays explore them, searching and stooping and poking for anything to sell.'

These last quotations [in Calvino's original Italian essay] were taken from the Italian translation in Einaudi's 'Struzzi' series, but my first quote above, about the chimneys, came from the version by Filippo Donini in Garzanti's 'I Grandi Libri' series. Donini's translation seems to reflect the book's spirit more accurately in some of the more subtle passages, even though it is more old-fashioned in other respects, such as the Italianisation of first names. In that quotation it was a question of rendering the gap between the humble pleasures of the terrace and the chimneys of the City, which were seen as haughty 'nobili dame' (dowagers): in Dickens no descriptive detail is ever otiose, rather it is always an integral part of the dynamics of the story.

One other reason why this novel is considered a masterpiece is its highly complex portrait of society and of its class conflict. On this point there is agreement between the two introductions to the Italian translations: both in Piergiorgio Bellocchio's perceptive and intelligent preface to the Garzanti edition, and in Arnold Kettle's introduction to the Einaudi version, which concentrates entirely on this class aspect. Kettle's polemic is directed against George Orwell who in a famous 'class' analysis of Dickens' novels proved that for Dickens the target was not so much the evils of society as the evils of human nature.

[1982]

Gustave Flaubert, *Trois Contes*

Trois Contes is entitled *Tre racconti* in Italian, and we could not call them anything else, but the term *conte* (as opposed to *récit* or *nouvelle*) underlines the link with oral narrative, with the marvellous and naive, in short with the folktale. This connotation applies to all three tales: not just to *The Legend of St Julien the Hospitaller* which is one of the first examples of a modern writer adopting the 'primitive' taste of medieval and popular art, and to *Hérodias*, which is a historical reconstruction that is erudite, visionary and aesthetically appealing, but also to *Un Coeur Simple* (*A Simple Heart*), where contemporary daily reality is experienced by a poor serving woman of simple spirit.

The three stories of *Trois Contes* are almost a distillation of all of Flaubert, and since they can be read in an evening I strongly recommend them to all those who want to pay homage, swift though it may be, to the sage of Croisset on the occasion of his centenary. (For the centenary Einaudi is reissuing them in the excellent translation by Lalla Romano.) In fact, those with even less time can omit *Hérodias* (its presence in the volume has always seemed to me rather dispersive and redundant) and concentrate all their attention on *A Simple Heart* and *The Legend of St Julien*, starting out from their fundamentally visual quality.

There is a history of visibility in the novel – of the novel as the art of making persons and things *visible* – which coincides with some of the phases of the history of the novel itself, though not with all of them. From Madame de Lafayette to Benjamin Constant the novel explores the human mind with prodigious accuracy, but these pages are like closed shutters which prevent anything else from being seen. Visibility in the novel begins with Stendhal and Balzac, and reaches in Flaubert the ideal rapport between word and image (supreme economy with maximum effect). The crisis of visibility in the novel will begin about half a century later, coinciding with the advent of the cinema.

A Simple Heart is a tale all about things that are seen, consisting of simple, light sentences in which something always happens: the moon on the Normandy meadows shining on the recumbent cattle, two women and two children passing by, a bull emerging from the mist charging head down, Félicité throwing earth in his eyes to allow the others to escape over a hedge; or the port at Honfleur with the derricks lifting the horses before lowering them into the boats, her nephew the cabin-boy whom Félicité manages to see for a second before he is immediately hidden again by a sail; and above all Félicité's little bedroom, crammed with objects, souvenirs of her own life and of that of her masters, where a holy water font in coconut wood stands alongside a block of blue soap, and over everything dominates the famous stuffed parrot, which is almost emblematic of what life has not given to the poor serving woman. We see all these things through Félicité's own eyes: the transparency of the sentences is the only possible medium to represent her purity and natural nobility in accepting both the good and the bad things in life.

In *The Legend of St Julien the Hospitaller* the visual world is that of a tapestry or a miniature in a manuscript or stained-glass window in a cathedral, but we experience it *from the inside* as if we too were figures that had been embroidered, illuminated or composed of coloured glass. The tale is dominated by a profusion of animals of every kind, typical of Gothic art. Stags, deer, falcons, wood grouse, storks: Julien the hunter is pushed towards the animal world by a bloody instinct and the tale treads the tenuous line between cruelty and compassion, until we finally seem to have entered the very heart of this zoomorphous world. In an extraordinary passage Julien finds himself suffocated by everything that is feathery, hairy or scaly, the forest all around him turns into a crowded, tangled bestiary of all fauna, including the most exotic (there are even parrots, as though in distant homage to old Félicité). At that point the animals are no longer the privileged targets of our sight, rather it is we ourselves who are captured by the animals' gaze, by that firmament of eyes staring at us: we feel as if we are crossing to the other side and seem to see the human world through the round, impassive eyes of an owl.

Félicité's eye, the owl's eye, Flaubert's eye. We realise that the real theme of this man who was so apparently closed up in himself was the identification with the Other. In the sensual embrace of Saint Julien and the leper we can discern the difficult goal towards which Flaubert's asceticism tends, emblematic of his programme for life and for relating to the world. Perhaps *Trois Contes* is the testimony of one of the most extraordinary spiritual journeys ever accomplished outside any religion.

[1980]

Leo Tolstoy, *Two Hussars*

It is not easy to understand how Tolstoy constructs his narratives. What other fiction writers make explicit – symmetrical patterns, supporting structures, counterbalances, link sequences – all remain hidden in Tolstoy. But hidden does not mean non-existent: the impression Tolstoy conveys of transferring 'life' just as it is on to the page ('life', that mysterious entity to define which we have to start from the written page) is actually merely the result of his artistry, that is to say an artifice that is more sophisticated and complex than many others.

One of the texts in which Tolstoyan 'construction' is most visible is *Two Hussars*, and since this is one of his most characteristic tales – at least of the early, more direct Tolstoy – as well as being one of the most beautiful, by observing how it is made we can learn something about the way the author worked.

Written and published in 1856, *Dva Gusara* appears to be a reevocation of what was by then a bygone age, the beginning of the nineteenth century. Its main theme is that of vitality, a thrusting, unrestrained vitality which is seen as something distant, lost, mythical. The inns where the officers on a new posting wait for a change of horses for the sledges, and fleece each other at cards, the balls given by the local provincial nobility, the wild nights 'with the gypsies': it is in the upper classes that Tolstoy represents and mythicises this violent, vital energy, as though it were the natural, but now lost, foundation beneath Russian military feudalism.

The entire story hinges on a hero for whom vitality is the sole reason for success, popularity and power, a vitality that finds in itself, in its very disregard for rules, in excesses, its own morality and consistency. The character of Count Turbìn, the Hussar officer who is also a great drinker, gambler, womaniser and dueller, is simply the concentration within the one character of the vital energy spread throughout society. His power as a mythical hero consists in his achieving positive outcomes for that force which in society displays only its destructive potential: for this is a world of cheats, despoilers of the public purse, drunkards, boasters, scroungers, libertines, but also one in which a warm, reciprocal tolerance turns all conflicts into games and festivity. This genteel civility barely masks a brutality worthy of the barbarian hordes; for the Tolstoy who wrote *Two Hussars* barbarism was the immediate predecessor of aristocratic Russia, and in this barbarity lay its truth and health. A good illustration is the apprehension with which, at the ball held by the aristocrats of K., the entrance of Count Turbìn is viewed by the hostess of the ball.

However, Turbìn combines within himself both violence and lightness: Tolstoy always makes him do things which he should not do, but endows his every movement with a miraculous rightness. Turbìn is capable of borrowing money from a snob with no intention of giving it back, in fact he insults and maltreats him; he can seduce in a twinkling a poor widow (his creditor's sister) hiding himself in her carriage, and casually compromising her by parading around wearing her late husband's fur coat. But he can also perform acts of selfless gallantry, such as coming back from his sledge-ride to give her a kiss as she sleeps and then leaving again. Turbìn is capable of telling everyone to their face what they deserve: he calls a cheat a cheat, then forcibly strips him of his ill-gotten gains and returns them to the poor fool who had allowed him to defraud him in the first place, and donates the money that is left over to the gypsy women.

But this is only half the story, the first eight chapters out of sixteen. In chapter 9 there is a jump of twenty years: we are now in 1848, Turbìn has died some time before in a duel, and his son is in his turn now an officer in the Hussars. He too reaches K., on his march to the front, and meets some of the characters from the earlier story: the foolish cavalryman, the poor widow, now an elderly matron resigned to her fate, as well as her young daughter, to make the young generation symmetrical to the old. The second part of the tale, we immediately notice, is a mirror image of the first, only everything is inverted: instead of a winter of snow, sledges and vodka, we have a mild spring with gardens in the moonlight; as opposed to the wild early years of the century with their orgies in the caravanserai at the staging posts, we are in mid-nineteenth century, a settled epoch of knitting and peaceful ennui in the calm of the family (for Tolstoy this was the present, but it is difficult for us to put ourselves in his perspective).

The new Turbìn is part of a more civilised world, and is ashamed of the wild reputation his father left behind. Whereas his father had beaten and maltreated his servant but had established a sort of bond and trust with him, the son does nothing but grumble and complain about his servant: he too oppresses him but in a strident, effeminate manner. There is also a card game in this half, but played in the family home for just a few roubles, and the young Turbìn with his petty calculations has no scruples about taking money off his landlady, while at the same time playing footsie with her daughter. He is as mean-spirited as his father had been overbearing and generous, but above all he is vague and incompetent. His courting of the girl is a series of misunderstandings, his nocturnal seduction is nothing but a clumsy advance which leaves him looking ridiculous, and even the duel which this is about to cause dies away as daily routine prevails.

In this story about military ethos written by the greatest writer of open warfare, one has to admit that the great absentee is war itself. And yet it is a war story: of the two Turbìn generations, the aristocratic and the militaristic, the first was the one that defeated Napoleon, the second the one that suppressed the revolutions in Poland and Hungary. The verses that Tolstoy places as the epigraph to the tale take on a polemical overtone, attacking History with a capital H, which usually only takes account of battles and tactics, ignoring the substance of which human existences are made. This is already the polemic that Tolstoy will develop ten years later in *War and Peace*. Even though here we never leave the officers' world, it will be his development of this same subject that will lead Tolstoy to set up as the real protagonists of History the masses of peasants turned ordinary soldiers as opposed to the great military leaders.

Tolstoy is not, then, so much interested in exalting the Russia of Alexander I over that of Nicolai I as in seeking out the 'vodka' of the story (see the story's epigraph), the human fuel. The opening of the second half (chapter 9) – which acts as a parallel to the introduction, and its nostalgic, rather clichéd, flashbacks – is not inspired by a generic lament for times past, but by a complex philosophy of history, and a weighing up of the cost of progress. 'Of the old world much that was beautiful and much that was ugly had disappeared, and in the new world much that was beautiful had developed. But much, much more that was monstrous and immature had surfaced under the sun in the new world.'

That fullness of life which is so much praised in Tolstoy by experts on the author is in fact – in this tale as much as in the rest of his oeuvre – the acknowledgement of an absence. As in the most abstract of narrators, what counts in Tolstoy is what is not visible, not articulated, what could exist but does not.

[1973]

Mark Twain, *The Man That Corrupted Hadleyburg*

Mark Twain was not just well aware of his role as a writer of popular entertainment but also proud of it. 'I have never tried in even one single instance to help cultivate the cultivated classes,' he writes in 1889, in a letter to Andrew Lang. 'I was not equipped for it, either by native gifts or training. And I never had any ambition in that direction, but always hunted for bigger game – the masses. I have seldom deliberately tried to instruct them, but have done my best to entertain them. To simply amuse them would have satisfied my dearest ambition at any time.'

As a statement of the writer's social ethic, Twain's remarks here at least have the merit of being sincere and verifiable, much more so than many other statements whose didactic pretensions and ambitions first obtained but subsequently lost credit over the last hundred years. He was genuinely a man of the people, and the idea of having to lower himself to their level from any pedestal in order to address his public is completely foreign to him. Today recognising his status as the folk-writer, or storyteller of his tribe – that enormously extended tribe which provincial America was in his youth – means that we acknowledge his achievement as a writer who not only entertained but also amassed a stock of material for constructing the myths and folktales of the United States, a whole battery of narrative instruments which the nation needed to develop an image of itself.

However, as a statement of aesthetics, it is more difficult to deny its overt anti-intellectualism. Even the critics who have raised Mark Twain to the position he deserves in the American literary pantheon start from the premiss that the one thing that his spontaneous and rather ungainly talent lacked was an interest in form. And yet, Twain's great and lasting success was a stylistic one, and a success, in fact, of historical importance: the entry into literature of the spoken language of America, with the strident, narrating voice of Huckleberry Finn. Was this an unconscious achievement, a purely chance discovery? His whole oeuvre, despite its uneven, undisciplined quality, points in the opposite direction, as can be clearly seen today, now that the various forms of verbal and conceptual humour – from clever replies to 'nonsense' – are being seriously studied as basic elements in the creative act. The humorist Mark Twain stands before us as a tireless experimenter and manipulator of linguistic and rhetorical tricks. At the age of twenty, when he had not yet chosen the pseudonym that was to enjoy such fame and was writing for a small Iowa paper, his first success had been the language full of grammatical and spelling howlers contained in the letters of a character who was a complete caricature.

Precisely because he had to write continually on demand for newspapers, Mark Twain was always searching for new stylistic inventions which would allow him to derive humorous effects from any subject, and the upshot is that although today we are not impressed by his tale *The Jumping Frog of Calaveras County*, when he retranslates the story from a French version this time it does amuse us.

He was a trickster in writing, not out of any intellectual need but through his vocation to be an entertainer of a public that was anything but sophisticated (and let us not forget that apart from writing he was also an extremely busy lecturer and itinerant public talker, always ready to gauge the effects of his gags against the instant reactions of his listeners). Twain follows procedures that are after all not so different from those of avant-garde writers who make literature out of literature: give him any written text and he will start to play around with it until another story emerges. But it has to be a text that has nothing to do with literature: a report to the Ministry on the supplies of canned meat sent to General Sherman, the letters of a Nevada senator replying to his voters, the local polemics in Tennessee newspapers, the regular features in a farming weekly, a German manual of instructions for avoiding thunderbolts, even an income tax return.

Conditioning everything is his choice of the prosaic over the poetic: by staying faithful to this principle, he was the first to give a voice and a shape to the dense materiality of American daily life – particularly in the masterpieces of his river saga, *Huckleberry Finn* and *Life on the Mississippi* – yet on the other hand he tends, in many of his short stories, to turn this quotidian heaviness into an abstract linearity, a mechanical game, a geometric shape. (A similar stylisation will be found, thirty or forty years later, translated into the silent language of mime, in Buster Keaton's gags.)

The stories whose main theme is money are the best examples of this two-way tendency: they represent a world which only thinks in economic terms, in which the dollar is the sole *deus ex machina* at work, and at the same time they prove that money is something abstract, a mere cipher for a calculation which exists only on paper, something to gauge a value that is in itself unattainable, a linguistic convention which does not refer to any palpable reality. In *The Man That Corrupted Hadleyburg* (1899), the mirage of a bag of gold coins tips an austere provincial town down the slope of moral degradation; in *The $30,000 Bequest* (1904) a non-existent legacy is spent in people's imagination; in *The £1,000,000 Bank-Note* (1893), a banknote of this excessive denomination attracts wealth without needing to be invested or even changed. Money had played an important role in nineteenth-century fiction: the motive force of Balzac's narrative, the true test of feeling in Dickens; but in Mark Twain money is a game of mirrors, causing vertigo over a void.

In this his most famous short story, the protagonist is the little town of Hadleyburg, 'honest, narrow, self-righteous, and stingy'. Its nineteen most respected notables form a microcosm of the entire citizenry, and these nineteen in turn are embodied by Mr Edward Richards and his wife, the couple whom we follow in their inner changes or rather in the revelation of their real selves to themselves. All the rest of the population acts as a chorus, a chorus in the proper sense of the word in that they accompany the development of the plot singing refrains, and they have a chorus-leader or voice of civic conscience who is known anonymously as 'the saddler'. (Every now and again an innocent loafer appears on the scene, Jack Halliday, but this is the only concession to 'local colour', a fleeting echo of the Mississippi saga.)

Even the settings are reduced to the minimum necessary for the story's mechanism to function: a prize falls on Hadleyburg as though from the heavens – 160 pounds of gold, worth $40,000. No one knows who sent it or who is meant to receive it, but in reality, as we learn right from the start, it is not a gift at all but an act of revenge, a trick to reveal those champions of self-righteousness as so many hypocrites and charlatans. The trick is played with a bag, a letter in an envelope to be opened immediately, another letter in an envelope to be opened later, plus nineteen identical letters sent by post and various postscripts and other missives (the texts of letters always play an important part in Twain's plots). All these concern a mysterious phrase, a genuine magic formula: whoever discovers it will get the bag of gold.

The presumed donor, but in fact the real avenger, is a character whom nobody knows: he wants to take revenge for an offence (never specified) done to him (impersonally) by the town. This indeterminacy surrounds him like a supernatural aura, his invisibility and omniscience turning him into a kind of god: nobody remembers him but he knows all of them and can predict their reactions.

Another character made mysterious by indeterminacy (and by invisibility, as he is dead) is Barclay Goodson, a Hadleyburg citizen different from all the rest, the only one able to challenge public opinion, and the only one capable of the unheard-of gesture of giving twenty dollars to a stranger ruined by gambling. We are not told anything else about him, and the reason for his fierce opposition to the town is left in the dark.

Between the mysterious donor and the dead beneficiary the town intervenes, in the shape of its nineteen notables, the Symbols of Incorruptibility. Each of them claims – and almost convinces himself of it – to be if not the dead Goodson, at least the person that Goodson chose as his heir.

This is how Hadleyburg is corrupted. The greed to possess an unclaimed bag of gold dollars easily outweighs every scruple of conscience and quickly leads to lying and cheating. If one thinks about how mysterious, shadowy and indefinable the presence of sin is in Hawthorne and Melville, Mark Twain's seems a simplified and rather basic version of Puritan morality, with a doctrine of fall and grace that is no less radical, only here it has become a clear and rational rule for good health, like remembering to use your toothbrush.

But even Twain has his reticences: if there is a shadow over the uprightness of Hadleyburg it is that of the sin committed by the Reverend Burgess, but it is spoken of only in the vaguest of terms as 'the thing'. In fact Burgess has not committed this sin and the only one who knows this – but he was careful not to say it – is Richards, who perhaps committed it himself? (But we are also left in the dark about this.) Now when Hawthorne *does not say* what sin has been committed by the pastor who goes around with a dark veil over his face, his silence envelops the whole story, but when it is Mark Twain who *does not say*, this is simply a sign that this is a mere detail which does not serve any function in the story.

Some biographers say that Mark Twain was subject to strict, preemptive censorship by his wife Olivia, who exercised her right to be moral supervisor over his writings. (They say also that sometimes he studded the first version of a story with scurrilous and blasphemous expressions, so that his wife's rigorous eye would discover an easy target on which to vent her spleen, leaving the substance of the text intact.) But we can be sure that even more severe than his wife's censorship was his own self-censorship which was so inscrutable as to border on innocence.

For the notables of Hadleyburg, as for the Fosters in *The $30,000 Bequest,* the temptation to sin takes the insubstantial shape of an estimate of capital and dividends; but we need to be clear that their sin is a sin because this is money which does not exist. When figures with three or six zeros are exchangeable in a bank, money becomes the test and the reward of virtue: no suspicion of guilt touches Henry Adams in *The £1,000,000 Bank-Note* (curiously enough, the same name as the first critic of the American mentality), who speculates on a Californian mine under the protection of a genuine banknote, though it is one that cannot be spent. He remains unsullied, like the hero of a fairy-tale or of one of those 1930s films in which democratic America still shows that it believes in the innocence of wealth, just as in the Golden Age of Mark Twain. Only when we look down into the bottom of the mines (both real and psychological ones) will we suspect that the real flaws are different.

[1972]

Henry James, *Daisy Miller*

Daisy Miller came out in instalments in 1878 and was published as a book in 1879. It was one of the few stories (perhaps the only one) by Henry James that one can say enjoyed instant popular acclaim. Certainly in the context of the rest of his work, which is typified by evasiveness, by what is not said, by reticence, this stands out as one of his clearest tales, with a female character who is full of life and explicit aspirations to symbolise the openness and innocence of young America. And yet it is also a story that is no less mysterious than others by this introverted writer, steeped as it is in the themes that appear, though always in chiaroscuro, throughout his entire oeuvre.

As with many of James' short stories and novels, *Daisy Miller* takes place in Europe, a Europe that is also in this tale the touchstone against which America measures itself. An America reduced to a single, typical specimen: the colony of carefree American tourists in Switzerland and Rome, that world to which James himself belonged in his youth after turning his back on his native land but before putting down roots in Britain, his ancestral homeland.

Far from their own society and the practicalities that determine the rules of behaviour, they are immersed in a Europe which represents on the one hand the attractions of culture and nobility, and on the other a world that is promiscuous and somewhat unhealthy, which they must keep at a distance. In such circumstances these Americans of James are prey to an insecurity that makes them double their puritan rigour and the safeguards of convention. Winterbourne, the young American studying in Switzerland, is destined – according to his aunt – to make mistakes since he has been living in Europe too long and does not know how to distinguish his 'decent' compatriots from those of low social extraction. But this uncertainty about social identity applies to all of them – these voluntary exiles in whom James sees a reflection of himself – whether they are 'stiff' or emancipated. Stiff rigour, both American and European, is represented by Winterbourne's aunt, who not by chance has taken up residence in Calvinistic Geneva, and by Mrs Walker, in a sense the aunt's foil, who is down in the softer atmosphere of Rome. The emancipated ones are the Miller family, who are cut adrift in a European pilgrimage which has been imposed on them as a cultural duty concomitant with their status. Provincial America, perhaps with new millionaires of plebeian origin, is exemplified in three characters: a dyspeptic mother, a petulant young boy, and a beautiful girl whose only strengths are her lack of culture and her spontaneous vitality, but who is the only one who manages to fulfil herself as an autonomous moral being, and to construct for herself a kind of freedom, however precarious.

Winterbourne glimpses all this, but too much of him (and of James) is in thrall to society's taboos and the dictates of caste, and above all too much of him (and all of James) is afraid of life (in other words, of women). Although at the beginning and the end there is a hint of the young man having a relationship with a foreign woman, from Geneva, right in the middle of the tale Winterbourne's fear at the prospect of a real confrontation with the opposite sex is openly stated; and in this character we can easily recognise a youthful self-portrait of Henry James and of the fear of sex which he never denied.

That imprecise presence which 'evil' was for James – vaguely connected with sinful sexuality or more visibly represented by the breaking of a class barrier – exercised over him a feeling of horror mixed with fascination. Winterbourne's mind – that is to say that syntactical construction which is all hesitation, delay and self-irony – is divided: one part of him ardently hopes that Daisy is 'innocent' in order to make up his mind to admit to being in love with her (and it will be the post-mortem proof of her innocence that will reconcile him to her, like the hypocrite he is), while the other part of him hopes to recognise in her an inferior creature relegated to a lower class, whom he might no longer 'be at pains to respect'. (And apparently this is not at all because he feels impelled to 'disrespect' her but perhaps only for the satisfaction of thinking of her in these inferior terms.)

The world of 'evil' that competes for Daisy's soul is represented first by the courier Eugenio, then by the urbane signor Giovanelli, the dowry-hunting Roman, and in fact by the whole city of Rome with its marble, moss and malarial miasma. The most poisonous gossip which the European Americans aim at the Miller family are the constant, dark allusions to the courier who travels with them and who, in the absence of Mr Miller, exercises a vaguely defined authority over mother and daughter. Readers of *The Turn of the Screw* will know just how much the world of domestic staff can embody for James the shapeless presence of 'evil'. But this courier (the English term is more precise than our 'maggiordomo' and does not really have an Italian equivalent: the courier was the servant who accompanied his masters on long journeys and who had to organise both their travel and their accommodation) could also be quite the opposite (for the little one sees of him), that is to say the only one in the family who represents the father's moral authority and respect for manners. But already the fact that he has an Italian name prepares us for the worst: we will see that the descent of the Millers into Italy is a descent into the underworld (as fatal, though perhaps less fated than Professor Aschenbach's visit to Venice, in the story which Thomas Mann will write thirty-five years later).

Unlike Switzerland, Rome has no natural power of landscape, protestant traditions and austere society, that could inspire self-control in American girls. Their rides in carriages to the Pincio is a vortex of gossip, in the midst of which one cannot tell whether the American girl's honour has to be protected in order to save face in front of Roman counts and marquises (the heiresses of the Mid-West are now starting to want coats-of-arms) or to avoid descending into the morass of promiscuity with an inferior race. This presence of danger becomes identified not so much with the gallant Signor Giovanelli (for he too, like Eugenio, could be the protector of Daisy's virtue, were it not for his humble origins), but much more with a silent but nevertheless crucial character in the tale's mechanism: malaria.

The marshes that surrounded nineteenth-century Rome would, every evening, breathe their deadly exhalations all over the city: this was the 'danger', an allegory of all possible dangers, the deadly fever that was ready to seize girls who went out in the evening on their own or not suitably accompanied. (Whereas going out at night in a boat on the salubrious waters of Lake Geneva would not have presented such risks.) Daisy Miller is sacrificed to malaria, that obscure Mediterranean deity: neither the puritanism of her compatriots nor the paganism of the natives had succeeded in winning her over, and it is for this very reason that she is condemned by both groups to be sacrificed right in the middle of the Colosseum, where the nocturnal miasmas gather in an enveloping, impalpable swarm like the sentences in which James always seems to be about to say something which he then omits.

[1971]

Robert Louis Stevenson,
The Pavilion on the Links

The Pavilion on the Links is above all a story of misanthropy: youthful misanthropy, born of self-satisfaction and savagery, misanthropy which in a young man actually means misogyny, and which spurs the protagonist to ride alone over the Scottish moors, sleeping in a tent and existing on porridge. But a misanthrope's solitude does not open up many narrative possibilities: the narrative develops from the fact that there are two misanthropic, or misogynistic, young men, hiding from each other, spying on each other, in a landscape which by its very nature evokes solitude and savagery.

We can say, then, that *The Pavilion on the Links* is the story of the relationship between two men who resemble each other, two brothers almost, bound by their common misanthropy and misogyny. It is also the story of how their friendship is transformed, for reasons which remain mysterious, into enmity and strife. But traditionally in the novel rivalry between two men presupposes a woman. And a woman who forces a change of heart in two misogynists must be the object of a love that is uncontrollable and unconditional, one that forces the two to outdo each other in chivalry and altruism. It must therefore be a woman threatened by danger, by enemies before whom the two ex-friends now turned enemies find themselves united and on the same side once more, even though still rivals in love.

We can, then, add that *The Pavilion on the Links* is a huge game of hide-and-seek played by adults: the two friends hide from and spy on each other, and the prize in their game is the woman. In addition, the two friends and the woman on one side hide from and spy on their mysterious enemies on the other, and the prize in their game is the life of a fourth character who has no other role but that of hiding, in a landscape which appears to be the perfect setting for hide and seek.

So, then, *The Pavilion on the Links* is a story that emerges from a landscape. From the desolate dunes of the Scottish coasts the only story that can emerge is one of people who hide and seek. But in order to bring out a landscape's contours there is no better method than that of introducing an extraneous, incongruous element. That is why Stevenson brings on to the Scottish moors and quicksands to threaten his characters none other than that murky, Italian secret society, the Carbonari, with their black conical hats.

Through this series of definitions and deductions I have tried to isolate not so much the secret nucleus of this story – which, as is often the case, contains more than one – as the mechanism which guarantees its hold over the reader, that fascination which never wanes despite the rather chaotic mixing of the different story plans that Stevenson takes up and then abandons. Of these, the most powerful is certainly the first one, the psychological tale about the relationship between the two friends/enemies, perhaps a first draft for the enemy brothers in *The Master of Ballantrae*, and which here hints vaguely at an ideological divide between Northmour, a Byronic free-thinker, and Cassilis, the champion of Victorian virtues. The second is the love story, and it is the weakest of all, saddled as it is with the two very conventional characters who are involved: the girl who is the model of every virtue, and the father who is a fraudulent bankrupt, driven by squalid avarice.

It is the third plot which triumphs, the one that is typically novelistic, which takes for its theme the elusive conspiracy which spreads its tentacles everywhere, a theme which has never been out of fashion from the nineteenth century to our own day. It triumphs for various reasons: firstly because Stevenson's hand which with just a few strokes suggests the menacing presence of the Carbonari – from the finger squeaking down the rain-soaked window to the black hat skimming over the quicksands – is the same hand that, more or less at the same time, was recounting the approach of the pirates to the 'Admiral Benbow' inn in *Treasure Island*. In addition, the fact that the Carbonari, however hostile and frightening they may be, enjoy the author's sympathy, in line with British romantic traditions, and are clearly in the right against the universally loathed banker, introduces into the complex game that is already being played this internal contrast, which is more convincing and effective than the others: the two friendly rivals, bound together by honour to defend Huddlestone, nevertheless in their conscience are on the side of the enemy, the Carbonari. And finally it triumphs because it immerses us more than ever in the spirit of childhood games, with sieges, sallies, and attacks by rival gangs.

The great resource that children have is that they know how to derive from the space that they have available for their games all the magic and emotion they need. Stevenson has retained this gift: he starts with the mystique of that elegant pavilion rising up in the middle of a natural wilderness (a pavilion 'Italian in design': perhaps this qualification already hints at the imminent intrusion of an exotic, unfamiliar element?); then there is the secret entry into the empty house, the discovery of the table already set, the fire ready for lighting, the beds prepared, though there is not a soul to be seen . . . a fairy-tale motif transplanted into an adventure story.

Stevenson published *The Pavilion on the Links* in the *Cornhill Magazine*, in the issues for September and October 1880; two years later, in 1882, he included it in his *New Arabian Nights*. There is one glaring difference between the two editions: in the first, the story appears as a letter and testament which an old father, as death closes in, leaves for his sons in order to reveal a family secret to them: namely, how he met their mother, who is already dead. In the rest of the text the narrator addresses the readers with the vocative, 'my dear sons', calls the heroine 'your mother', 'your dear mother', 'the mother of my sons' and calls that sinister character, her father, 'your grandfather'. The second version, in book form, goes straight into narration from the first sentence: 'I was a great solitary when I was young'; the heroine is called 'my wife' or by her name, Clara, and the old man is called 'her father' or Huddlestone. This shift usually means a completely different style, indeed a completely different kind of story; instead the corrections are minimal: the excision of the preamble, of the addresses to the sons, and of the more grief-stricken references to the mother. Everything else remains exactly the same. (Other corrections and cuts concern old Huddlestone, whose infamous reputation in the first version, instead of being attenuated later through familial piety, as one might have expected, was actually accentuated – perhaps because the conventions of the theatre and the novel made it quite natural that an angelic heroine should have a horribly avaricious father, whereas the real problem was making acceptable the terrible end of a blood relative, without the comfort of Christian burial, which could be justified only if this relative was thoroughly evil.)

According to M. R. Ridley, the editor of the recent, 'Everyman's Library' edition, *The Pavilion on the Links* really must be considered a flawed work: the characters fail to arouse any interest in the reader, and only the first version, which has the narrative start from the heart of a family secret, manages to communicate any sympathy and suspense. That is why, contrary to the rule that demands that the last edition of a work corrected by the author be definitive, Ridley reissues the text of the *Cornhill* version. I have not followed Ridley's practice. In the first place I disagree with his value judgment: I consider this tale, particularly in the *New Arabian Nights* edition, one of Stevenson's finest. Secondly, I would not be so sure about the order in which these versions were written: I am more inclined to think of different layers of writing reflecting the uncertainties of the young Stevenson. The opening the author chooses as definitive is so direct and full of pace that it is easier to imagine Stevenson starting writing with its dry, objective thrust, perfectly suited to an adventure story. As he progresses in the tale, he realises on the one hand that the relations between Cassilis and Northmour are so complex as to require a psychological analysis much deeper than the one he intended to embark on, and on the other that the love story with Clara was turning out rather cold and conventional. Consequently he goes back and starts the story all over again, enveloping it in a smoke-screen of family affections: this is the version he publishes in the magazine; then dissatisfied with these mawkish overlays, he decides to cut them, but discovers that to keep the female character at a distance the best solution is to have her known from the start and to wrap her in reverential respect. That is why he adopts the formula 'my wife' instead of 'your mother' (except for one point where he forgets to alter it and garbles the text somewhat). This is all conjecture on my part, which only manuscript research could confirm or disprove: from a comparison of the two printed versions the only certain fact to emerge is the hesitancy of the author. His hesitancy is somehow consonant with the game of hide and seek with himself which he plays in this story about a childhood which he would like to prolong, even though he knows full well that it is over.

[1973]

Conrad's Captains

Joseph Conrad died thirty years ago, on 3 August 1924, in his country house at Bishopsbourne near Canterbury. He was sixty-six and had spent twenty years as a seaman and thirty years writing. He was already a success in his own lifetime, but his real fame in terms of European criticism began only after his death. In December 1924 a whole issue of *La Nouvelle Revue Française* was devoted to him, with articles by Gide and Valéry: the remains of the old captain, a veteran of long sea voyages, were lowered into the sea with a guard of honour comprising France's most sophisticated and intellectual literati. By contrast, in Italy, the first translations were only available in the red canvas bindings of Sonzogno's Adventure Library, though Emilio Cecchi had already singled him out to readers of more refined tastes.

Those few, bare facts are sufficient to indicate the different kinds of appeal that the figure of Conrad has inspired. He had lived a life of practical experience, travel and action, and he possessed the prolific creativity of the popular novelist, but also the fastidious attention to style of the disciple of Flaubert, as well as having links with the chief exponents of international Decadentism. Now that his critical fortune has been established in Italy, at least judging by the number of translations available (Bompiani is publishing the collected works, both Einaudi and Mondadori are bringing out translations of individual books, either in hardback or in paperback, while Feltrinelli's Universale Economica has recently published two of his works), we are in a position to define what this writer has meant and still means for us.

I believe there were many of us who turned to Conrad driven by a recidivist taste for adventure-stories – but not just for adventure stories, also for those authors for whom adventures are only a pretext for saying something original about man, while the exotic events and countries serve to underline more clearly man's relationship with the world. On one bookshelf of my ideal library Conrad's place is next to the aery Stevenson, who is nevertheless almost his opposite in terms of his life and his literary style. And yet on more than one occasion I have been tempted to move him onto another shelf, one less accessible for me, the one containing analytical, psychological novelists, the Jameses and Prousts, those who tirelessly recover every crumb of sensation we have experienced. Or maybe even alongside those who are more or less aesthetes *maudits*, like Poe, full of displaced passions; always presuming that Conrad's dark anxieties about an absurd universe do not consign him to the shelf (not yet properly ordered or finally selected) containing the 'writers of the crisis of modernism'.

Instead I have always kept him close to hand, alongside Stendhal, who is so unlike him, and Nievo, who has nothing in common with him at all. For the fact is that though I never believed in a lot of what he wrote, I have always believed that he was a good captain, and that he brought into his stories that element which is so difficult to write about: the sense of integration with the world that comes from a practical existence, the sense of how man fulfils himself in the things he does, in the moral implicit in his work, that ideal of always being able to cope, whether on the deck of a sailing ship or on the page of a book.

This is the moral substance of Conrad's fiction. And I am happy to discover that it is also there, in its pure form, in a work of non-fiction, *The Mirror of the Sea*, a collection of pieces on maritime topics: the techniques of mooring and setting sail, anchors, sails, cargo weights and so on. (*The Mirror of the Sea* has been translated into Italian – for the first time, I believe, and in beautiful Italian prose – by Piero Jahier, who must have had enormous fun, as well as agonising difficulty, translating all those nautical terms: it appears in volumes 10–11 of the complete works being published by Bompiani, which also contains the magnificent tales of *'Twixt Land and Sea*, which has already appeared in the same translation in Einaudi's Universale series.)

Who else but Conrad in these pieces has ever been able to write about the tools of his trade with such technical precision, such passionate enthusiasm, and in such an unrhetorical, unpretentious way? Rhetoric only comes out at the end with his exaltation of British naval supremacy, and his reevocation of Nelson and Trafalgar, but this also highlights a practical and polemical basis to these essays, which is always present when Conrad discusses the sea and ships, just when one thinks he is absorbed in contemplation of metaphysical profundities: he constantly stressed his regret for the passing of the ethos of the age of sailing ships, always rehearsed the myth of the British Navy whose age was now on the wane.

This was a typically English polemic, because Conrad was English, chose to be English and succeeded: if he is not situated in an English social context, if one considers him merely an 'illustrious visitor' in that literature, as Virginia Woolf defined him, one cannot give an exact historical definition of the man. That he was born in Poland, called Teodor Konrad Nalecz Korzieniowski, and possessed a 'Slav soul' and a complex about abandoning his native land, and resembled Dostoevsky despite hating him for nationalistic reasons, are facts on which much has been written but which are not really of much interest to us. Conrad decided to enter the British Merchant Marine at the age of twenty, and English literature at the age of twenty-seven. He did not assimilate the family traditions of English society, nor its culture or religion (he was always averse to the latter); but he integrated with English society through the Merchant Navy, and made it his own past, the place where he felt mentally at home, and had nothing but contempt for whatever seemed to him contrary to that ethos. It was that quintessentially English personage, the gentleman captain, that he wanted to represent in his own life and in his creative works, though in widely differing incarnations, ranging from the heroic, romantic, quixotic and exaggerated to the over-ambitious, flawed and tragic. From MacWhirr, the impassive captain in *Typhoon*, to the protagonist of *Lord Jim* who tries to escape being obsessed by a single act of cowardice.

Lord Jim goes from being a captain to being a merchant: and here we find an even wider range of Europeans trafficking in the Tropics and ending up as outcasts there. These too were types Conrad had known during his naval experience in the Malaysian archipelago. The aristocratic etiquette of the maritime officer and the degradation of the failed adventurers are the two poles between which his human sympathies oscillate.

This fascination for pariahs, vagabonds and madmen is also evident in a writer far removed from Conrad, but more or less a contemporary, Maksim Gorki. And it is curious to note that an interest in this kind of humanity, so steeped in irrational, decadent complacency (an interest that was shared by a whole epoch of world literature, down to Knut Hamsun and Sherwood Anderson) was the terrain in which the British conservative as much as the revolutionary Russian found the roots of their robust and rigorous conception of man.

This has brought us round to the question of Conrad's political ideas, of his fiercely reactionary spirit. Of course at the root of such an exaggerated, obsessive horror for revolution and revolutionaries (which led him to write whole novels against anarchists, without ever having known one, not even by sight) lay his upbringing as an aristocratic, land-owning Pole, and the milieu in which he lived as a young man in Marseilles, amidst Spanish monarchist exiles and American ex-slavers, shipping contraband arms for Don Carlos. But it is only by situating him in the English context that we can recognise in his stance a key historical configuration similar to Marx's Balzac and Lenin's Tolstoy.

Conrad lived through a period of transition for British capitalism and colonialism: the transition from sail to steam. His world of heroes was based on the culture of the small shipowners' sailing ships, a world of rational clarity, of discipline at work, of courage and duty as opposed to the sordid spirit of profit. The new fleet of steamships owned by huge companies seemed to him squalid and worthless, like the captain and the officers of the 'Patna' who push Lord Jim into betraying himself. So, whoever still dreams of the old virtues either becomes a kind of Don Quixote, or surrenders, dragged down to the other pole of humanity in Conrad: the human relics, the unscrupulous commercial agents, the bureaucratic, colonial outcasts, all of Europe's human dregs which were starting to fester in the colonies, and whom Conrad contrasts with the old romantic merchant-adventurers like his own Tom Lingard.

In the novel *Victory*, which takes place on a desert island, there is a fierce game of chase, which involves the unarmed, Quixote character Heyst, the squalid desperadoes, and the battling woman Lena, who accepts the struggle against evil, is eventually killed, but achieves a moral triumph over the chaos of the world.

For the fact is that in the midst of that aura of dissolution which often hovers over Conrad's pages, his faith in man's strengths never falters. Though far removed from any philosophical rigour, Conrad sensed that crucial moment in bourgeois thought when optimistic rationalism shed its final illusions and a welter of irrationalism and mysticism was unleashed on the world. Conrad saw the universe as something dark and hostile, but against it he marshalled the forces of man, his moral order, his courage. Faced with a black, chaotic avalanche raining down on him, and a conception of the world which was laden with mystery and despair, Conrad's atheistic humanism holds the line and digs in, like MacWhirr in the middle of the typhoon. He was an incorrigible reactionary, but today his lesson can only be fully understood by those who have faith in the forces of man, and faith in those men who recognise their own nobility in the work they do, and who know that that 'principle of fidelity' which he held dear cannot be applied solely to the past.

[1954]

Pasternak and the Revolution*

Halfway through the twentieth century the great Russian nineteenth-century novel has come back to haunt us, like King Hamlet's ghost. That is the feeling that *Doctor Zhivago* by Boris Pasternak (Milan: Feltrinelli, 1957) arouses in us, his first European readers. The reaction is a literary one, then, not a political one. Yet the term 'literary' is still not adequate. It is in the relationship between the reader and the book that something really happens: we fling ourselves into reading with the hunger for questions that typified our early reading, in fact just like when we first tackled the Russian classics, and we were not looking for this or that type of 'literature', but an explicit and general discussion of life, capable of putting the particular in direct relation to the universal, and of containing the future in its portrayal of the past. In the hope that it can tell us something about the future we rush towards this novel which has come back from the grave, but the shade of Hamlet's father, as we know, wants to intervene in today's problems, though always wanting to relate them back to the time when he was alive, to what happened before, to the past. Our encounter with *Doctor Zhivago*, which has been so dramatic and emotional, is similarly tinged with dissatisfaction and disagreement. At last, a book with which we can argue! But at times, right in the middle of a dialogue, we notice that each of us is talking about something different. It is difficult to talk with our fathers.

Even the systems that the great ghost uses to arouse our emotions are those of his own time. Hardly ten pages into the novel, one character is already grappling with the mystery of death, man's purpose in life and the nature of Christ. But the surprising thing is that the appropriate climate for sustaining such weighty topics has already been created, and the reader is plunged back into that notion of Russian literature as something totally bound up with explicit exploration of the big questions, a notion which in recent decades we have tended to set aside, ever since, that is, we stopped considering Dostoevsky as Russian literature's central figure but more as a gigantic outsider.

This first impression does not stay with us for long. To come towards us, the ghost knows full well how to find the battlements we most like to stalk: those of objective narrative, full of facts and persons and things, from which the reader can extract a philosophy only bit by bit, at great personal labour and risk; not those of novelised intellectual debate. This vein of earnest philosophising certainly courses throughout the book, but the vastness of the world which is portrayed in it is able to support much more than this. And the principal tenet of Pasternak's thought – that Nature and History do not belong to two different orders but form a *continuum* in which human lives find themselves immersed and by which they are determined – can be articulated better through narration than through theoretical propositions. In this way these reflections become one with the broad canvas of all the humanity and nature in the novel, they do not dominate or suffocate it. The result is that, as happens with all genuine storytellers, the book's meaning is not to be sought in the sum of the ideas enunciated but in the totality of its images and sensations, in the flavour of life, in its silences. And all the ideological proliferations, these discussions which constantly flare up and die down, about nature and history, the individual and politics, religion and poetry, as though resuming old conversations with friends long gone, create a deep echo chamber for the strictly humble events the characters undergo, and come forth (to adopt a beautiful image used by Pasternak for the revolution) 'like a sigh which has been held back too long'. Pasternak has breathed into his whole novel a desire for the kind of novel which no longer exists.

And yet we could say, paradoxically, that no book is more typical of the USSR than *Doctor Zhivago*. Where else could it have been written except in a country in which girls still wear pigtails? Those boys and girls of the start of the century, Yura, Misha Gordon and Tonja, who form a triumvirate 'based on an apologia for purity', probably also have the same fresh, distant faces as the Young Communists that we met so often on our delegation visits. On those visits we often saw the Soviet people's enormous reserves of energy, which had been spared the dizzying strains (the pointless phases of fashion, but also the urge for new discoveries, trials and truths) experienced by Western consciences in the last forty years (in culture, the arts, morale, and way of life), and we wondered what fruit would come forth from their constant and exclusive concentration on their own classics if it were ever confronted with a lesson in reality which was as harsh, solemn and historically new as ever could be. This book by Pasternak is a first response to that question. It is not a young man's response, which was more what we expected, but that of an elderly man of letters, which is all the more significant, perhaps, because it shows us the unexpected direction taken by Pasternak on his interior journey in his long period of silence. This last survivor of the Westernising, avant-garde poets of the 1920s has not detonated in the 'thaw' a display of stylistic fireworks long held in reserve; after the end of the dialogue with the international avant-garde, which had been the natural space for his poetry, he too has spent the years reconsidering the nineteenth-century classics of his own country, and he too has been directing his gaze at the unsurpassable Tolstoy. However, his reading of Tolstoy is quite different from the official literary line, which all too easily pointed to him as the canonical model. And he has also reread his own years of experience in a different way from the official line. What emerges from this is a book far removed from the rehashed nineteenth-century fiction which is 'socialist realism', but it is also, unfortunately, the most harshly negative book as regards socialist humanism. Do we have to repeat that stylistic choices do not come about by chance? that if the avant-garde Pasternak concerned himself with the problems of the revolution, the Tolstoyan Pasternak could not but turn to a nostalgia for the pre-revolutionary past? But this too would be only a biased judgment. *Doctor Zhivago* is and is not a nineteenth-century novel written today, just as it is and is not a book of nostalgia for the pre-revolutionary period.

From the bloody years of the Russian and Soviet avant-garde, Pasternak has conserved their aspiration towards the future, the emotional questioning on how history is made; and he has written a book which, like a late fruit from a great tradition which has now ended, reaches us at the end of its lonely itinerary and manages to be a book contemporary with the more important works of modern Western literature, to which it gives an implicit assent.

In fact I believe that today a book structured 'as in the nineteenth century', containing a plot covering many years, with huge descriptions of society, must of necessity lead to a nostalgic, conservative vision. This is one of the many reasons why I disagree with Lukács: his theory of 'perspectives' can be turned back against his own favourite genre. I believe that it is no accident that our age is the age of the short story, or short novel, of autobiographical testimony. Today a genuinely modern narrative can only bring its poetic charge to bear on the times (whatever they be) in which we live, showing their worth as a decisive and infinitely significant moment. It therefore has to be 'in the present', with a plot that takes place before our eyes, unified in time and action as in Greek tragedy. And conversely whoever wants today to write the novel of 'an epoch', unless this is pure rhetoric, ends up writing a book whose poetic tension weighs on 'the past'.[1] Pasternak does the same, but not quite: his position as regards history is not so easy to reduce to such simple definitions; and his is not an 'old-fashioned' novel.

As far as technique goes, to situate *Doctor Zhivago* 'before' the twentieth-century deconstruction of the novel does not make sense. There are two major ways of deconstructing it, and they are both present in Pasternak's book. The first is to fragment realistic objectivity into an immediacy of sensations or into an impalpable dust-cloud of memory; the second is to make the plot technique part of the plot itself, so that it is considered in its own right, like a geometric outline, which then leads to parody, and to the ludic 'novel within the novel'. Pasternak takes this playing with the 'novelistic' to its ultimate consequences: he constructs a plot of continual coincidences, across all of Russia and Siberia, in which about fifteen characters do nothing but bump into each other, as though they were the only ones there, like Charlemagne's knights in the abstract geography of Renaissance chivalric poems. Is this just the writer having fun? It is meant to be something more, at the outset; it is intended to represent the network of destinies which bind us without our knowing, the disintegration of history into a complex mingling of human stories. 'They were all together, close by, and some did not know the others, others never got to know each other, and some things remained for ever unknown, while others waited for the next opportunity, the next meeting before coming to fruition' (Italian tr., p.157; English tr., p.113). But the emotion aroused by this discovery does not last long: and the constant series of coincidences in the end merely shows the author's consciousness of his conventional use of the novel form.

Given this convention, and its overall structure, Pasternak enjoys total freedom in writing the book. Some parts he sketches in fully, others he leaves only in outline. At times a minute chronicler of the days and months, at others suddenly changing gear, he covers several years in a few lines: for instance, in the epilogue, where in twenty pages of great density and vigour, he runs before our eyes the epoch of 'purges' and the Second World War. Similarly, amongst the characters there are some whom he constantly flits over, not bothering to give us a deeper knowledge of them: even Zhivago's wife, Tonya, is in this category. In short, this is an 'impressionistic' type of narrative. Impressionistic even in psychology: Pasternak refuses to give us a precise justification for his characters' behaviour. For instance, why is the conjugal harmony between Lara and Antipov suddenly shattered, and he finds no other way out except to leave for the front? Pasternak says many things about it, but none is either sufficient or necessary: what counts is the general impression of contrast between the two characters. He is not interested in psychology, character, situations, but in something more general and direct: *life*. Pasternak's prose is simply a continuation of his verse.

As far as their basic core myths are concerned, there is a strict unity between Pasternak's lyrics and *Doctor Zhivago*: the movement of nature which contains and informs every other event, act or human emotion, and an epic élan in describing the spatter of rainstorms and the melting of snow. The novel is the logical development of this élan, for the poet tries to include in a single discourse nature and human history, both private and public, to provide a total definition of life: the smell of the limes and the noise of the revolutionary crowds as Zhivago's train travels towards Moscow in 1917 (Part V, chapter 13). Nature is no longer the romantic source of symbols for the poet's inner world, a kind of dictionary for his subjective thoughts; it is something which exists before, and after, and everywhere, which man cannot change but can only try to understand, by science and poetry, and to be worthy of it.[2] Pasternak continues Tolstoy's polemic against history ('Tolstoy did not push his thoughts to their conclusion . . .', p.591; 406): it is not great men who make history, but it is not made by small men either; history moves like the plant realm, like a wood changing in springtime.[3] From this derive two fundamental aspects of Pasternak's conception: the first is his sense of the sacrality of history, seen as a solemn coming into being, transcending man, uplifting even in its tragicity; the second is an implicit lack of trust in what man *does*, in his capacity to construct his own destiny, in his deliberate modification of nature and society. Zhivago's experience leads to contemplation, to the exclusive pursuit of interior perfection.

We who, as direct or indirect descendants of Hegel, understand history and man's relationship with the world in a different, if not diametrically opposite, way, find it difficult to agree with Pasternak's 'ideological' passages. But the narrative parts, inspired by his moving vision of history-nature (particularly in the first half of the novel), communicate that aspiration towards the future which we recognise as something with which we can identify.

The mythical moment for Pasternak is the 1905 revolution. The long poems written during his 'committed' phase, in 1925–27, dealt with that epoch,[4] and *Doctor Zhivago* starts from there. It was a time when the Russian people and the intelligentsia entertained very different potential and hopes: politics, morality and poetry all marched together without any order but at the same pace. ' "Our lads are firing", thought Lara. And she was not referring only to Nika and Pasha, but to the whole city which was firing. "Good, honest lads", she thought. "They are good, that's why they're firing" ' (p.69; 55). The 1905 revolution contained for Pasternak all the myths of youth and all the points of departure for a certain kind of culture; it is a peak from which he surveys the jagged terrain of this first half-century and he sees it in perspective, sharp and detailed in the nearer slopes, and, as we move towards today's horizon, smaller and less focused in the mist, with only the odd sign standing out.

The revolution is the key moment for Pasternak's essential poetic myth: nature and history become one. In this sense, the heart of the novel, the point where it reaches its peak in terms of style and thought, is part V, the revolutionary days of 1917, at Melyuzeyevo, a little hospital city full of back streets:

> *Yesterday I went to a night-time rally. An extraordinary spectacle. Mother Russia is on the move, cannot stay still, is walking, does not know where she is, is talking and knows how to express herself. And it is not only the men who are talking. The trees and the stars have met up and are talking, the nocturnal flowers are philosophising and the stone houses are holding rallies.*
> *(p.191; 136)*

At Melyuzeyevo we see Zhivago living a moment of suspended happiness, between the fervour of revolutionary life and the idyll, still only hinted at, with Lara. Pasternak conveys this state in a wonderful passage (p.184; 131) about nocturnal noises and perfumes, in which nature and human bustle mingle together, as in the houses of Verga's Aci Trezza, and the tale unravels without needing anything to happen, composed entirely of the relationship between the facts of existence, as in Chekhov's 'The Steppe', the story that is the prototype for so much modern narrative.

But what does Pasternak mean by revolution? The novel's political ideology is summed up in that definition of socialism as the realm of authenticity, which the author puts into the mouth of his protagonist, in spring 1917:

Everyone has been reanimated, reborn, everywhere there are transformations, upheavals. One could say that two revolutions have taken place within each one of us: our own, individual, one and the other general revolution. Socialism seems to me to be a sea into which all these single, individual revolutions have to flow like rivulets, the sea of everyone's life, the sea of everyone's authenticity. The sea of life, I say, of that life that you can see in paintings, of life as geniuses understand it, creatively enriched. Today, though, men have decided not to experience life through books any more, but in themselves, not in the abstract, but in actual practice. (p.191; 136)

An ideology of 'spontaneity', as we would say in political jargon: and we well understand the subsequent disillusionment. But it does not matter that these words (and the other excessively literary ones which Zhivago utters when applauding the Bolsheviks' seizure of power in October) will be proved bitterly wrong several times in the course of the novel: its positive pole always remains that ideal of a society of authentic beings, glimpsed in the springtime of the revolution, even when the portrayal of reality emphasises more and more the negative character of that reality.

Pasternak's objections to Soviet communism seem to me to move in two directions: against the barbarism, the ruthless cruelty unleashed by the civil war (we shall return to this topic, which has a preponderant role in the novel); and against the theoretical and bureaucratic abstractions in which the revolutionary ideals become frozen. This second polemic, which is the one that most interests us, is not objectified in characters, situations or imagery,[5] but only in occasional reflections. And yet there is no doubt that the really negative pole is this one, implicitly or explicitly. Zhivago returns to the town in the Urals after spending several unwilling years with the partisans, and sees the walls covered with posters:

What were these words? from the year before? from two years before? Once in his life he had been elated by the incontrovertibility of that language, the linearity of that thought. Was it possible that he would have to pay for that careless enthusiasm by having nothing in front of him now for the rest of his life except those cries and claims, which never changed in the course of the years, in fact with the passing of time they became less and less vital, more and more incomprehensible and abstract? (p.497; 343)

We must not forget that the revolutionary enthusiasm of 1917 actually stemmed from protests against a period of 'abstraction', that of the First World War:

War was an artificial break in life, as though one could delay existence even for a moment: what an absurd idea! The revolution broke out almost unintentionally, like a sigh held back too long. (p.192; 136)

(It is easy to see in these lines – written, I believe, after the Second World War – that Pasternak is probing sore points which are much more recent.)

Against the reign of abstraction there is a hunger for reality, for 'life', which pervades the whole book; that hunger for reality which allows him to greet the Second World War, 'its real horrors, its real danger and its threat of a real death', as 'something positive compared with the inhuman domination by abstractions' (p.659; 453). In the Epilogue, which takes place during that very war, *Doctor Zhivago* – like the novel of alienation it becomes – throbs once more with the passion of involvement which had animated it at the beginning. In that war Soviet society becomes genuine again, tradition and revolution are once more present side by side.[6]

Pasternak's novel thus also manages to take in the Resistance, in other words the epoch which for the younger generation in the whole of Europe corresponds to what 1905 was for Zhivago's contemporaries: the point from which all roads started out. It is worth pointing out that this period retains even in the Soviet Union the value of an active 'myth', of the image of a real nation as opposed to an official nation. The unity of the Soviet people at war, on which Pasternak's book closes,[7] is also the reality which is the starting point for younger Soviet writers, who hark back to it and contrast it with abstract, ideological schematisation, as though wanting to affirm a socialism that belongs 'to everyone'.[8]

However this appeal to a real unity and spontaneity is the only link which we can discern between the elderly Pasternak's ideas and those of the younger generations. The image of a socialism 'for everyone' can only start from a confidence in the new forces generated and developed by the revolution. And this is precisely what Pasternak denies. He declares and proves that he does not believe in the people. His notion of reality is shaped more and more in the course of the book like an ethical and creative ideal based on a private, family-centred individualism: man's relations with himself and his neighbour are restricted to the circle of his affections (and beyond that on cosmic relations, with 'life'). He never identifies with the classes who are born to consciousness, and whose very errors and excesses can be welcomed as the first signs of an autonomous awakening, as the signs, always pregnant with meaning for the future, of life, against abstraction. Pasternak restricts his support and compassion to the world of the intelligentsia and the bourgeoisie (even Pasha Antipov, who is a workers' son, has studied, is an intellectual), all the others are bit-parts, there to make up the numbers.

The proof of this is his language. All the proletarian characters speak in the same way, the rather childish, folksy, picturesque chatter of the *muzhik* in Russian classic novels. A recurring theme in *Doctor Zhivago* is the anti-ideological nature of the proletariat, and the ambivalence of its stances, in which the most diverse strains of traditional morality and prejudice are fused together with historical forces which it never fully comprehends. This theme allows Pasternak to sketch some really very attractive figures (Tiverzin's old mother, protesting against the charge by the Czar's cavalry and at the same time against her revolutionary son; or the cook Ustin'ja insisting on the truth of the miracle of the deaf-mute against the commissar from the Kerensky government) and it culminates in the grimmest apparition of the whole book, the partisan witch. But by then we are already in another climate: as the avalanche of civil war gathers pace, this crude proletarian voice is heard louder and louder, taking on a single name: barbarism.

The barbarism inherent in today's world is the great theme of contemporary literature: modern narratives drip with the blood of all the slaughter which our half-century has witnessed, and their style affects the immediacy of cave-graffiti, while their morality aims to rediscover humanity through cynicism, ruthlessness or atrocity. It feels natural for us to place Pasternak in this literary context, to which the Soviet writers of the civil war in fact belonged, from Sholokhov to the early Fadeyev. But whereas in most contemporary literature violence is accepted as something one has to go through to get beyond it poetically, to explain it and to cleanse oneself of it (Sholokhov tends to justify and ennoble it, Hemingway to confront it as a testing ground for virility, Malraux to aestheticise it, Faulkner to consecrate it, Camus to empty it of significance), Pasternak expresses only weariness in the face of violence. Can we salute him as the poet of non-violence, which our century has never had? No, I should not say that Pasternak makes poetry out of his own rejection of violence: he records it with the weary bitterness of someone who has had to witness it all too often, who cannot talk of anything but atrocity upon atrocity, recording each time his dissent, his own role as outsider.[9]

The fact remains that although so far we have found also represented in *Doctor Zhivago* our own idea of reality, not just the author's, nevertheless in the account of his long enforced stay with the partisans the book, far from expanding to a wider, epic dimension, restricts itself to Zhivago-Pasternak's point of view, and drops in poetic intensity. One could say that up until the magnificent journey from Moscow to the Urals Pasternak seemed to want to explore a universe in all its good and evil, representing the motivations of all the sides involved; but after that his vision becomes one-sided, simply piling up events and negative verdicts, a sequence of violence and brutality. The author's emphatic partisanship necessarily elicits our own emphatic partisanship as readers: we can no longer separate our aesthetic judgment from our historical and political one.

Perhaps that was exactly what Pasternak intended, to make us reopen questions that we tend to consider closed: by we I mean we who accepted the mass revolutionary violence of the civil war as necessary, though we did not accept as necessary the bureaucratic running of society and the fossilisation of ideology. Pasternak takes the discussion back to revolution-ary violence, and subsumes under it the subsequent bureaucratic and ideological inflexibility. Against all the most widespread negative analyses of Stalinism, nearly all of which start from Trotsky's or Bukharin's position, that is to say they talk of the system's *degeneration*, Pasternak starts from the mystical-humanitarian world of pre-revolutionary Russia,[10] to end up with a condemnation not only of Marxism and revolutionary violence, but of politics as the main testing ground for the values of contemporary humanity. In short, he ends up with a rejection of everything, but this in turn borders on an acceptance of everything. His sense of the sacred qualities of history-nature dominates everything, and the advent of barbarism acquires (even in Pasternak's wonderfully restrained style) a kind of halo, as though it were a new millennium.

In the Epilogue, the laundry girl Tanya tells her story. (This is the final surprise, worthy of a serialised novel, with its allegorical touch: she is the illegitimate daughter of Yuri Zhivago and Lara, whom Yuri's brother, General Yevgraf Zhivago, goes in search of through the battlefields.) The style is primitive, elementary, so much so that it resembles that of a lot of American narrative; and a crude, adventurous episode from the civil war resurfaces from memory like a text from a book on ethnology which has become twisted, illogical and exaggerated like a folktale. And the intellectual Gordon brings the curtain down on the book with these emblematic and enigmatic words:

> *This is how it happened many times in history. What had been lofty and noble in conception, has become crude matter. Thus did Greece become Rome, thus the Russian Enlightenment became the Russian Revolution. If you think of Blok's phrase, 'We, the children of Russia's terrible years', you will instantly see the difference in the times. When Blok said this, we must understand it in a metaphorical, figurative way. The 'children' were not literally the sons, but the creatures, the products, the* intelligentsia; *and the terrors were not terrible, but providential, apocalyptic, which is quite different. But now all that was metaphorical has become literal: the sons are literally the sons, and the terrors are genuinely terrible, that's the difference. (p.673; 463)*

That is how Pasternak's novel ends: without him being able to detect in this 'crude matter' a spark of anything 'lofty and noble'. The 'lofty and noble' elements were entirely concentrated in the late Yuri Zhivago, who in his increasing asceticism manages to reject everything, reaching a crystalline purity of spirit which leads him to live like a beggar, after abandoning medicine and earning his living for a while writing small volumes of philosophical and political reflections which 'sold out to the last copy' (!), until finally he dies of a heart attack in the tram.

So Zhivago takes his place in that gallery – so crowded in contemporary Western literature – of heroes of negation, those who refuse to integrate, the *étrangers*, the outsiders.[11] But I would not say that he has a particularly prominent artistic place there: the *étrangers*, though they are hardly ever rounded characters, are always strongly defined in the extreme situation in which they move. By comparison Zhivago remains a shadowy character;

and it is that part 15,[12] the one which deals with his last years, in which we expect an assessment of his life, that strikes us for the disproportion between the importance that the author would like to attribute to Zhivago and his insubstantial presence in the novel.

In short, I have to say that the thing with which I least agree in *Doctor Zhivago* is that it is the story of Doctor Zhivago, in other words that it can form part of that vast sector of contemporary narrative called the intellectual biography. I am not speaking so much about the explicit autobiography, whose importance is far from diminished, but of those professions of faith in narrative form which have at their centre a character who is a spokesman for a particular philosophy or poetics.

Who is this Zhivago? Pasternak is convinced that he is a person of boundless fascination and spiritual authority, but in fact the reasons we like him are all to be found in his status as an average man. It is his discretion and mildness, his always sitting, as it were, on the edge of his chair, the fact that he always lets himself be persuaded by externals, and be overcome by love bit by bit.[13] Instead, the halo of sanctity that Pasternak at a certain point wants him to wear weighs heavily on him; we readers are asked to worship Zhivago, which we cannot do, since we do not share his ideas or choices, and this ends up by undermining even that all too human sympathy which we feel for the character.

The story of another life runs through the novel from beginning to end: that of a woman, who appears to us as a rounded, distinct character (even though she says very little about herself, and her story is narrated more from the outside than from within) in the terrible events we see her live through, in the resolution which she draws from them, in the sweetness that she manages to spread around her. This is Lara, Larisa: she is the great character of the book. We find that by shifting the axis of our reading so that Lara's story, not Zhivago's, remains at the novel's centre, we place *Doctor Zhivago* in the full light of its literary and historical significance, reducing to secondary ramifications its imbalances and digressions.

The life of Lara is in its linearity a perfect story of our times, almost an allegory of Russia (or of the world), of the possibilities which gradually opened up for her (or it), or which were all presented to her (or it). Three men revolve around Larisa. The first is Komarovskij, the unscrupulous racketeer who has made her live from childhood with an awareness of the brutality of life, who represents vulgarity and unscrupulousness, but also a basic, concrete practicality, the unostentatious chivalry of a man who is sure of himself (he never fails her, not even after Lara tries to kill the impurity of her previous links with him by firing a revolver at him). Komarovskij who personifies everything that is base about the bourgeoisie, but whom the revolution spares, making him – still through dubious means – still a sharer in power. The other two men are Pasha Antipov, the revolutionary, the husband who leaves Lara so as to have no obstacles to his solitary determination to be a moral but ruthless subversive, and Yuri Zhivago, the poet, the lover whom she will never have entirely for herself, because he has surrendered totally to the things and opportunities of life. Both occupy the same level of importance in her life, and the same poetic importance, even though Zhivago is constantly in the spotlight, and Antipov hardly ever. During the civil war in the Urals, Pasternak shows us both men as though they were already destined for defeat: Antipov-Strel'nikov, the Red partisan commandant, terror of the Whites, has not joined the Party and knows that as soon as the fighting is over he will be outlawed and eliminated; and Doctor Zhivago, the reluctant intellectual, who does not want to or is not able to be part of the new ruling class, knows he will not be spared by the relentless revolutionary machine. When Antipov and Zhivago face each other, from the first encounter on the armed train to the last one, when they are both being hunted in the villa at Varykino, the novel reaches its peak of poignancy.

If we retain Lara as the novel's protagonist, we see that the figure of Zhivago, relegated to the same level as Antipov, is no longer overpowering, he no longer tends to turn the epic account into 'the story of an intellectual', and the long narrative about the doctor's partisan experiences is then confined to a marginal digression which does not now outweigh and crush the linearity of the plot.

Antipov, the enthusiastic and ruthless applier of the revolution's laws, under which he knows he himself will perish, is an imposing figure of our times, full of echoes of the great Russian tradition, portrayed with clarity and simplicity. Lara, a hard but delightful heroine, is and remains his woman even when she is and remains Zhivago's woman. In the same way – or rather in an inexplicable and indefinable way – she is and remains Komarovskij's former woman. It is by him, after all, that she is taught the fundamental lesson: it is because she has learned the rough taste of life from Komarovskij, from the smell of his cigar, from his gross, philanderer's sensuality, from his arrogance at being simply physically stronger, that Lara knows more than Antipov and Zhivago, the two naïve idealists of violence and non-violence respectively; and it is for this reason that she is more important than they are, she more than they represents life, and we come to love her more than them, to follow her and seek her out amidst Pasternak's elusive periods which never reveal her to us in her entirety.[14]

I have tried in this way to bring out the emotions, questions, disagreements that the reading of a book like this – or rather the struggle with it – arouses in someone who is concerned with the same set of problems, and who admires the immediacy of its representation of life, without sharing its fundamental thesis: history as transcending humanity. On the contrary I have always sought the exact opposite in literature and in thought: an active involvement of man with history. Not even the operation that was a crucial part of our literary education, of separating the 'poetic' elements from the author's ideological world, works here. This idea of history-nature is that same idea that gives *Doctor Zhivago* the quiet solemnity that fascinates me as well. How can I define my relationship with this book?

An idea which is realised artistically can never be without meaning. But being meaningful does not correspond at all to uttering a truth. It means indicating a crucial point, a problem, a source of alarm. Kafka, thinking he was writing metaphysical allegory, described contemporary man's alienation in a way that has never been surpassed. But Pasternak, so terribly *realistic*? On closer inspection, this cosmic realism of his consists of one single lyric moment through which he filters the whole of reality. It is the lyric moment of man seeing history – either admiring or execrating it – as a distant sky above his head. That in today's Soviet Union a great poet should elaborate such a vision of man's relations with the world – the first vision in many years to have developed autonomously, not in conformity with official ideology – has a deep historical and political significance. It confirms that the ordinary man has had very little sense of having history in his control, of creating socialism, and expressing within it his own liberty, responsibility, creativity, violence, interest or disinterest.[15]

Perhaps Pasternak's importance resides in this warning: history – whether in the capitalist or socialist world – is not yet history enough, it is not yet a conscious construct of human reason, it is still too much a succession of biological phenomena, of brute nature, not a realm of liberties.

In this sense Pasternak's idea of the world is *true* – true in the sense of assuming the negative as a universal criterion, just as Poe's and Dostoevsky's and Kafka's ideas were true in this way – and his book has the superior *utility* of great poetry. Will the Soviet world know how to make use of it? Will socialist literature in the world be able to elaborate a response to it? This can be done only by a world which is in a ferment of self-criticism and creativity, and only by a literature which can develop an even stricter adherence to things. From today onwards, *realism* means something deeper. (But has it not always meant that?)

[1958]

Notes

* Page references to *Doctor Zhivago* in this essay are both to the Italian edition (Milan: Feltrinelli, 1957) and to the standard English translation, *Doctor Zhivago*, translated by Max Hayward and Manya Harari (London: Collins Harvill, 1988).

1. Even in the nineteenth century, on closer inspection, it was often nostalgia for the past that enlivened the mimesis of the great novels, but it was a nostalgia with a critical, even revolutionary, approach towards the present, as Marx and Lenin clearly showed with, respectively, Balzac and Tolstoy.

2. Someone should study and analyse this surrender of man to nature (which is no longer felt as an *alterity*), which has been constantly expressed in recent years: from Dylan Thomas' poetry to the paintings of the 'aformalists'.

3. There seem to me to be two uses of the word 'history' in Pasternak: the one used here means history assimilated into nature, and the other means history as the realm of the individual, founded by Christ. Pasternak's 'Christianity' – particularly as expressed in the aphorisms of uncle Nikolai Nikolaevich and his disciple Misha Gordon – has nothing to do with Dostoevsky's terrible religiosity, but belongs in the context of a symbolic, aestheticising reading and dynamic interpretation of the Gospels, in which Gide had also indulged (the only difference being that here it rests on a more profound sense of human compassion).

4. Italian translations of the poems 'The Year 1905' and 'Lieutenant Schmidt', by Angelo Maria Ripellino, are in Boris Pasternak, *Poesie* (Turin: Einaudi, 1957).

5. In fact we never manage to see the communists clearly, face to face. The

cocaine-addicted partisan commander, Liverij, is not a fleshed-out character. Much is said about Antipov the father and Tiverzin, two old workers, now Bolshevik chiefs, but we are never told how they exist, what they think, why they have become bureaucratic ogres after being fine revolutionary workers at the beginning of the book. And Yuri's brother, Yevgraf Zhivago, who appears to be a communist of some authority, a *deus ex machina* who descends every now and again down from the heaven of his mysterious authority: who is he? what does he do? what does he think? what is his significance? The rich gallery of Pasternak characters also has some empty frames.

6. In these pages on the Second World War there is also the indirect, distant appearance of the only 'positive communist hero' of the book: a woman (p.656; 451). And she is (as we learn from another fleeting reference on p.627; 431) the daughter of a Tikhonovite priest. While still a child, in order to eliminate the shame of her father being in prison, she becomes 'a childishly passionate follower of what seemed to her to be the least dubious elements of communism'. When the war comes, she has herself parachuted beyond the Nazi lines, performs a heroic partisan action and ends up being hanged: 'they say that the Church counts her among the saints.' Is Pasternak trying to tell us that Russia's ancient religiosity lives on in the communists' spirit of sacrifice? The juxtaposing of the two attitudes is not new; and to those of us who espouse a totally secular communism it has been rather hard to take. But the tone of the story of Christina Orletsova, contained in just a few lines of the novel, links up immediately in our memory with the tone – in fact identical in human attitude, though existing in different faiths and ideals – of the *Lettere dei condannati a morte della Resistenza* (*Letters of the (Italian and European) Martyrs of the Resistance*).

7. There is still a final chapter, barely a page long, about our times, with a little optimistic fanfare, but it is stuck on, rather sugary in tone, almost as if it were not by Pasternak at all, or as if the author wanted to show that he had written it with one hand tied behind his back.

8. See my article on Viktor Nekrasov's *In His Home Town*, in *Notiziario Einaudi*, 5:1–2 (January-February 1956).

9. This anguish at the civil war reminds me of Cesare Pavese's *Prima che il gallo canti* (*Before the Cock Crows*). The second story, *La casa in collina* (*The House on the Hill*), seemed to me, when it appeared in 1948, to have a tone of resignation; but rereading it today, I think that in it Pavese went further than anyone else down the road of a moral conscience engaging with history, and all this in an area which has nearly always been the preserve of the others, of mystical and transcendental conceptions of the world. In Pavese too we find the same terrified compassion for any blood spilled, even enemy blood, of those who died without knowing why; but just as Pasternak's pity is the latest

incarnation of a Russian tradition of mystical relations with one's neighbour, Pavese's pity is the most recent incarnation of a tradition of stoic humanism, which has influenced so much of Western culture. In Pavese too we find: nature and history, but on opposite sides; nature is the countryside of the first discoveries of childhood, the perfect moment, outside history, the 'myth'; history is war, which 'will never end', which 'ought to bite deeper into our blood'. Like Zhivago, Pavese's Corrado is an intellectual who does not want to escape the responsibilities of history: he lives on the hill because it has always been his hill, believing that the war does not concern him. But the war populates that world of nature with the presence of others, of history: evacuees, partisans. Nature too is history and blood, wherever he turns his eyes: his flight is an illusion. He discovers that even his previous life was history, with his own responsibilities and failings: 'Every man who dies resembles the man that survives and asks him to account for it.' Man's active involvement with history stems from the necessity of making sense of the bloody march of man. 'After shedding his blood we must placate it.' Man's real historical and civic commitment is in this 'placating', in this 'accounting for it'. We cannot be outside history, we cannot refuse to do everything in our power to give a reasonable and humane stamp to the world, all the more so, the more the world presents itself to us as senseless and vicious.

10. We really need, from the subject specialists, an analysis of Pasternak's cultural roots, of the way he develops many of the key discourses relating to Russian culture.

11. *The Outsiders* is the title of a book about this type of literary character, written by a young, rather confused Englishman, Colin Wilson, who has risen to undeserved fame in his native land.

12. The exceptions are the chapters evoking Zhivago's final wanderings through Russia, the horrific march amongst the rats: all the journeys in Pasternak are wonderful. Zhivago's story is exemplary as an Odyssey of our time, with his uncertain return to Penelope obstructed by rational Cyclops and rather unassuming Circes and Nausicaas.

13. Some of these qualities make this imaginary doctor-author resemble (and many have already noted this) a real doctor-writer from the previous generation, Chekhov; Chekhov the man, with the force of his sense of balance, as we can see from his letters (soon to be published by Einaudi). But in other ways Chekhov is the exact opposite of Zhivago: the plebeian Chekhov, for whom refinement is a wild flower with its natural grace, whereas Zhivago is refined both in terms of his birth and his origins, looking down on ordinary people; the mystical-symbolist Zhivago and the agnostic Chekov, who did pay homage with a couple of short stories to mystic symbolism, but these are such isolated examples in an oeuvre which is the

exact opposite of any mysticism, that they can be considered as a mere tribute to a fashion.

14. In the end they obliterate her from us, dispatching her hurriedly to a Siberian concentration camp; this too is a 'historical' death, not a private one like Zhivago's.

15. Perhaps the period on which Pasternak's book dwells most is the very one to which this argument applies least. In writing, Pasternak reflected on to the past his consciousness of the present. Probably, in the portrait of the doctor held prisoner by the partisans, who while still regarding himself as their enemy still works with them and ends up fighting alongside them, Pasternak wanted to express the situation in his homeland under Stalin. But these are all conjectures: we would really need to know above all whether Pasternak ended Zhivago's story deliberately in 1929, or whether, after starting a story that was meant to come down to our own times, he realised at that point that he had already fully expressed everything he wanted to say.

The World is an Artichoke

The world's reality presents itself to our eyes as multiple, prickly, and as densely superimposed layers. Like an artichoke. What counts for us in a work of literature is the possibility of being able to continue to unpeel it like a never-ending artichoke, discovering more and more new dimensions in reading. It is for this reason that I maintain that amongst all the important and brilliant authors about whom we have spoken in these days, perhaps only Gadda deserves the name of a great writer.

La cognizione del dolore (Acquainted with Grief) is on the surface the most subjective work imaginable: it is almost nothing but an outpouring of pointless despair. Yet in reality it is a book packed with objective and universal meanings. *Quer pasticciaccio brutto de via Merulana (That Awful Mess on Via Merulana)*, on the other hand, is totally objective, a portrait of life as it swarms around, but it is at the same time a deeply lyrical book, a self-portrait hidden between the lines of a complex design, as in those children's games where they have to discern amidst the tangles of a wood the image of a hare or the hunter.

On *La cognizione del dolore (Acquainted with Grief)* Juan Petit said something very perceptive today: that the key emotion in the book, the ambivalent love-hatred for the mother, can be understood as a love-hate for his own country and his own social milieu. The analogy can be extended. Gonzalo, the protagonist, who lives in isolation in the villa overlooking the village, is the bourgeois who sees that the landscape of places and values that he once loved has been completely overturned. The obsessive motif of his fear of thieves expresses the conservative's sense of alarm at the uncertainty of the times. To face up to the threat of burglars a body of night vigilantes is set up which should return security to the villa's owners. But this organisation is so suspect, so dubious, that it ends up by becoming for Gonzalo an even graver problem than the fear of thieves. The references to Fascism are constant but they are never so precise as to freeze the narrative into a purely allegorical reading and to prevent other possible interpretations.

(The vigilante service should be formed by war veterans, but Gadda continually casts doubts upon their much vaunted patriotic merits. Let us recall one of the basic nuclei of Gadda's oeuvre, not just of this book: having fought in the First World War, Gadda saw it as the moment when the moral values which had come to the fore in the nineteenth century found their highest expression, but also as the beginning of their end. One might say that for the First World War Gadda felt both a possessive love and at the same time a shock-induced terror from which neither his inner spirit nor the external world would ever be able to recover.)

His mother wants to enlist in the vigilante service but Gonzalo obstinately opposes her. On to this disagreement, on the surface purely a question of form, Gadda manages to graft an unbearable tension, as in a Greek tragedy. Gadda's greatness resides in his ability to tear through the triviality of anecdote with flashes of a hell that is at the same time psychological, existential, ethical and historical.

The close of the novel, the fact that the mother wins out by joining the night-time vigilantes, that the villa is ransacked – it seems – by the guards themselves, and that in the thieves' attack the mother loses her life, could suggest a narrative that ends within the closed circle of a fable. But it is easy to realise that Gadda was less interested in this closure than in the creation of tremendous tension, which is expressed in all the details and digressions of the story.

I have sketched out one interpretation along historical lines: now I should like to attempt an interpretation in philosophical and scientific terms. Gadda's cultural background was positivism, he had a degree in engineering from the Milan Politecnico, he was obsessed with the problems and terminology of the practical and natural sciences, so he lived through the crisis of our times as the crisis of scientific thought, moving from the security of rationalism and nineteenth-century belief in progress to the awareness of the complexity of a universe which gave no reassurance and was beyond all possibility of expression. The central scene in *La cognizione* is when the village doctor comes to see Gonzalo, a confrontation between a confident nineteenth-century image of science and the tragic self-awareness of Gonzalo, of whom we are given a merciless and grotesque physiological portrait.

In his enormous output, published and unpublished, and made up for the most part of works a mere ten or twenty pages long, amongst which is some of his best writing, I will mention a piece written for the radio in which Gadda the engineer discusses modern buildings. He begins with the classical composure of a Bacon or a Galileo describing how modern houses are made with reinforced concrete; but his technical precision gradually gives way to mounting irritation and colourful language when he explains how the walls in modern houses cannot contain the noise; he then moves on to a physiological section on how noises react on the encephalon and the nervous system; and finishes with verbal pyrotechnics which express the exasperation of the neurotic victim of noise in a huge urban block of flats.

I believe that this piece of prose represents not only the entire range of Gadda's stylistic capabilities, but also the full gamut of his cultural significance, his kaleidoscopic range of philosophical stances from the most rigorous technical-scientific rationalism to this descent into the darkest and most hellish abyss.

[1963]

Carlo Emilio Gadda, the *Pasticciaccio*

What Carlo Emilio Gadda had in mind when in 1946 he began writing *Quer pasticciaccio brutto de via Merulana* (*That Awful Mess on Via Merulana*), was a detective novel but also a philosophical novel. The detective plot was inspired by a crime that had recently taken place in Rome. The philosophical novel was based on a concept enunciated in the very first pages: nothing can be explained if one simply looks for a single cause for every effect, since every effect is determined by a multiplicity of causes, each one of which in turn has many other causes behind it; hence every event (for example, a crime) is like a vortex into which different currents flow, each one moved by different springs, none of which can be overlooked in the search for the truth.

A vision of the world as 'a system of systems' was expounded in a philosophical notebook found amongst Gadda's papers after his death (the *Meditazione milanese*). The author, starting from his favourite philosophers, Spinoza, Leibniz and Kant, had constructed his own 'discourse on method'. Every element in a system is in turn a system itself; every single system is linked to a genealogy of systems; every change in an element implies the alteration of the entire system.

But what counts even more is how this philosophy of knowledge is reflected in Gadda's style: in the language, which is a dense amalgam of popular and erudite expressions, of interior monologue and studied prose, of various dialects and literary quotations; and in narrative composition, in which minimal details take on giant proportions and end up by occupying the whole canvas and hiding or obscuring the overall design. That is what happens in this novel, in which the detective story is gradually forgotten:

maybe we are just on the point of discovering who committed the murder and why, but the description of a hen and the excrement it deposits on the earth become more important than the solution of the mystery.

What Gadda wants to convey is the boiling cauldron of life, the infinite stratification of reality, the unravellable knot of knowledge. When this image of universal complexity, which is reflected in the slightest object or event, reaches its ultimate paroxysm, it is pointless for us to speculate whether the novel was destined to remain unfinished, or whether it could have gone on ad infinitum, opening up new vortices inside every episode. The thing that Gadda really wanted to convey was the congested superabundance of these pages through which one single, complex object, organism and symbol, takes shape, the city of Rome.

Because we must immediately point out that this novel is not intended to be just a mixture of a detective and a philosophical novel, but also a novel about Rome. The Eternal City is the book's real protagonist, in its social classes from the most middling of the middle classes to the criminal underworld, in the words of its dialect (and of its variety of dialects, particularly southern ones, which bubble up in this melting-pot), in its extrovert nature and in its darkest subconscious, a Rome in which the present mixes with the mythical past, in which Hermes or Circe is evoked in connection with the most trivial incidents, in which characters who are domestics or petty thieves are called Aeneas, Diomedes, Ascanius, Camilla, or Lavinia, like the heroes and heroines in Virgil. The noisy, down-at-heel Rome of neorealist cinema (which was enjoying its heyday at that very time) acquires in Gadda's book a cultural, historical and mythical depth that neorealism neglected. And even the Rome of art history comes into play, with references to Renaissance and Baroque painting (like the passage on the saints' bare feet, with their enormous big toes).

The novel of Rome, written by a non-Roman. In fact Gadda was from Milan and identified closely with the middle class of his native city, whose values (practicality, technical efficiency, moral principles) he felt were being overturned by the predominance of another Italy, a cheating, noisy, unscrupulous Italy. But even although his stories and his most autobiographical novel (*La cognizione del dolore* (*Acquainted with Grief*)) are rooted in Milanese society and dialect, the work which brought him to the attention of the wider public is this book written mostly in Roman dialect, in which Rome is seen and understood with an almost physical involvement in even its most infernal aspects, like a witches' sabbath. (And yet, by the time he wrote the *Pasticciaccio*, Gadda had only known Rome from having lived there for a few years in the 1930s, when he had found employment as overseer of the heating systems in the Vatican.)

Gadda was a man of contradictions. An electro-technical engineer (he had used his professional skills for about ten years, mostly abroad), he sought to control his hypersensitive and nervous temperament by means of a scientific, rational mentality, but only succeeded in making it worse; and he used his writing to give vent to his irritability, phobias, and outbursts of misanthropy, which he tried to suppress in real life by donning the mask of a gentleman from a bygone age full of courtesy and good manners.

He was considered by the critics as a revolutionary in terms of narrative structure and language, an expressionist or follower of Joyce (a reputation which he enjoyed right from the start even in the most exclusive literary circles, and which was reinforced when the young writers of the new avant-garde in the 1960s acknowledged him as their model). And yet as far as his personal literary tastes were concerned, he was devoted to the classics, and tradition (his favourite author was the sedate and wise Manzoni) and his models in the art of the novel were Balzac and Zola. (He possessed some of the basic qualities of nineteenth-century realism and naturalism, such as the portrayal of characters, milieus and situations through physical details, and through bodily sensations, such as savouring a glass of wine at lunch, with which this book opens.)

Fiercely satirical towards the society of his day, and driven by a quite visceral hatred for Mussolini (as is proved by the sarcasm with which this book evokes Mussolini's tough-jawed look), Gadda in political terms was totally alien from any form of radicalism, a moderate law-and-order man, respectful of the laws, nostalgic for the sound administration of yesteryear, a good patriot whose formative experience had been the First World War which he had fought and suffered in as a scrupulous officer, constantly indignant at the damage which can be caused by improvised solutions, incompetence, or being overambitious. In the *Pasticciaccio*, whose action is supposed to take place in 1927, at the beginning of Mussolini's dictatorship, Gadda does not simply go in for a facile caricature of Fascism: he analyses in great detail what effects are produced on the daily administration of justice by the failure to respect the division of Montesquieu's three powers of the state (the reference to the author of *L'Esprit des lois* is explicit).

This continual need for something concrete and detailed, this appetite for reality is so strong as to create a kind of congestion, hypertension and even blockages in Gadda's writing. His characters' voices, sensations, and the dreams of their subconscious are mixed up with the author's constant presence, with his bursts of intolerance, his sarcasms and the dense network of cultural references. As in a ventriloquist's performance, all these voices overlay each other in the one discourse, sometimes with changes of tone, modulations, and falsetto notes all in the same sentence. The novel's structure is altered from within, through the excessive richness of the material represented and the excessive intensity with which the author overloads it. The existential and intellectual trauma of this process are all left implicit, while comedy, humour, grotesque transformations all form the natural means of expression of this man who always lived most unhappily, tormented by neuroses, by the difficulty of his relations with others, and by the terror of death.

He did not set out with plans of innovations in form to revolutionise the structure of the novel: his dream was to construct solid novels obeying all the rules, but he never managed to bring them to completion. He kept them in their unfinished state for years, and would decide to publish them only when he had given up all hope of completing them. One feels that just a few pages more would have been enough to round off the plot of *La cognizione del dolore* or the *Pasticciaccio*. Other novels he cut up into short stories and it is no longer possible to reconstitute them by reassembling their various fragments.

The *Pasticciaccio* tells of a double police investigation into two crimes, one trivial, the other horrific, which took place in the same building in the centre of Rome: a widow looking for some consolation is robbed of her jewels, and a married woman, who is inconsolable because she cannot have children, is stabbed to death. This obsession with failed maternity is very important in the novel: Signora Liliana Balducci surrounded herself with girls whom she considered her adopted daughters until for one reason or another she would leave them. The figure of Liliana, who dominates even as a victim, and the atmosphere of the gynoecium which she spreads around her opens up a shadowy perspective on femininity, that mysterious force of nature before which Gadda expresses his confusion in pages in which considerations of female physiology are combined with geographical and genetic metaphors and with the legend of the origins of Rome, which guaranteed its continuity through the rape of the Sabine women. Traditional anti-feminism which reduces the woman solely to her procreative function is expressed here in very crude terms: is this to ape

Flaubert's dictionary of 'idées reçues', or because the author shares these views? In order to define the problem more precisely we have to bear in mind two circumstances, one historical, the other relating to the author's psychology. When Mussolini was in power, the Italians' main duty, hammered home by the insistent official propaganda, was to have children for the fatherland; only the mothers and fathers of many children were considered worthy of respect. This apotheosis of procreation made Gadda, a bachelor oppressed by a paralysing shyness at any female presence, suffer and feel excluded, and left him hovering between attraction and repulsion.

Attraction and repulsion inform the description of the female corpse with its throat horrifically cut, in one of the virtuoso passages of the book, like a Baroque painting of the martyrdom of some saint. The police commissioner, Francesco Ingravallo, invests a particular interest in the enquiry into the crime, for two reasons: first, because he knew (and desired) the woman; and second, because he is a Southerner brought up on philosophy and driven by a passion for science as well as sensitivity for everything that is human. It is he who theorises about the multiplicity of causes which go to determine an effect, and amongst these causes (since his reading apparently also includes Freud) he always includes sex, in some form or other.

If Inspector Ingravallo is the author's philosophical spokesman, there is also another character with whom Gadda identifies at a psychological and poetic level: one of the tenants, the retired civil servant Angeloni, who because of the awkwardness with which he replies to questioning instantly becomes a suspect, even though he is the most harmless person in the world. Angeloni, an introverted, melancholy bachelor, who takes lonely walks through the streets of ancient Rome, is prone only to temptations of gluttony, or perhaps of one other vice: he is in the habit of ordering prosciutto and cheese from delicatessens which are delivered to his door by boys in short trousers. The police are looking for one of these boys, who is probably an accomplice in the robbery and perhaps also in the murder. Angeloni, who clearly lives in fear of being accused of homosexual proclivities, jealous as he is of his respectability and privacy, stumbles under questioning with his omissions and contradictions and ends up by being arrested.

More serious suspicions fall on a nephew of the murdered woman, who has to explain how he comes to possess a gold pendant containing a precious stone, a jasper which has replaced an opal, though this seems very much a red herring. The enquiries into the robbery, on the other hand, seem to gather more promising clues, moving from the capital to the villages on the Alban hills (consequently becoming the domain of the carabinieri rather than the city police) in the search for a gigolo electrician, Diomede Lanciani, who used to visit the obsessive widow of the many jewels. In this village world we pick up the traces of various girls on whom Signora Liliana lavished her maternal care. And it is there that the carabinieri find, hidden in a bed-pan, the widow's stolen jewels as well as another jewel which had belonged to the murdered woman. The descriptions of the jewels (as with the previous description of the pendant with its opal or jasper) are not only virtuoso performances by a master of style but they add another level to the reality portrayed: besides the linguistic, phonetic, psychological, physiological, historical, mythical, gastronomic levels, we have this mineral, underworld level, about hidden treasures, involving geological history and the powers of inanimate matter in the squalid business of a crime. And it is around the possession of jewels that Gadda tightens the knots of the psychology and psycho-pathology of his characters: the violent envy of the poor along with what Gadda defines as 'the typical psychosis of frustrated women' which leads the unfortunate Liliana to load her 'children' with jewels.

We could have been helped some way towards the solution of the mystery by a chapter which was chapter 4 in the first version of the novel (published in instalments in the monthly Florentine review *Letteratura*, in 1946), if the author had not eliminated it when he published it as a book (with Garzanti in 1957) precisely because he did not want to reveal his hand too early. In it the inspector interrogated Liliana's husband about the relationship which he had had with Virginia, one of their ambitious adopted children, whose character was marked by lesbian tendencies (the Sapphic atmosphere around Signora Liliana and her gynecium was stressed), by a lack of morality, greed for money and social ambitions (she had become her adoptive father's lover only to blackmail him), and by violent fits of hatred (she would utter dark threats while slicing the roast meat with the kitchen knife).

Is Virginia the murderer, then? Any doubt we might have had is eliminated if one reads an unpublished document which was discovered and published recently (*Il palazzo degli ori* (*The Apartment Building of Riches*), Turin: Einaudi, 1983). This is a film script which Gadda wrote at the same time as the first draft of the novel: either shortly before it, or shortly afterwards, apparently. In it the whole plot is developed and clarified in every particular. (We also learn that the robbery was committed not by Diomede Lanciani but by Enea Retalli, who in order to avoid arrest opens fire on the carabinieri and is shot dead.) The script (which bears no relation to the film which Pietro Germi made from the novel in 1959 and in which Gadda had no part) was never taken up by producers or directors, and no wonder: Gadda had a rather naïve idea of writing for cinema, based on continual fade-outs to reveal characters' thoughts and background detail. For us it makes very interesting reading as a rough sketch for the novel, but it fails to generate any real tension either in its action or its psychology.

In brief, the problem is not 'Who dunnit?', for already in the novel's opening pages we are told that what causes the crime is the whole 'force-field' which establishes itself around the victim; it is the 'compulsion on destiny' emanating from the victim, her circumstances in relation to others' circumstances, that spins the web of events: 'that system of forces and probabilities which surrounds every human being and which is usually called destiny.'

[1984]

Eugenio Montale,
'Forse un mattino andando'

When I was young I used to enjoy learning poetry off by heart. We studied many poems at school – and today I wish we had studied many more – which have subsequently stayed with me all my life, in a kind of unconscious, mental recital of them which resurfaces many years later. After secondary school, I continued learning some on my own for a few years: poets who were at that time not included in school syllabuses. Those were the years when *Ossi di seppia* (*Cuttlefish Bones*) and *Le occasioni* (*The Occasions*) began to circulate in Italy in the grey covers of Einaudi's books. So, around the age of eighteen, I learnt several of Montale's poems by heart: some of them I have now forgotten, others I have continued to carry with me to this day.

Rereading Montale today naturally takes me back to that repertoire of poems deep in my memory ('che si sfolla' (which empties)). An analysis of what has remained and what has been cancelled (or 'scancellato', to use the local form of 'cancellato' retained by Montale), and a study of how my memory has varied or even deformed the verses, would lead me to an in-depth exploration of those poems and of the relationship that I have established with them over the years.

But I would like to choose a poem, which though it has long stayed in my memory and bears the scars of that stay, lends itself better to a totally contemporary, objective reading rather than leading to a search for the conscious or unconscious autobiographical echoes that Montale's poems, particularly the early ones, arouse in me. I am going to choose, therefore, 'Forse un mattino andando in un'aria di vetro' ('Perhaps One Morning Walking in an Air of Glass'), one of the poems that has continued to go round more than most on my mental turntable, and which comes back to me every time without any tremor of nostalgia, as though I were reading it for the first time.

'Forse un mattino' is an 'osso di seppia' (cuttlefish-bone) which stands out from the others not so much because it is a 'narrative' poem (the typical narrative poem by Montale is 'La folata che alzò l'amaro aroma' ('The Gust that Stirred the Bitter Aroma'), where the subject of the action is a gust of wind and the action itself is simply the realisation of the absence of a person, so the narrative movement resides in contrasting an inanimate subject which is present with a human object who is absent), but because it is without objects, natural symbols, or a particular landscape, it is a poem of abstract imagination and thought of a kind that is rare in Montale.

But I notice that (and this distances it even more from the others) my memory had corrected a bit of the poem: as far as I am concerned the sixth line begins 'alberi case strade' (trees houses streets) or 'uomini case strade' (men houses streets) not 'alberi case colli' (trees houses hills), which only now rereading the text after 35 years do I see is the right reading. That means that by substituting 'strade' (streets) for 'colli' (hills), I am setting the action very much in a city landscape, perhaps because the word 'colli' sounds too vague for me, or because the presence in the poem of 'uomini che non si voltano' (men who don't turn round) suggests the rush of passers-by. In short, I see the disappearance of the world as the disappearance of the city rather than of nature. (I now notice that my memory was only grafting on to this poem the image of the verse 'Ciò non vede la gente nell'affollato corso' (the people on the crowded street do not see this), which appears four pages before this, in a companion piece to this poem.)

If we look closely, we shall see that what sets off the 'miracle' is something natural or rather atmospheric, the dry, crystalline transparency of the winter air, which makes things so clear as to create an effect of unreality, almost as though the halo of haze which usually covers the landscape (here once again I am setting Montale's poetry, the early Montale's poetry, in the usual coastal landscape, assimilating it into the Ligurian landscape of my own memory) is identifiable with the density and weight of existence. No, that's not quite it: it is the concreteness of this invisible air, which seems in fact like glass, with a self-sufficient solidity of its own, which in the end settles on the world and makes it vanish. The glass-air is the real element in this poem, and the city in which I place it is a city of glass, which becomes more and more diaphanous until it eventually disappears. It is the definite nature of the air that leads to a sense of emptiness (whereas in Leopardi it is the indeterminacy which reaches the same effect). Or to be more precise, there is a sense of being suspended which is caused by that opening 'Forse un mattino' (Perhaps one morning), which is not so much indeterminacy as a careful equilibrium, 'andando *in* un'aria di vetro' (walking *in* an air of glass), as though we were walking in the air, in the fragile glass of air, in the cold light of morning, until we realise that we are suspended in the void.

The sense of suspension and at the same time of concreteness continues in the second line because of the oscillating rhythm, with that 'compìrsi' which the reader is continually tempted to pronounce 'còmpiersi', but notices each time that the whole line rests on that prosaic 'compìrsi' which dulls any emphatic overtone in stating the miracle. This is a line which my ear has always been fond of precisely because when you say it mentally it needs some help, it seems to have one foot too many, but it is not in fact one too many: often my memory tends to discard the odd syllable. The most vulnerable area of the line in terms of memory is that 'rivolgendomi' (turning round) which sometimes I abbreviate to 'voltandomi' (turning) or 'girandomi' (spinning), thus disrupting the rhythm of all the successive accents.

Of all the reasons that cause a poem to stick in the memory (first almost asking you to commit it to memory, then allowing itself to be memorised) metrical peculiarities play a decisive role. I have always been attracted by Montale's use of rhyme: two-syllable words ('parole piane') rhyming with three-syllable ones ('parole sdrucciole'), imperfect rhymes, rhymes in unusual positions like 'Il saliscendi bianco e nero dei / [balestrucci dal palo]' (the black and white rise and fall of the little swallows from the pole) where 'dei' rhymes with 'dove piú non sei' (where you are no more). The surprise in the rhyme is not just a question of sound: Montale is one of the few poets who knows the secret of using rhyme to lower the tone, not to raise it, with unmistakable repercussions on meaning. Here the word 'miracolo' (miracle) which closes the second line is attenuated by rhyming with 'ubriaco' (drunk), and the whole quatrain seems to stay teetering on the edge, vibrating eerily.

The 'miracle' is Montale's first theme, which he never abandons: it is the 'maglia rotta nella rete' (broken skein in the net), 'l'anello che non tiene' (the link that does not hold) in the opening poem, but this poem is one of the few occasions on which that *other* truth which the poet presents beyond the solid wall of the empirical world is revealed in a definable experience. We could say that it is about nothing more nor less than the unreality of the world, if that definition did not risk making hazy and generic something which is conveyed to us in precise terms. The unreality of the world is the basis particularly of Oriental philosophies, religions and literatures, but this poem moves in a different epistemological area, one of clarity and transparency, just as though it were a mental 'aria di vetro' (air of glass). Merleau-Ponty has many fine pages in his *Phenomenology of Perception* on cases in which the subjective experience of space separates from the objective experience of the world (at night in the dark, in dreams, under the influence of drugs, when suffering from schizophrenia etc.). This poem could be one of Merleau-Ponty's examples: space separates from the world and presents itself to us as just space, empty and limitless. The poet greets this discovery favourably, as a 'miracle', as the acquisition of a truth as opposed to the 'inganno consueto' (usual illusion), but it also makes him suffer a terrifying vertigo: 'con un terrore di ubriaco' (with a drunk's terror). Not even the 'aria di vetro' (air of glass) can support man's footsteps any more: that balanced opening with 'andando' (going), after the sudden turning around, becomes a kind of staggering without anything to hold on to.

The 'di gitto' (instantly) which closes the first line of the second quatrain limits the experience of the void in temporal terms to an instant. The walking movement resumes again inside a landscape that is solid but now fleeting: we realise that the poet is merely following one of many vectorial lines along which the other men present in this space also move, 'gli uomini che non si voltano' (the men who do not turn round). The poem thus ends on a multiple movement of people along uniform straight lines.

The doubt still remains whether these other men had also disappeared in the instant when the world disappeared. Amongst the objects which come back 'ad accamparsi' (to position themselves) there are trees but no men (though my memory's variations lead to different philosophical outcomes); so the men might have remained there; just as the disappearance of the world stays external to the poet's self, so it could spare every other person from that experience and judgment. The background void is studded with units, populated by so many point-like selves which if they turned round would discover the deception, but they continue to appear to us as backs moving, confident of the solidity of their trajectory.

We could see here the opposite situation from that of 'Vento e bandiere' ('Wind and Flags'), where the lability is all on the part of the human presence while 'Il mondo esiste . . .' (The world exists . . .) in a time that will never come back. Instead here only the human presence persists while the world and its values fade away; the human presence is a subject in a desperate condition because it is either the victim of deception or the holder of the secret of the void.

My reading of 'Forse un mattino' could now be considered to have reached its conclusion. But it has sparked off inside me a series of reflections on visual perception and the appropriation of space. A poem lives on, then, also through its power to emanate hypotheses, digressions, associations of ideas in distant areas, or rather to recall and hook on to itself ideas from different sources, organising them in a mobile network of cross-references and refractions, as though viewed through a crystal.

The 'vuoto' (void) and the 'nulla' (nothing) are 'alle mie spalle' (behind my back). This is the key point of the poem. It is not an indeterminate sense of dissolution: rather it is the construction of an epistemological model which is not easy to refute and which can coexist within us with other more or less empirical models. The hypothesis can be enunciated in very simple and rigorous terms: given the bipartite division of the space surrounding us into a visual field in front of our eyes and an invisible one behind our backs, the first is defined as the screen of deceptions and the second as the void which is the real substance of the world.

It would be legitimate to expect that having established that behind him is the void, the poet would also extend this discovery in other directions; but in the rest of the poem there is nothing to justify this generalisation, whereas the bipartite model of space is never denied by the text, on the contrary it is reaffirmed by the tautologous third line: 'il nulla alle mie spalle, il vuoto dietro / di me' (nothing behind my back, the void behind me). When I knew this poem only by memory, this tautology at times perplexed me, so I tried a variant: 'il nulla a me dinanzi, il vuoto dietro / di me' (nothing in front of me, the void behind me); that is to say, the poet turns round, sees the void, turns back round again and the void has spread to all sides. But on reflection I realised that part of the poetic richness was lost if the discovery of the void was not located specifically 'dietro' (behind).

The division of space into an anterior and posterior visual field is not only one of the most elementary human operations in terms of categories. It is a basic fact common to all animals, which starts very early in the biological scale, with the appearance of living beings which no longer develop according to radial symmetry but along bipolar lines, with the organs which relate to the outside world placed at one end of the body: a mouth and some nerve ends, some of which will become organs of sight. From that point on the world is identified with the anterior field, and complementary to this there is an unknowable zone, a zone of *non-world*, of void, located behind the observer. As it moves and adds together the successive visual fields, the living being successfully constructs a complete and coherent circular world, but this is always an inductive model, evidence of which will never be conclusive.

Man has always suffered from the lack of eyes on the back of his neck, and his attitude to knowledge can only be problematic because he can never be sure what is behind him; in other words, he cannot check if the world continues between the extreme points he manages to see by stretching out his pupils to right and left. If he is not immobilised he can turn his neck and his whole body to confirm that the world also exists there, but this is also the confirmation that his visual field is still what he has in front of him, extending to a width of so many degrees and no more, while behind his back there is a corresponding arc in which at that moment the world might not exist. In short, we wheel round on ourselves putting before our eyes our visual field and we never manage to see what the space which our visual field excludes is like.

The protagonist of Montale's poem succeeds through a combination of factors both objective (air of glass, arid air) and subjective (receptivity to an epistemological miracle), in turning round so fast as to manage, let's say, to cast his eye on the place where his visual field has not yet reached: and he sees nothing, the void.

I discovered the same set of problems more positively (or negatively, at any rate with the opposite sign) in a legend from the Wisconsin and Minnesota wood-dwellers, cited by Borges in his *Fantastic Zoology*. There is an animal called the 'hide-behind' which when you go for wood in the forest is always behind you, following you everywhere: you turn around, but however quick you are the hide-behind is quicker still and has moved behind you already; you will never find out what it looks like but it is always there. Borges does not cite his sources, and it could be that he invented this legend himself; but that would not take anything away from its hypothetical force which I would say is genetic, categorical. We could say that Montale's man is the one who has managed to turn round and see what the hide-behind looks like: and it is more frightening than any other animal, it is the void.

Continuing with these free-wheeling digressions, one could argue that the context of this whole discourse precedes a fundamental anthropological revolution in the twentieth century: the invention of the rear-view mirror in cars. Motorised man should feel reassured of the existence of the world behind him, in the sense that he possesses an eye that can look backwards. I am talking of car-mirrors in particular, not of mirrors in general, because in ordinary mirrors the world behind us is seen as adjacent to or complementary to our own person. What ordinary mirrors confirm is the presence of the observing subject, in relation to which the world is merely a secondary backdrop. Such mirrors perform an operation that objectifies the self, along with the imminent danger, which is the point of the myth of Narcissus, of being drowned in the self and of the subsequent loss of both the self and the world.

Instead the great discovery of this century is the daily use of a mirror positioned in such a way as to exclude the self from vision. Motorised man can be considered a new biological species more because of this mirror than because of the motor car itself, since his eyes see a road which progressively gets shorter in front of him and longer behind him, in other words he can take in with one look two opposite visual fields without the encumbrance of the image of himself, as though he were nothing but an eye hovering over the whole world.

But, on closer inspection, the hypothesis of 'Forse un mattino' is not really undermined by this revolution in perception techniques. If the 'inganno consueto' (usual illusion) is whatever we have in front of us, this deception extends to that portion of the anterior field of vision which, because it is enclosed in the mirror, claims to represent the posterior visual field. Even if the 'I' of 'Forse un mattino' was *driving* along in an air of glass and was to turn round in the same receptive condition, he would see beyond the car's rear window not the landscape receding into the distance in the mirror, with the white lines on the tarmac, the stretch of road just past, the cars he thinks he has overtaken, but an empty abyss that knows no bounds.

In any case, in Montale's mirrors – as Silvio D'Arco Avalle has shown in 'Gli orecchini' ('The Earrings') and 'Vasca' ('Pool') and stretches of water in other poems – images are not reflected but rather surface 'di giú' (from down there), coming towards the observer.

In reality, the image we behold is not something which the eye records, or which resides in the eye: it is something which takes place entirely in the brain, following stimuli transmitted by optic nerves, but which only acquire shape and sense in one part of the brain. That part is the 'screen' against which the images stand out, and if I succeed by turning round, that is by turning myself round within myself, in *seeing* beyond that part of my brain, that is to say in understanding what the world is like when my sense perceptions are not attributing to it the colour and shape of trees, houses, hills, I will be groping in a darkness that has no dimensions or objects, and contains only a dust-cloud of cold, shapeless vibrations, shadows on a badly tuned radar system.

The reconstruction of the world takes place 'as though on a screen', a metaphor that can only summon up the cinema. Our native poetic tradition has habitually used the word 'schermo' (screen) in the sense of 'a shelter which obscures vision' or 'diaphragm', and if we wanted to risk claiming that this is the first time that an Italian poet uses 'schermo' in the sense of 'surface on which images are projected', I do not think the risk of error would be very high. This poem, datable to somewhere between 1921 and 1925, clearly belongs to the cinema age, in which the world now runs before us like the outlines on a film: trees, houses, hills, stretch out on a canvas backdrop which is two-dimensional, and the speed with which they appear ('di gitto' (instantly)) and the listing of them conjure up a sequence of images in movement. It is not said whether they are images which are projected, their 'accamparsi' (positioning themselves, placing themselves in the field, occupying a field – here the *visual field* is actually alluded to) might not actually refer to a real source or matrix for the image, they might emerge directly from the screen (as we saw happen with the mirror), but the cinema spectator's illusion is also that the images come from the screen.

The illusion of the world was traditionally conveyed by poets and dramatists using metaphors of the theatre; the twentieth century replaces the world as theatre with the world as cinema, a vortex of images on a white screen.

★　★　★

Two distinct speeds run through the poem: the speed of the mind that perceives the intuition and the speed of the world flashing by. Understanding is all a question of being fast enough to turn around suddenly to surprise the hide-behind, a dizzying turning around on oneself, and in that dizziness lies knowledge. The empirical world, on the other hand, is the familiar succession of images on the screen, an optical illusion like the cinema, where the speed of the photograms convinces you of their continuity and permanence.

There is a third rhythm which triumphs over the other two and it is that of meditation, the motion of someone absorbed in thought and suspended in the morning air, the silence in which the secret is kept, which has been plucked in that flash of intuitive motion. A substantial analogy connects this 'andare zitto' (silent walking) with the nothing, the void which we know is the beginning and end of everything, and with the 'aria di vetro / arida' (arid air of glass) which is its less deceptive outward manifestation. Apparently this motion is no different from that of the 'uomini che non si voltano' (the men who do not turn round), who have perhaps, each in his own way, also understood, and amongst whom the poet finally loses himself. And it is this third rhythm, which takes up the lightness of the opening notes but at a more solemn pace, that stamps its concluding seal on the poem.

[1976]

Montale's Cliff

To talk about a poet on the front page of a newspaper is a risky business: you have to make a 'public' discourse, stressing his vision of the world and of history, and the moral lessons implicit in his poetry. Everything you say may be true, but then you realise that it could apply equally to a different poet, that your discussion has failed to capture the unmistakable note of this poet's verse. Let me try, therefore, to remain as close as possible to the essence of Montale's poetry when I try to explain how today the funeral of this poet, who was so averse to any ceremonials and so remote from the image of 'the national bard', is an event with which the whole country can identify. (This fact is also the more peculiar in that the great openly declared 'religions' in the Italy of his lifetime never could count him amongst their followers, on the contrary he never spared the sarcasm he directed against every 'cleric, red or black'.)

I would like to say this first of all: Montale's poetry is unmistakable for the precision and uniqueness of its verbal expression, its rhythm and the imagery it conjures up: 'il lampo che candisce / alberi e muri e li sorprende in quella / eternità d'istante' (the flash that whitens / trees and walls and surprises them in that / eternity of an instant). I am not going to speak about the richness and versatility of his lexis, a gift which other Italian poets also possessed to a high degree, and which is often linked to a copious, even redundant quality, in other words to something that is at the opposite extreme from Montale. Montale never wastes his shots, he goes for the unique expression at the right moment and isolates it in all its irreplaceability: '. . . Turbati / discendevamo tra i vepri. / Nei miei paesi a quell'ora / cominciano a fischiare i lepri' (Disturbed, we came down through the thornbushes. / In my region the hares begin to whistle at that time).

I will come straight to the point. In an age of generic and abstract words, words that are used for everything, words that are used not to think and not to say, a linguistic plague which is spreading from the public sphere to the private, Montale was the poet of exactness, of justified lexical choices, of sureness in terminology, which he used to capture the uniqueness of the experience described: 'S'accese su pomi cotogni, / un punto, una cocciniglia, / si udí inalberarsi alla striglia / il poney, e poi vinse il sogno' (a tiny point, a ladybird lit up on quinces, a pony was heard rearing at the curry-comb, then I fell into a dream).

But this precision is used to tell us what? Montale talks to us of a world like a vortex, spun by a wind of destruction, with no solid ground for our feet to stand on, the only aid being the individual's morality which teeters over the edge of an abyss. This is the world of the First and Second World Wars, maybe even of the Third. Or perhaps the First is still a little bit outside the frame (in the cinemathèque of my historical memory it is the subtitles of Ungaretti's spare lines that run under those already rather faded photograms); and it is the precariousness of that world as it appeared to the young men of just after the First World War that forms the backdrop to *Ossi di seppia* (*Cuttlefish Bones*). Similarly it would be the anticipation of another catastrophe that would make up the atmosphere of *Le occasioni* (*The Occasions*), while the catastrophe itself and its ashes would be the central theme of *La bufera* (*The Storm*). *La bufera* is the finest book to have emerged from the Second World War, and even when it is talking about something else it is really talking about the War. Everything is implicit in it, even our postwar anxieties, right down to today's fears: the atomic catastrophe ('e un ombroso Lucifero scenderà su una proda / del Tamigi, del Hudson, della Senna / scuotendo l'ali di bitume semi-mozze dalla fatica, a dirti: è l'ora' (and a shadowy Satan will disembark on the bank of the Thames, the Hudson, the Seine, shaking his bitumen wings half-worn by the effort, to tell you: the time has come)), and the horror of the concentration camps of the past and the future ('Il sogno del prigioniero' ('The Prisoner's Dream')).

But it is not Montale's direct representations and clearly-stated allegories that I want to emphasise: the historical situation in which we live is seen as a cosmic one; even the tiniest presences of nature become reshaped, under the poet's daily observation, into a vortex. Instead I would stress the rhythm of the verse, its metre, its syntax, all of which contain this movement in themselves, from the beginning to the end of his three great collections. 'I turbini sollevano la polvere / sui tetti, a mulinelli, e sugli spiazzi / deserti, ove i cavalli incappucciati / annusano la terra, fermi innanzi / ai vetri luccicanti degli alberghi' (The whirlwinds raise the dust up on to the roofs, in little sandstorms, and the empty piazzas, where the hooded horses sniff the ground, stationary before the sparkling hotel windows).

I mentioned the individual morality that withstands the historical or cosmic apocalypse that could at any moment cancel the fragile trace of human kind: but it must be said that in Montale, though he is far removed from any communion with others or outburst of solidarity, the interdependence of each person with other people's lives is always present. 'Occorrono troppe vite per farne una' (Too many lives are needed to make one) is the memorable conclusion to a poem from *Le occasioni*, where the shadow of the hawk in flight gives a sense of the destruction and renaissance that pervades every biological or historical continuum. But the help which can come from nature or man is always an illusion except when it is a tiny rivulet which surfaces 'dove solo / morde l'arsura e la desolazione' (where only heat and desolation bite); it is only by going up the rivers until they become as slender as hair that the eel finds the safe place for procreation; it is only 'a un filo di pietà' (at a thin stream of pity) that the porcupines of Monte Amiata can slake their thirst.

This difficult heroism carved out of the inner aridity and precariousness of existence, this antiheroic heroism was Montale's reply to the problem of poetry in his generation: how to write poetry after (and against) D'Annunzio (and after Carducci, and Pascoli, or at least a certain side of Pascoli), the problem which Ungaretti solved with the inspiration of the single word in all its purity, and Saba with the recovery of an inner sincerity which embraced also pathos, affection, sensuality: those were hallmarks of humanity that Montale the man rejected, or considered could not be articulated.

There is no message of consolation or encouragement in Montale unless one accepts the consciousness of a hostile, greedy universe. It is on this arduous road that his discourse continues that of Leopardi, even though their voices sound so different. Just as, when compared with Leopardi's atheism, Montale's strain of atheism is more problematic, fraught as it is with constant supernatural temptations that are however immediately undermined by his basic scepticism. If Leopardi dismisses the consolations of Enlightenment philosophy, the proposals of consolation for Montale come from contemporary irrationalisms which he weighs up one by one and then drops with a shrug of his shoulders, constantly reducing the surface of the rock on which his feet rest, the cliff to which Montale the shipwreck obstinately clings.

One of his themes which becomes more and more insistent with the passing of time, is the way in which the dead are present in us, the uniqueness of each person that we refuse to allow to perish: 'il gesto d'una / vita che non è un'altra ma se stessa' (the gesture of a life, which is not another's life but itself). These lines are from a poem in memory of his mother, where the birds come back, the dead, against a sloping landscape: these are part of the repertoire of positive images in his poetry. Today I could find no better frame for his memory than these same lines: 'Ora che il coro delle coturnici / ti blandisce nel sonno eterno, rotta / felice schiera in fuga verso i clivi / vendemmiati del Mesco . . .' (Now that the chorus of rock partridges soothes you in eternal sleep, a broken but happy crowd fleeing towards the freshly vintaged slopes of Cape Mesco).

As well as continuing to read 'inside' his books. This will certainly guarantee his survival: because however much they are read and reread, his poems capture the reader at the start of the page but are never fully exhausted.

[1981]

Hemingway and Ourselves

There was a time when for me – and for many others, those who are more or less my contemporaries – Hemingway was a god. And they were good times, which I am happy to remember, without even a hint of that ironic indulgence with which we look back on youthful fashions and obsessions. They were serious times and we lived through them seriously and boldly and with purity of heart, and in Hemingway we could also have found pessimism, an individualistic detachment, a superficial involvement with extremely violent experiences: that was all there too in Hemingway, but either we could not see it in him or we had other things in our head, but the fact remains that the lesson we learnt from him was one of a capacity for openness and generosity, a practical commitment – as well as a technical and moral one – to the things that had to be done, a straightforward look, a rejection of self-contemplation or self-pity, a readiness to snatch a lesson for life, the worth of a person summed up in a brusque exchange, or a gesture. But soon we began to see his limitations, his flaws: his poetics, his style, to which I had been largely indebted in my first literary works, came to be seen as narrow, too prone to descending into mannerism. That life of his – and philosophy of life – of violent tourism began to fill me with distrust and even aversion and disgust. Today, however, ten years on, assessing the balance of my apprenticeship with Hemingway, I can close the account in the black. 'You didn't put one over on me, old man,' I can say to him, indulging for the last time in his own style, 'you did not make it, you never became a *mauvais maître*.' The aim of this discussion of Hemingway, in fact – now that he has won the Nobel Prize for Literature, a fact that means absolutely nothing, but which is as good an occasion as any other for putting down on paper ideas that have been in my head for some time – is to try to define both what Hemingway meant for me, and what he is now, what moved me away from him and what I continue to find in his not others' works.

At that time what pushed me towards Hemingway was an appeal that was both poetic and political, a confused urge towards an active antifascism, as opposed to purely intellectual antifascism. Actually, to be truthful, it was the twin constellation of Hemingway and Malraux that attracted me, the symbol of international antifascism, the international front in the Spanish Civil War. Fortunately we Italians had had D'Annunzio to inoculate us against certain 'heroic' inclinations, and the rather aestheticising base to Malraux' works soon became apparent. (For some people in France, such as Roger Vailland, who is also a very nice guy, a bit superficial but genuine enough, the Hemingway-Malraux double-bill was a formative factor.) Hemingway too has had the label of D'Annunzian attached to him, and in some cases not inappropriately. But Hemingway's style is always dry, he hardly ever gets sloppy or pompous, his feet are on the ground (or almost always: I mean, I cannot take 'lyricism' in Hemingway: *The Snows of Kilimanjaro* is for me his worst work), he sticks to dealing with things: all features that are at the opposite extreme from D'Annunzio. And in any case, we should be careful with these definitions: if all you need to be called a D'Annunzian is to like the active life and beautiful women, long live D'Annunzio. But the problem cannot be framed in these terms: the myth of Hemingway the activist comes from another side of contemporary history, much more relevant to today and still problematic.

Hemingway's hero likes to identify with the actions that he carries out, to be himself in the totality of his actions, in his commitment to manual or at any rate practical dexterity. He tries not to have any other problems, any other concerns except that of knowing how to do something well: being good at fishing, hunting, blowing up bridges, watching bullfights the way they should be watched, as well as being good at making love. But around him there is always something he is trying to escape, a sense of the vanity of everything, of desperation, of defeat, of death. He concentrates on the strict observance of his code, of those sporting rules that he always feels he should impose on himself everywhere and that carry the weight of moral rules, whether he finds himself fighting with a shark, or in a position besieged by Falangists. He clings to all that, because outside it is the void and death. (Even though he never mentions it: for his first rule is understatement.) One of the best and most typical of his tales in the 45 short stories in *The Big Two-Hearted River* is nothing more than an account of every single action done by a man who goes fishing on his own: he goes up the river, looks for a good place to pitch his tent, makes himself some food, goes into the river, prepares his rod, catches some small trout, throws them back into the river, catches a bigger one, and so on. Nothing but a bare list of actions, fleeting but clear-cut images in between, and the odd generic, unconvincing comment on his state of mind, like 'It was a good feeling'. It is a very depressing tale, with a sense of oppression too, of vague anguish besetting him on all sides, no matter how serene nature is and how caught up he is in his fishing. Now the story in which 'nothing happens' is not new. But let's take a recent example from nearer home: *Il taglio del bosco* (*The Cutting of the Woods*) by Cassola (all he has in common with Hemingway is his love of Tolstoy) which describes the actions of a woodcutter, against the background of his endless grief for the death of his wife. In Cassola the two poles of the story are the work on one side and a very precise feeling on the other: the death of a loved one, a situation which can apply to everyone, at any time. The format is similar in Hemingway, but the content is completely different: on one side a commitment to a sport, which has no other sense beyond the formal execution of the task, and on the other something unknown, nothingness. We are in an extreme situation, in the context of a very precise society, in a very precise moment of the crisis of bourgeois thought.

Hemingway, famously, did not care for philosophy. But his poetics has anything but accidental connections with American philosophy, linked as the latter is so directly to a 'structure', to a milieu of activity and practical concepts. The Hemingway hero's fidelity to a sporting and ethical code, the only certain reality in an unknowable universe, corresponds to neopositivism which proposes rules of thought inside a closed system, which has no other validity outside itself. Behaviourism, which identifies man's reality with the paradigms of his behaviour, finds its equivalent in Hemingway's style, which in its bare list of actions, its lines of brief dialogue, eliminates the unreachable reality of emotions and thoughts. (On Hemingway's code of behaviour, and on characters' 'inarticulate' conversation, see the intelligent observations in Marcus Cunliffe, *The Literature of the US* (Penguin Books, 1954), pp. 271 ff.)

All around is the *horror vacui* of existentialist nothingness. *Nada y pues nada y nada y pues nada*, thinks the waiter in 'A Clean, Well-Lighted Place', while 'The Gambler, the Nun and the Radio' ends with the conclusion that everything is 'the opium of the people', in other words an illusory shelter from a general malaise. These two stories (both from 1933) can be regarded as the texts of Hemingway's loose 'existentialism'. But it is not on these more explicitly 'philosophical' statements that we can rely, so much as on his general way of representing the negative, the senseless, the despairing elements of contemporary life, right from the time of *Fiesta* (1926) with its eternal tourists, sex-maniacs and drunkards. The emptiness of the dialogues with their pauses and digressions, whose most obvious predecessor must be the 'talking of other things' by Chekhov's characters when they are on the verge of desperation, reflects the problematics of twentieth-century irrationalism. Chekhov's petty bourgeois characters, defeated in everything except their consciousness of human dignity, stand their ground as the storm approaches and retain their hope for a better world. Hemingway's rootless Americans are inside the storm, body and soul, and the only defence they have against it is trying to ski well, to shoot lions well, establish the right relationship between a man and a woman, and between a man and another man, techniques and virtues which certainly will be useful in that better world except that they do not believe in it. Between Chekhov and Hemingway comes the First World War: reality is now seen as a huge massacre. Hemingway refuses to join the side of the massacre, his antifascism is one of those clear, indisputable 'rules of the game' on which his conception of life is based, but he accepts massacres as the natural scenario of contemporary man. The apprenticeship of Nick Adams – the autobiographical character in his earliest and most poetic stories – is a training course to help him tolerate the brutality of the world. It begins in *Indian Camp* where his father, the doctor, operates on a pregnant Indian woman with a fishing pen-knife, while her husband, unable to stand the sight of suffering, silently slits his own throat. When the Hemingway hero wants a symbolic ritual to represent this conception of the world the best he can come up with is the bullfight, thus starting down the road towards the primitive and the barbaric, which leads to D. H. Lawrence and a certain kind of ethnology.

It is this jagged cultural panorama that is Hemingway's context, and here we might bring in for comparison another writer who is often named in this context, Stendhal. This is not an arbitrary choice, but is suggested by Hemingway's admission of admiration for him, and justified by a certain analogy in their chosen sobriety of style – even though this is much more skilful, Flaubertian, in the more modern writer – and by certain parallels in key events and places in their lives (that 'Milanese' Italy they both loved). Stendhal's heroes are on the border between eighteenth-century rationalist lucidity and Romantic *Sturm und Drang*, between an Enlightenment education of the sentiments and the Romantic exaltation of amoral individualism. Hemingway's heroes find themselves at the same crossroads a hundred years later, when bourgeois thought has been impoverished, past its best – which instead has been inherited by the new working class – and yet is still developing as best it can, between blind alleys and partial and contradictory solutions: from the old Enlightenment trunk American technicist philosophies branch off, while the Romantic trunk brings forth its final fruits in existential nihilism. Stendhal's hero, though a product of the Revolution, still accepted the world of the Holy Alliance and submitted to the rules of his own hypocritical game, in order to fight his own individual battle. Hemingway's hero, who has also seen open up the great alternative of the October Revolution, accepts the world of imperialism and moves amongst imperialism's massacres, also fighting a battle with lucidity and detachment, but one which he knows is lost from the outset because he is on his own.

Hemingway's fundamental intuition was to have realised that war was the most accurate image, the *everyday* reality of the bourgeois world in the imperialist age. At the age of eighteen, even before America joined the war, he managed to reach the Italian front, just to see what war was like, first as an ambulance driver, then in charge of a canteen shuttling on bike between the trenches on the river Piave (as we learn from a recent book by Charles A. Fenton, *The Apprenticeship of Ernest Hemingway* (Farrar and Strauss, 1954)). (A long essay could be written on how much he understood about Italy, and how already in 1917 he was able to recognise the country's 'fascist' face and on the opposite side the people's face, as he portrayed them in his best novel, *A Farewell to Arms* (1929); and also on how much he still understood of 1949 Italy and portrayed in his less successful, but still in many respects interesting, novel, *Across the River and Into the Trees*; but also on how much he never understood, never managing to escape from his tourist shell.) His first book (published in 1924 then expanded in 1925), whose tone was set by his memories of the Great War and those of the massacres in Greece which he witnessed as a journalist, is entitled *In Our Time*, a title which by itself does not tell us much, but which takes on a cutting ironic tone if it is true that he wanted to echo a line from *The Book of Common Prayer*: 'Give us peace in our time, O Lord.' The flavour of war conveyed in the brief chapters of *In Our Time* was decisive for Hemingway's development, just as the impressions described in the *Tales of Sebastopol* were crucial for Tolstoy. And I don't know whether it was Hemingway's admiration for Tolstoy that led him to seek out the experience of war, or vice versa. Of course, the manner of being at war described by Hemingway is not the same as in Tolstoy, nor as in another admired author, who wrote a minor classic, the American Stephen Crane. This is war in distant lands, viewed with the detachment of a foreigner: Hemingway thus prefigures the spirit of the American soldier in Europe.

If the poet who celebrated British imperialism, Kipling, still had a precise link with his adopted country, so that his India also became a fatherland for him, in Hemingway (who unlike Kipling did not want to 'celebrate' anything but only to report facts and things) we find the spirit of America roaming the world without any clear motive, following the lead of its expanding economy.

But Hemingway interests us more not for his testimony of the reality of war or for his condemnation of massacres. Just as no poet identifies totally with the ideas which he represents, so Hemingway is not to be identified solely with the cultural crisis which is his context. Leaving aside the limits of behaviourism, that identification of man with his actions, his being able to cope or not with the duties that have been imposed on him, is still a valid and correct way of conceiving of existence, a way which can be adopted by a more industrious humanity than Hemingway's heroes, whose actions are almost never a *job* – except in 'exceptional' jobs, such as shark-fishing, or having a precise duty in a struggle. We do not really know what to do with his bullfights, for all the technique they require; but the clear, precise seriousness with which his characters know how to light a fire in the outdoors, cast a rod, position a machine gun, that is of interest and use to us. We can do without all of the more flashy and famous sides of Hemingway, in return for those moments of perfect integration of man with the world in the things he does, for those moments when man finds himself at peace with nature though still struggling with it, in harmony with humankind even in the fire of battle. If someone one day manages to write poetically about the relationship of the worker with his machinery, with the precise operations of his labour, he will have to go back to these moments in Hemingway, attaching them from their context of touristic futility, brutality or boredom, and restoring them to the organic context of the modern productive world from which Hemingway has taken and isolated them. Hemingway has understood how to live in the world with open, dry eyes, without illusions or mysticism, how to be alone without anguish and how it is better to be in company than to be alone: and, in particular, he has developed a style which expresses fully his conception of life, and which though sometimes betraying its limitations and defects, in its more successful moments (as in the Nick Adams stories) it can be considered the driest and most immediate language, the least redundant and pompous style, the most limpid and realistic prose in modern literature. (A Soviet critic, J. Kashkin, in a fine article which came out in a 1935 issue of *International Literature*, and which was quoted in the proceedings of the symposium edited by John K. M. McCaffery, *Ernest Hemingway: the Man and his Work* (The World Publishing Company, 1950) compares the style of those tales to that of Pushkin the novelist.)

In fact there is nothing more remote from Hemingway than the hazy symbolism, and religious-based exoticism with which he is associated by Carlos Baker in his *Hemingway, the Writer as Artist* (Princeton University Press, 1952, recently translated into Italian by G. Ambrosoli for Guanda). This volume contains extremely precious information and quotations from unpublished letters by Hemingway to Baker himself, to Fitzgerald and others, and it also has an excellent bibliography (missing from the Italian translation), as well as useful individual analyses, for instance of Hemingway's polemical relationship with – not his adherence to – the 'lost generation' in *Fiesta*; but the book is based on flimsy critical formulas, like the opposition between 'Home' and 'Not-home', between 'Mountain' and 'Plain', and it talks of 'Christian symbolism' in *The Old Man and the Sea*.

Less ambitious and less philologically interesting is another American book: Philip Young's brief *Ernest Hemingway* (Rinehart, 1952). Young too, poor soul, has to go to considerable lengths to prove that Hemingway was never a Communist, that he is not 'un-American', that one can be crude and pessimistic without being 'un-American'. But the general outlines of his critical approach show us the Hemingway we know, attributing a fundamental value to the Nick Adams stories, and placing them in the tradition inaugurated by that wonderful book – wonderful for its language, the richness of life and adventure it contains, its sense of nature, its involvement with the social problems of its time and place – which is Mark Twain's *Huckleberry Finn*.

[1954]

Francis Ponge

'Kings do not touch doors. They do not know that pleasure of pushing open in front of you, slowly or brusquely, one of those big familiar rectangular panels, and turning back to close it in its place again – holding a door in your arms.'

'. . . the pleasure of grabbing, at the belly of one of those tall obstacles to a room, its porcelain knob; the rapid duel in which you hold back your step for the instant it takes for the eye to open and the whole body to adapt to its new surroundings.'

'With a friendly hand you hold onto it still, before decisively pushing it back and closing yourself in another room – a feeling of enclosure which is reenforced by the click of the handle's powerful, but well-oiled spring.'

This brief text is entitled *The Pleasures of the Door* and is a good example of Francis Ponge's poetry: taking the most humble object, the most everyday action, and trying to consider it afresh, abandoning every habit of perception, and describing it without any verbal mechanism that has been worn by use. And all this, not for some reason extraneous to the fact in itself (for, say, symbolism, ideology or aesthetics), but solely in order to reestablish a relationship with things as things, with the difference between one thing and another, and with the difference of everything from us. Suddenly we discover that existing could be a much more intense, interesting and *genuine* experience than that absent-minded routine to which our senses have become hardened. This makes Francis Ponge, I believe, one of the great sages of our times, one of the few *fundamental* authors to whom we should turn so as not to continue going round in circles.

How? By allowing our attention to rest, for instance, on one of those wooden trays used by fruitsellers. 'At every street corner leading to the major markets it shines still with the unpresumptuous brightness of plain wood. Still brand new, and slightly surprised at finding itself in an ungainly position, thrown out with the rubbish never to return, this object is in reality one of the most charming objects around – on whose fate, however, one should not dwell too long.' That final qualification is a typical Ponge move: it would be hopeless if, once our sympathy had been aroused for this lowest and lightest of objects, we should insist too much on sympathising; that would ruin everything, that little grain of truth that we had just garnered would be instantly lost.

He does the same with a candle, a cigarette, an orange, an oyster, a piece of boiled meat, and bread: this inventory of 'objects' extending to the vegetable, animal and mineral worlds is contained in the slim volume which first made Francis Ponge famous in France (*Le Parti pris des choses* (*The Voices of Things*), 1942) and which Einaudi has now published (*Il partito preso delle cose*) with a useful, accurate introduction by Jacqueline Risset and a facing Italian translation of the French original. (A translation of a poet's work with the original on the opposite page can have no better function than to stimulate readers into attempting their own versions.) A tiny book ideally suited to being slipped into your pocket or put by your bedside table next to the clock (since the book is by Ponge, the very physicality of the book as object cries out for the same treatment). This ought also to be the opportunity for this discreet, retiring poet to find new acolytes in Italy. Instructions for use are: a few pages every evening will provide a reading which is at one with Ponge's method of sending out words like tentacles over the porous and variegated substance of the world.

I used the word acolytes to denote the unconditional and rather jealous devotion which has hitherto characterised his following both in France (where over the years it has included very different if not opposite characters from himself, from Sartre to the young members of the *Tel Quel* group) and in Italy (where his translators have included Ungaretti and Piero Bigongiari: the latter has been for years his most competent and enthusiastic exponent, having edited back in 1971 a wide selection of his works in Mondadori's Specchio series, entitled *Vita del testo*).

Despite all this, Ponge's moment (he has just turned eighty, having been born, in Montpellier, on 27 March 1899) has still to come, I am convinced, both in France and in Italy. And since this appeal of mine is addressed to

Ponge's many potential readers who as yet know nothing of him, I should immediately say something that should have been stated at the outset: that this poet writes entirely in prose. Short texts, ranging from half a page to six or seven, in his early period; though lately his texts have expanded to reflect that process of constantly moving closer to the truth, which is what writing means for him: his description of a piece of soap, for example, or a dried fig, have expanded into books in their own right, and his description of a meadow has become *La Fabrique du pré* (*Making A Meadow*).

Jacqueline Risset rightly contrasts Ponge's work with two other basic trends in contemporary French literature which describes 'things': Sartre (in a couple of passages in *La Nausée*) looking at a root, or at a face in the mirror, as though they were totally divorced from any reference to or meaning for humanity, and summoning up a disturbing and distraught vision; and Robbe-Grillet who established a kind of 'non-anthropomorphic' writing, describing the world in absolutely neutral, cold, objective terms.

Ponge (who chronologically precedes both of them) is 'anthropomorphic' in the sense that he wants to identify with things, as if man came out of himself to experience what it is like to be a thing. This involves a struggle with language, constantly pulling it and folding it back like a sheet which is in some places too short, in others too long, since language always tends to say too little or too much. It recalls Leonardo da Vinci's writing: he too tried to describe in brief texts which he laboriously wrote and rewrote, the flaring up of fire and the scraping of a file.

Ponge's sense of proportion and discretion – which is at the same time the sign of his practicality – is reflected in the fact that in order to talk about the sea he has to take as his theme the shores, beaches and coasts. The infinite never enters his pages, or rather it enters them when it encounters its own borders and only at that point does it really start to exist (*Sea Shores*): 'Profiting from the reciprocal distance which prevents coasts from linking up with each other except via the sea or by tortuous twists and turns, the sea allows every shore to believe that it is heading towards it in particular. In reality, the sea is courteous with all of them, actually more than courteous: it can show maximum enthusiasm and successive passions for each shore, keeping in its basin an infinite store of currents. It only ever marginally exceeds its own limits, it imposes its own restraint on its waves, and like the jelly-fish which it leaves for fishermen as a miniature image or sample of itself, it does nothing but ecstatically prostrate itself before all its shores.'

His secret is with every object or element to fix on its decisive aspect, which is nearly always the one we usually consider least, and to construct his discourse around that. To define water, for instance, Ponge homes in on its irresistible 'vice', which is gravity, its tendency to descend. But doesn't every object, for example a wardrobe, obey the force of gravity? This is where Ponge by distinguishing the very different way a wardrobe adheres to the ground, manages to see – almost from the inside – what it is to be liquid, the rejection of any and every shape in order simply to obey the obsessive idea of its own gravity . . .

A cataloguer of the diversity of things (*De Varietate Rerum* is how the work of this new, understated Lucretius has been defined), Ponge also has a couple of themes to which, in this first collection, he constantly returns, hammering away at the same cluster of images and ideas. One is the world of vegetation, paying particular attention to the shape of trees; the other is that of molluscs, particularly seashells, snails, and shells in general.

With trees, it is their comparison with man that constantly emerges in Ponge's discourse. 'They have no gestures: they simply multiply their arms, hands, fingers – like a Buddha. And in this way, doing nothing, they get to the bottom of their thoughts. They hide nothing from themselves, they cannot harbour a secret idea, they open out entirely, honestly and without restrictions. Doing nothing else, they spend all their time complicating their own shape, perfecting their own bodies towards greater complexity for analysis . . . Animate beings express themselves orally, or with mimetic gestures which however instantly disappear. But the vegetable world expresses itself in a written form that is indelible. It has no way of going back, it is impossible to have a change of mind: in order to correct something, the only thing it can do is to add. Like taking a text that has already been written and *published* and correcting it through a series of appendices, and so on. But one also has to say that plants do not ramify *ad infinitum*. Each one of them has a limit.'

Must we conclude that things in Ponge always refer back to a spoken or written discourse, to words? Finding a metaphor of writing in every written text has become too obvious a critical exercise for it to yield any further benefit here. We can say that in Ponge language, that indispensable medium linking subject and object, is constantly compared with what objects express outside language, and that in this comparison it is reassessed and redefined – and often revalued. If leaves are the trees' words, they only know how to repeat the same word. 'When in spring . . . they think they can sing a different song, to come out of themselves, to extend to the whole of nature and to embrace it, they still transmit, in thousands of copies, the same note, the same word, the same leaf. *One cannot escape from the tree by solely arboreal means.*'

(If there is a negative value, or something damned, in Ponge's universe, where it seems as if everything is saved, it is repetition: the sea's waves breaking on the shore all decline the same noun, 'a thousand important lords and ladies all with the same name are thus admitted on the same day to be presented by the prolix and prolific sea.' But multiplicity is also the principle of individualisation, of diversity: a pebble is 'a stone at the stage when for it the age of the person, the individual begins, that is to say the age of the word.')

Language (and work) as the person's secretions is a metaphor which recurs several times in the texts on snails and seashells. But what counts even more (in *Notes for a Seashell*) is his eulogy of the proportion between the shell and its mollusc inhabitant, as opposed to the disproportion of man's monuments and palaces. This is the example the snail sets us by producing its own shell: 'What their work consists of does not involve anything that is extraneous to them, to their necessities or their needs. Nothing that is disproportionate to their physical being. Nothing that is not necessary and essential for them.'

That is why Ponge calls snails saintly. 'But saintly in what? In their precise obedience to their own nature. Know yourself, then, first of all. And accept yourself as you are. Along with your flaws. In proportion with your own measure.'

Last month I ended an article on another – very different – sage's testament (Carlo Levi's) with a quotation: Levi's eulogy of the snail. Here I am now ending this essay with Ponge's eulogy of the snail. Could the snail be the ultimate image of contentment?

[1979]

Jorge Luis Borges

Jorge Luis Borges' critical acclaim in Italy goes back some thirty years now: it began in 1955, the date of the first Italian translation of *Ficciones* (*Fictions*), which appeared under the title of *La biblioteca di Babele* (*The Library of Babel*), published by Einaudi, and culminates today with the publication of the collected works in Mondadori's Meridiani series. If I remember correctly, it was Sergio Solmi who, after reading Borges' stories in French, spoke enthusiastically about them to Elio Vittorini, who immediately suggested doing an Italian edition and found an enthusiastic and congenial translator in Franco Lucentini. Since then Italian publishers have been competing with each other to publish the Argentine writer's works in translations which now Mondadori has gathered together along with several other texts which have never been translated before. This will be the most comprehensive edition of his *Opera omnia* to date: the first volume, edited by Borges' faithful friend Domenico Porzio, is published this very week.

This popularity with publishers has been accompanied by a literary-critical acclaim which is both the cause and the effect of the former. I am thinking of the admiration for Borges expressed by even those Italian writers who are furthest from him in terms of their poetics; of the in-depth analyses that have been carried out in order to reach a critical definition of his world; and also, especially, of the influence he has had on creative literature in Italian, on literary taste and even on the very idea of literature: we can say that many of those who have been writing in the last twenty years, starting with those who belong to my own generation, have been profoundly shaped by him.

How can we explain this close encounter between our culture and an oeuvre which embraces a wide range of literary and philosophical legacies, some familiar to us, others very unfamiliar, and which modulates them into a key which is definitely as remote as could be from our own cultural inheritance? (Remote, at least in those days, from the paths trodden by Italian culture in the 1950s.)

I can only reply by relying on my memory, trying to reconstruct what the Borges experience has meant for me from the beginning down to today. The starting point, indeed the fulcrum, of this experience was a pair of books, *Fictions* and *The Aleph*, in other words that particular genre which is the Borgesian short story, before I moved on to Borges the essayist, who is not easily distinguishable from the narrator, and then Borges the poet, who often contains the nucleus of narrative, or at least a nucleus of thought, a pattern of ideas.

I will start with the major reason for my affinity with him, that is to say my recognising in Borges of an idea of literature as a world constructed and governed by the intellect. This is an idea that goes against the grain of the main run of world literature in this century, which leans instead in the opposite direction, aiming in other words to provide us with the equivalent of the chaotic flow of existence, in language, in the texture of the events narrated, in the exploration of the subconscious. But there is also a tendency in twentieth-century literature, a minority tendency admittedly, which had its greatest supporter in Paul Valéry – and I am thinking in particular of Valéry the prosewriter and thinker – and which champions the victory of mental order over the chaos of the world. I could try to trace the outlines of an Italian vocation in this direction, from the thirteenth century through the Renaissance and seventeenth century down to the twentieth century, in order to explain that the discovery of Borges was for me like seeing a potentiality that had always only been toyed with now being realised: seeing a world being formed in the image and shape of the spaces of the intellect, and inhabited by a constellation of signs that obey a rigorous geometry.

But perhaps to explain the consensus that an author arouses in each of us, we should start, rather than from grand classifications by category, from motives more precisely connected with the art of writing. Amongst these I would put in first place his economy of expression: Borges is a master of concision. He manages to condense into texts which are always just a few pages long an extraordinary richness of ideas and poetic attraction: events which are narrated or hinted at, dizzying glimpses of the infinite, and ideas, ideas, ideas. How this density is conveyed without any sense of congestion, in his limpidly clear, unadorned and open sentences; how this style of brief, tangential narration leads to the precision and concreteness of his language, whose originality is reflected in the variety of rhythm, of syntactic movement, of always unexpected and surprising adjectives; all this is a stylistic miracle, which is without equal in the Spanish language, and for which only Borges knows the secret recipe.

Reading Borges, I have often been tempted to draw up a poetics of concise writing, proclaiming its superiority over prolixity, and contrasting the two mentalities that are reflected in the favouring of one tendency over the other, in terms of temperament, idea of form and tangibility of content. For the moment I will simply say that the true vocation of Italian literature, just like any literature that values the poetic line in which each word is irreplaceable, is more recognisable in brevity than in prolixity.

In order to write briefly, Borges' crucial invention, which was also what allowed him to invent himself as a writer, was something that in retrospect was rather simple. What helped him overcome the block that had prevented him, almost until he was forty, from moving from essays to narrative prose was to pretend that the book he wanted to write had already been written, written by someone else, by an unknown invented author, an author from another language, another culture, and then to describe, summarise or review that hypothetical book. Part of the legend that surrounds Borges is the anecdote that the first, extraordinary, story that he wrote using this formula, 'The Approach to Almotasim', when it first appeared in the journal *Sur*, convinced readers that it was a genuine review of a book by an Indian author. Similarly, all Borges' critics regularly point out that each text of his doubles or multiplies its own space through other books cited from an imaginary or real library, works that are either classical or erudite or simply invented. What I am most interested in stressing here is that with Borges we see the birth of literature raised to the second degree, as it were, and at the same time literature as derived from the square root of itself: a 'potential literature', to borrow a term that would later be fashionable in France, but whose forerunners can all be found in *Fictions* in the ideas and formulae for those works which could have been written by Borges' own hypothetical Herbert Quain.

It has been said many times that for Borges only the written word has a full ontological reality and that the things of this world exist for him only inasmuch as they refer back to things which have been written. What I want to underline here is the circuit of values that characterises this relationship between the world of literature and that of experience. Lived experience is only valued for what it can inspire in literature or for what it in turn repeats from literary archetypes: for instance, there is a reciprocity between a heroic or daring enterprise in an epic poem and a similar deed actually happening in ancient or contemporary history which makes one want to identify or compare episodes and values from the written event with those from the real event. This is the context in which the moral problem resides, which is always present in Borges like a solid nucleus in the fluidity and interchangeability of his metaphysical scenarios. For this sceptic, who seems to sample philosophies and theologies impartially, only for their value in terms of spectacle or aesthetics, the moral problem is constantly restated in exactly the same terms from one universe to the next, in its elementary alternatives of courage or cowardice, violence caused or suffered, and the search for truth. In Borges' perspective, which excludes any psychological depths, the moral problem surfaces reduced almost to the terms of a theorem from geometry, in which individual destinies form an overall pattern which everyone has to recognise first before choosing. Yet it is in the rapid instant of real life, not in the fluctuating time of dreams, nor in the cyclical or eternal time of myths, that one's fate is decided.

At this point we should remember that Borges' epic is made up not only of what he read in the classics, but also of Argentine history, which in some episodes overlaps with his family history, with the daring deeds of military ancestors in the wars of the emerging nation. In 'Poema conjectural' ('Conjectural Poem'), Borges imagines in Dantesque style the thoughts of one of his ancestors on his mother's side, Francisco Laprida, as he lies in a marsh, wounded after a battle, hunted down by the tyrant Rosas' gauchos: Laprida recognises his own fate in that of Buonconte da Montefeltro, as Dante portrays him in *Purgatorio* canto 5. Roberto Paoli has pointed out, in a detailed analysis of this poem, that more than Buonconte's death, which is explicitly cited, it is the preceding episode in the same canto that Borges draws on, the demise of Jacopo del Cassero. There could be no better exemplification than this, of the osmosis between what happens in literature and what happens in real life: the ideal source is not some mythical event that took place before the verbal expression, but a text which is a tissue of words and images and meanings, a harmonisation of motifs which find echoes in each other, a musical space in which a theme develops its own variations.

There is another poem which is even more significant for defining this Borgesian continuity between historical events, literary epics, poetic transformation of events, the power of literary motifs, and their influence on the collective imagination. And this too is a poem which concerns us closely, because it mentions the other Italian epic which Borges knows in detail, Ariosto's *Orlando Furioso*. The poem is entitled 'Ariosto and the Arabs'. In it Borges runs through the Carolingian and Arthurian epics which merge in Ariosto's poem, which skims over these elements of the tradition as though on the hippogriff. In other words it transforms them into a fantasy which is both ironic and yet full of pathos. The popularity of the *Orlando Furioso* ensured that the dreams of medieval heroic legends were transmitted to European culture (Borges cites Milton as a reader of Ariosto), right down to the moment when what had been the dreams of Charlemagne's enemies, that is to say the dreams of the Arab world, supersede them. *The Arabian Nights* conquer the imagination of European readers, taking the place that had once been held by the *Orlando Furioso* in the collective imagination. There is thus a war between the fantasy worlds of the West and the East which prolongs the historic war between Charlemagne and the Saracens, and it is in this later war that the Orient gains its revenge.

The power of the written word is, then, linked to lived experience both as the source and the end of that experience. As a source, because it becomes the equivalent of an event which otherwise would not have taken place, as it were; as an end, because for Borges the written word that counts is the one that makes a strong impact on the collective imagination, as an emblematic or conceptual figure, made to be remembered and recognised whenever it appears, whether in the past or in the future.

These mythical or archetypal motifs, which are probably finite in number, stand out against the infinite backdrop of metaphysical themes of which Borges is so fond. In every text he writes, in any way he can, Borges manages to talk about the infinite, the uncountable, time, eternity or rather the eternal presence or cyclical nature of time. And here I go back to what was said previously about his maximum concentration of meanings in the brevity of his texts. Take a classic example of Borges' art: his most famous story, 'The Garden of Forking Paths'. The surface plot is a conventional spy thriller, a tale of intrigue condensed into a dozen pages, which is then manipulated somewhat in order to reach the surprise conclusion. (The epics exploited by Borges can also take the form of popular fiction.) This spy-story also includes another tale, whose suspense is more to do with logic and metaphysics, and which has a Chinese setting: it is the quest for a labyrinth. Inside this second story in turn there is the description of an endless Chinese novel. But what counts most in this complex narrative tangle is the philosophical reflection on time it contains, or rather the definitions of the conceptions of time which are articulated one after another. At the end we realise that, underneath the appearance of a thriller, what we have read is a philosophical tale, or rather an essay on the idea of time.

The hypotheses about time which are put forward in 'The Garden of Forking Paths' are each contained (and almost hidden) in just a few lines. First there is an idea of constant time, a kind of subjective, absolute present ('I reflected that everything happens to a man in this very moment of now. Centuries and centuries, but events happen only in the present; countless men in the air, on land and sea, and everything that really happens, happens to me . . .'). Then an idea of time determined by will, the time of an action decided on once and for all, in which the future would present itself as irrevocable as the past. Lastly the story's central idea: a multiple, ramified time in which every present instant splits into two futures, so as to form 'an expanding, dizzying web of divergent, convergent and parallel times'. This idea of an infinity of contemporary universes, in which all possibilities are realised in all possible combinations, is not a digression from the story, but the very condition which is required so that the protagonist can feel authorised to commit the absurd and abominable crime which his spying mission imposes on him, certain that this will happen only in one of the universes but not in the others, or rather by committing the crime here and now, he and his victim can recognise each other as friends and brothers in other universes.

Such a conception of ramified time is dear to Borges because it is the one which dominates in literature: in fact, it is the condition which makes literature possible. The example I am about to quote takes us back again to Dante, and it is an essay by Borges on Ugolino della Gherardesca, to be precise on the line 'Poscia, piú che il dolor poté il digiuno' (Then what grief could not manage hunger did), and on what was described as a 'pointless controversy' on the possibility that Conte Ugolino committed cannibalism. Having examined the views of many critics, Borges agrees with the majority of them, who say the line must mean that Ugolino died through starvation. However, he adds that Dante without wanting us to believe it was true, certainly wanted us to suspect 'albeit with uncertainty and hesitation' that Ugolino could have eaten his own children. And Borges then lists all the hints of cannibalism in *Inferno* canto 33, starting with the opening image of Ugolino gnawing the skull of Archbishop Ruggieri.

This essay is significant for the general considerations on which it closes. In particular the idea (which is one of Borges' statements that comes closest to coinciding with structuralist methods) that a literary text consists solely of the succession of words of which it is composed, so 'on Ugolino we have to say that he is a textual construct, comprising about thirty *terzine*'. Then there is the idea that links with the notions maintained by Borges on many occasions, about the impersonality of literature, concluding that 'Dante did not know much more about Ugolino than what his *terzine* tell us'. And lastly the idea I really wanted to stress, the idea of ramified time: 'In real time, in history, whenever a man finds himself facing different alternatives, he opts for one, eliminating the others for ever; not so in the ambiguous time of art, which resembles that of hope and oblivion. Hamlet, in this literary time, is both sane and mad. In the darkness of the Tower of Hunger Ugolino devours and does not devour the bodies of his beloved children, and this wavering imprecision, this uncertainty is the strange matter of which he is made up. This was how Dante imagined him, in two possible death scenes, and how future generations imagine him.'

This essay is contained in a volume published in Madrid two years ago, and not yet translated into Italian, which collects Borges' essays and lectures on Dante: *Nueve ensayos dantescos* (*Further Essays on Dante*). His constant and passionate study of the founding text of Italian literature, his congenial appreciation of the poem, which has allowed him to make what he has inherited from Dante bear fruit both in his critical reflections and in his creative works, is one of the reasons, certainly not the least, why we celebrate Borges here and express once more with emotion and affection our gratitude for the intellectual nourishment he continues to give us.

[1984]

The Philosophy of Raymond Queneau

Who is Raymond Queneau? At first glance this might seem a strange question, since the image of this writer is well known to anyone with any knowledge of twentieth-century literature, and of French literature in particular. But if each one of us tries to put together the things we know about Queneau, this image immediately takes on intricate and complex outlines, embraces elements which are difficult to hold together; and the more defining traits we manage to highlight, the more we feel that we are missing others which are necessary to round out into a unitary figure the various planes of this multi-faceted polyhedron. This writer who seems always to welcome us with an invitation to put ourselves at our ease, to find the most comfortable and relaxed position, to feel on the same level as he is, as though we were about to play a round of cards with friends, is in reality someone with a cultural background that can never be fully explored, a background whose implications and presuppositions, explicit or implicit, one can never exhaust.

Of course Queneau's fame is based primarily on his novels about the rather uncouth and shady world of the Parisian *banlieue* or of provincial French towns, on his word-games involving the spelling of everyday, spoken, French. His is a narrative oeuvre which is extremely consistent and compact, reaching its apogee of comic elegance in *Zazie dans le métro* (*Zazie in the Metro*). Whoever remembers Saint-Germain-des-Prés in the early postwar period will include in this more popular image some of the songs sung by Juliette Gréco like 'Fillette, fillette' . . .

Other layers are added to this picture by those who have read his most 'youthful' and autobiographical novel, *Odile*: there we find his past links with the group of Surrealists surrounding André Breton in the 1920s (this account tells of his first, tentative approach towards them, his rather rapid distancing from them, their basic incompatibility, all in a series of merciless caricatures) against the backdrop of a rather unusual intellectual passion in a writer and poet: mathematics.

But someone might object that, leaving aside the novels and the collections of poetry, Queneau's most typical books are works which are unique in their own genre, such as *Exercices de style* (*Exercises in Style*), or *Petite Cosmogonie portative* (*The Portable Small Cosmogony*) or *Cent mille milliards de poèmes* (*One Hundred Million Million Poems*). In the first, an episode narrated in a few sentences is repeated 99 times in 99 different styles; the second is a poem in Alexandrines on the origin of the earth, chemistry, the origin of life, animal evolution and the development of technology; the third is a machine for composing sonnets, consisting of ten sonnets using the same rhymes printed on pages cut into horizontal strips, one line on each strip, so that every first line can be followed by a choice of ten second lines, and so on until the total of 10^{14} combinations is reached.

There is another fact which should not be overlooked, namely that Queneau's official profession for the last twenty-five years of his life was that of encyclopedia consultant (he was the editor of Gallimard's *Encyclopédie de la Pléiade*). The map we have been outlining is now quite jagged, and every piece of bio-bibliographical information which can be added to it only makes it even more complicated.

Queneau published three volumes of essays and occasional writings in his lifetime: *Bâtons, chiffres et lettres* (*Signs, Figures and Letters*) (1950 and 1965), *Bords* (*Borders*) (1963), and *Le Voyage en Grèce* (*The Journey to Greece*) (1973). These works, along with a certain number of uncollected pieces, can give us an intellectual outline of Queneau, which is the starting-point for his creative work. From the range of his interests and choices, all of them very precise and only at first sight rather divergent, emerges the framework of an implicit philosophy, or let us say a mental attitude and organisation which never settles for the easy route.

In our century Queneau is a unique example of a wise and intelligent writer, who always goes against the grain of the dominant tendencies of his age and of French culture in particular. (But he never – and he is a rare, or rather, unique example of this – allows himself through intellectual self-indulgence to be dragged into saying things which are later shown to be disastrous or stupid mistakes.) He combines this with an endless need to invent and to test possibilities (both in the practice of literary creation and in theoretical speculation) only in areas where the fun of the game – that distinctive hallmark of the human – guarantees that he will not go far wrong.

These are all qualities which make him still, both in France and in the world at large, an eccentric figure, but which perhaps in the not too distant future may reveal him to be a master, one of the few who will stay the course in a century in which there have been so many flawed maestros, or ones that have been only partially successful or inadequate or too well-intentioned. As far as I am concerned, without going farther afield, Queneau has assumed this magisterial role for some time now, even though – perhaps because of my excessive adherence to his ideas – I have always found it difficult to explain fully why. I am afraid that I will not succeed in explaining it in this essay either. Instead I would like him to explain it, in his own words.

The first literary battles in which we find Queneau's name embroiled were those which he fought in order to establish 'le néo-français', in other words to bridge the gap between written French (with its rigid rules of spelling and syntax, its monumental immobility, its lack of flexibility and agility) and the spoken language (with its inventiveness, mobility and economy of expression). On a journey to Greece in 1932, Queneau had convinced himself that that country's linguistic situation, characterised even in its written form by the split between the classicising (*kathareuousa*) and the spoken (*demotikê*) language, was no different from the French situation. Starting from this conviction (and from his studies of the peculiar syntax of American Indian languages such as Chinook), Queneau speculated on the advent of a demotic written French which would be initiated by himself and Céline.

Queneau did not opt for this choice for reasons of populist realism or vitality ('In any case I have no respect nor consideration for what is popular, the future, "life" etc.', he wrote in 1937). What inspired him was an iconoclastic approach to literary French (which, however, he did not want to abolish, but rather to conserve as a language in its own right, in all its purity, like Latin), and the conviction that all the great inventions in the field of language and literature emerged through transitions from the spoken to the written language. But there was more to it than this: the stylistic revolution he promoted derived from a context which was philosophical right from the start.

His first novel, *Le Chiendent* (*The Bark-Tree*) (translated into Italian as *Il pantano*, 1947, though the title literally means 'couch-grass', and figuratively 'spot of bother'), written in 1933 after the formative experience of Joyce's *Ulysses*, was intended to be not only a linguistic and structural tour-de-force (based on a structure that was numerological and symmetrical, as well as on a catalogue of narrative genres), but also a definition of existence and thought, nothing less than a novelised commentary on Descartes' *Discourse on Method*. The novel's action spotlights those things which are thought but not real, but which have influenced the reality of the world: a world which in itself is totally devoid of meaning.

It is in fact to challenge the endless chaos of the meaningless world that Queneau establishes the need for order in his poetics and for a truth within language. As the English critic Martin Esslin says, in an essay on Queneau:

> *It is in poetry that we can give meaning and measured order to the formless universe – and poetry depends on language, whose true music can only come from a return to its true rhythms in the living vernacular.*
>
> *Queneau's rich and varied oeuvre as poet and novelist is devoted to the destruction of ossified forms and the dazzling of the eye by phonetic spelling and authentic Chinook-type syntax. Even a casual glance at his books will show numerous examples of this kind: 'spa' for 'n'est-ce pas', 'Polocilacru' for 'Paul aussi l'a cru', 'Doukipudonktan' for 'D'où qu'il pue donc tant' . . .*[1]

'Le néo-français', inasmuch as it is an invention of a new correlation between the written and spoken word, is only one particular case of Queneau's general need to insert into the universe 'small areas of symmetry', as Martin Esslin says, a sense of order which only (literary and mathematical) invention can create, given that all of reality is chaos.

This aim will remain central in Queneau's oeuvre even when the battle for 'le néo-français' fades from his centre of interest. In the linguistic revolution he had found himself fighting on his own (the demons which inspired Céline turned out to be completely different) waiting for facts to prove him right. But it was the opposite that was happening: French was not evolving at all as he thought it would; even the spoken language was tending to ossify and the advent of television would determine the triumph of the learned norm over popular inventiveness. (Similarly in Italy, television has exercised a powerful unifying influence on the language, even though Italian was characterised much more strongly than in France by the multiplicity of local dialects.) Queneau realised this and in a statement in 1970 (in *Errata corrige*) he had no hesitation in admitting the inaccuracy of theories which in any case he had for some time now ceased to promote.

Of course it must be said that Queneau's intellectual role had never been limited to that one linguistic battle: right from the outset the front on which he campaigned was vast and complex. After he distanced himself from Breton, the members of the Surrealist diaspora to which he remained closest were Georges Bataille and Michel Leiris, even though his involvement in their journals and initiatives was always rather marginal.

The first journal on which Queneau collaborated with any continuity was *La Critique sociale*, in 1930–34, again with Bataille and Leiris: this was the journal of Boris Souvarine's Cercle Communiste Démocratique (Souvarine was a 'dissident' *avant-la-lettre*, who was the first in the West to explain what Stalinism would be). 'One has to recall here,' wrote Queneau some thirty years later, 'that *La Critique sociale*, founded by Boris Souvarine, was centred round the Cercle Communiste Démocratique, which was made up of former Communist militants who either had been expelled from or were in dispute with the party; this group had been joined by another small band of former Surrealists such as Bataille, Michel Leiris, Jacques Baron and myself, who all came from a very different background.'

Queneau's collaboration on *La Critique sociale* consisted in brief reviews, rarely to do with literature (though amongst these was one in which he invited readers to discover Raymond Roussel: 'his imagination combines the passion of the mathematician with the rationality of a poet'). But more often they were scientific reviews (on Pavlov, and the scientist Vernadsky who would later suggest to him a circular theory of sciences; or his review – included in this Italian translation of *Bâtons, chiffres et lettres* (*Signs, Figures and Letters*) (Turin: Einaudi, 1981) – of the book by an artillery officer on the history of equestrian caparisons, a work greeted by Queneau as revolutionary in its historical methodology). But he also appeared in it as co-author, with Bataille, of an article 'published', as he will clarify later, 'with our signatures in issue number 5 (March 1932) with the title "La critique des fondements de la dialectique hégélienne (A Critique of the Foundations of Hegelian Dialectic)". Georges Bataille really wrote the whole article: I only dealt with the passage on Engels and mathematical dialectic.'

This work on the application of dialectic to exact sciences in Engels (which Queneau later included in the 'Mathematics' section of his collected essays and which appears under this heading in the Italian translation) gives only a partial account of Queneau's quite considerable period spent studying Hegel. But this period of study can be more accurately reconstructed from something he wrote in his last years (and from which the two preceding quotations came), published in the journal *Critique*, in the issue dedicated to Georges Bataille. Here he recalls his late friend's article, 'Premières confrontations avec Hegel' (*Critique*, 195–196 (August –September 1966)), in which we see not only Bataille but also, and perhaps even more intensely, Queneau dealing with Hegel, a philosopher who is as alien as can be from the traditions of French thought. If Bataille read Hegel essentially to reassure himself that he was not at all Hegelian, for Queneau it was a more positive journey, in that it involved his discovery of André Kojève, and his adoption to a certain extent of Kojève's brand of Hegelianism.

I will come back to this point later on, but for the moment suffice it to say that from 1934 to 1939 Queneau was at the École des Hautes Études attending Kojève's lectures on *The Phenomenology of the Spirit*, which he would later edit and publish.[2] Bataille recalls: 'how many times did Queneau and I emerge drained from the tiny lecture hall: drained and exhausted . . . Kojève's lectures destroyed me, ground me down, killed me ten times over.'[3] (Queneau actually, with a hint of malice, remembers his fellow student as not very assiduous and sometimes rather sleepy.)

Editing Kojève's lectures certainly remains Queneau's most substantial academic and editorial undertaking, though the volume does not contain any original contribution by Queneau himself. However, on this Hegelian experience we have the precious evidence of his memoir on Bataille which is also indirectly autobiographical, where we see him participating in the most sophisticated polemics of French philosophical culture in those years. Traces of these arguments can be found throughout his fiction, which often seems to demand a reading which is sensitive to the erudite researches and theories which then preoccupied Parisian academic journals and institutions, though they are all transformed into a pyrotechnic display full of clowning grimaces and somersaults. The three works, *Gueule de Pierre*, *Les Temps mêlées* and *Saint Glinglin* (subsequently rewritten and collected as a trilogy under this last title) would repay a close analysis from this perspective.

We could say that if in the 1930s Queneau took an active part in the discussions both of the literary avant-garde and of academic specialists, while maintaining that restraint and discretion which will remain his stable character traits, to find the first articulation of his own ideas we have to wait for the years immediately preceding the Second World War, when his polemical presence finds expression in *Volontés*, a journal on which he collaborates from its first issue (December 1937) to its last (whose publication was prevented by the German invasion of May 1940).

This journal, edited by Georges Pelorson (and which also had Henry Miller on its editorial board) ran for the same length of time as the Collège de Sociologie run by Georges Bataille, Michel Leiris, Roger Callois (and also enjoyed the participation of Kojève, Klossowski, Walter Benjamin and Hans Mayer). The debates of this group are the background to the articles in the journal, especially those by Queneau.[4]

But Queneau's discourse follows a line that is very much his own and which can be summed up in this quotation from an article written in 1938: 'Another highly fallacious idea which nevertheless is very popular nowadays is the equivalence that has been established between inspiration, exploration of the subconscious and liberation; between chance, automatic reaction and freedom. Now *this* inspiration which consists in blindly obeying every single impulse is in reality a form of slavery. The classical writer composing a tragedy by observing a certain number of rules with which he is familiar is freer than the poet who writes down whatever flits through his head and is enslaved to other rules which he is not aware of.'

Leaving aside the contemporary polemic against Surrealism, here Queneau articulates a number of constants in his aesthetics and ethics: the rejection of 'inspiration', or romantic lyricism, of the cult of chance and automatic suggestion (Surrealism's idols), and instead the appreciation of a work that has been constructed, finished, completed (previously he had campaigned against the poetics of the incomplete, the fragment, the sketch). Not only this: the artist must be fully aware of the aesthetic rules which his work obeys, as well as of its particular and universal meaning, its function and influence. If one thinks of Queneau's method of writing, which appears only to follow the whims of improvisation and clowning, his theoretical 'classicism' might seem astonishing; and yet the text we are discussing ('What is Art?', along with its complementary piece, 'More and

Less', both written in 1938) has the status of a profession of faith which he never renounced (though the still rather youthful tone of aggression and exhortation would disappear in the later Queneau).

All the more reason, then, why we should be amazed that this anti-Surrealist polemic should lead Queneau (of all people!) to attack humour. One of his first pieces in *Volontés* is an invective against humour, which of course was linked to issues of the moment, even to contemporary mores (it is against the reductive and defensive premises of humour that he takes issue), but what counts here too is the *pars construens*: his praise for total comedy, the line that extends from Rabelais to Jarry. (Queneau would return to the topic of Breton's *humour noir* immediately after the Second World War, to see how well it had stood up in the experience of that horror; and again in a later note, he would take account of Breton's clarification of the moral implications of the question.)

Another recurrent target in his *Volontés* articles (and here what we need to try and square these with is his future role as encyclopedia director) was the endless mass of information which lands on top of contemporary man without forming an integral part of his existence, or being an essential necessity. ('The identity between what one is and what one really and truly knows . . . the difference between what one is and what one thinks one knows but does not really know.')

We can say, then, that Queneau's polemics in the 1930s go in two main directions: against poetry as inspiration and against 'false knowledge'.

Queneau's figure as 'encyclopedist', 'mathematician' and 'cosmologer' has therefore to be carefully defined. His 'wisdom' is characterised by a need for global knowledge and at the same time by a sense of limits, and a diffidence towards any type of absolute philosophy. In his outline for the circularity of sciences which he drafts in a work written between 1943 and 1948 (from natural sciences to chemistry and physics, and from these to mathematics and logic), the general tendency of sciences towards mathematisation is reversed and mathematics is transformed when it comes into contact with the problems posed by the natural sciences. This is consequently a line that can go in either direction and therefore can turn itself into a circle, at the point where logic is proposed as a model for the functioning of human intelligence, if what Piaget says is true: namely that 'logic is the axiomatisation of thought itself'. At this point Queneau adds: 'But logic is also an art, and turning things into rules is a game. The ideal constructed by scientists throughout the whole of this first half of the century is a presentation of science not as knowledge but as rules and method. They offer (indefinable) notions, axioms and instructions for use, in short a system of conventions. But is this not perhaps a game just as much as chess or bridge? Before proceeding to an examination of this aspect of science, we must dwell on this point: is science knowledge, does it help us to know anything? And given that (in this article) we are dealing with mathematics, what does one know in mathematics? Precisely nothing. And there is nothing to know. We do not know the point, the number, the group, the set, the function any more than we "know" the electron, life, human behaviour. We do not know the world of functions and differential equations any more than we "know" Daily, Concrete Life on Earth. Everything we know is a method accepted (agreed) as true by the scientific community, a method which has *also* the advantage of being linked to manufacturing techniques. But this method is also a game, or more precisely what is called a *jeu d'esprit*. Hence the whole of science, in its most complete form, presents itself to us both as technique and as a game. That is to say no more and no less than the way the *other* human activity presents itself: Art.'

This passage contains all of Queneau: his practice is to place himself constantly on the two contemporary dimensions of art (as technique) and play, against the backdrop of his radical epistemological pessimism. This is a paradigm which as far as he is concerned is equally suited to science and literature: hence the ease he displays in moving from one field to the other, and in containing them both in a single discourse.

We must not forget, however, that the 1938 article, cited above, 'What is Art?' opened with a denunciation of the bad influence on literature of any 'scientific' pretension; nor that Queneau had a place of honour ('Transcendent Satrap') in the 'Collège de Pataphysique', the group formed by Alfred Jarry's disciples, which in the spirit of that master, makes fun of scientific language turning it into caricature. ('Pataphysics' is defined as the 'science of imaginary solutions'.) In short we could say of Queneau what he himself said of Flaubert, talking of *Bouvard et Pécuchet*: 'Flaubert is *for* science only insofar as it is sceptical, restrained, methodical, prudent, human. He hates the dogmatists, the metaphysicists, the philosophers.'

In his prefatory essay to *Bouvard et Pécuchet* (1947), the result of years of study of this encyclopedic novel, Queneau expresses his sympathy for the two pathetic autodidacts, those researchers of the absolute in knowledge, and highlights Flaubert's shifts in attitude towards his book and its heroes. Without the peremptoriness of his youthful outbursts, but with that tone of discretion and pragmatism which would be characteristic of his maturity, Queneau identifies with the later Flaubert and seems to recognise in this book his own odyssey across 'false knowledge' and 'not concluding', in his search for the circularity of wisdom, guided by the methodological compass of his scepticism. (It is here that Queneau enunciates his idea of *The Odyssey* and *The Iliad* as the two alternatives in literature: 'every great work of literature is either an *Iliad* or an *Odyssey*.')

Between Homer, 'the father of all literature and all scepticism', and Flaubert who understood that scepticism and science are identical, Queneau accords positions of honour, first of all to Petronius, whom he considers as a contemporary and brother, then to Rabelais, 'who in spite of the chaotic appearance of his work, knows where he is going and directs his giants towards their final *Trinc* without being crushed by it', and finally to Boileau. That the father of French classicism should figure in this list, that his *Art poétique* should be considered by Queneau 'one of the greatest masterpieces in French literature', should not surprise us, if we think on the one hand of classical literature's ideal as awareness of the rules to follow, and on the other of his thematic and linguistic modernity. Boileau's *Le Lutrin* 'brings the epic to an end, completes *Don Quixote*, ushers in the novel in French and is a forerunner both of *Candide* and *Bouvard et Pécuchet*'.[5]

Amongst the moderns, in Queneau's Parnassus, we find Proust and Joyce. In the former it is the 'architecture' of *La Recherche* which interests him most of all, from the time when he was campaigning for the 'well constructed work' (see *Volontés*, 12 (1938)). The latter is seen as a 'classical author' in whom 'everything is determined, both the overall structure and the episodes, though nothing shows any sign of constraint'.

Although always ready to recognise his debt towards the classics, Queneau certainly did not stint in his interest in obscure and neglected authors. The very first academic work which he embarked on in his youth had been a piece of research on 'fous littéraires' (literary madmen), 'heterodox' authors, those considered mad by official culture: inventors of philosophical systems belonging to no school at all, of models of the universe devoid of any logic and of poetic universes lying outside any stylistic classification. Through a selection of such texts Queneau wanted to put together an

Encyclopedia of Inexact Sciences; but no publisher would consider the project and the author ended up using the material in his novel *Les Enfants du limon* (*The Children of Clay*).

On the aims (and disappointments) of this research, one should look at what Queneau wrote when introducing his only 'discovery' in this field, a discovery upheld by him subsequently as well: the precursor of science-fiction, De Fontenai. But his enthusiasm for the 'heterodox' has always stayed with him, whether it is the sixth-century grammarian Virgil of Toulouse, the eighteenth-century author of futuristic epics J.-B. Grainville, or Edouard Chanal, an unwitting French precursor of Lewis Carroll.

From the same family, certainly, is the utopian writer Charles Fourier, in whom Queneau took an interest on several occasions. One of these essays analyses the bizarre calculations of his 'series' which are the basis of the social projects in Fourier's Harmony. Queneau's intention here was to prove that Engels, when he put Fourier's 'mathematical epic' on the same level as Hegel's 'dialectical epic', was thinking of the utopian Charles not of his contemporary Joseph Fourier, the famous mathematician. After piling up proof after proof in support of his thesis, he concludes that perhaps his thesis does not stand up after all and that Engels really was talking about Joseph. This is a typical Queneau gesture: he is not so much interested in the triumph of his thesis, as in recognising a logic and consistency even in the most paradoxical argument. And we then find ourselves naturally thinking that Engels (on whom he wrote another essay) was also seen by Queneau as a genius of the same type as Fourier: an encyclopedic *bricoleur* or doodler, a foolhardy inventor of universal systems which he constructs with all the cultural materials he has at his disposal. And what about Hegel then? What attracts Queneau to Hegel to the point where he is prepared to spend years attending and then editing Kojève's lectures? What is significant is that in the same years Queneau also followed H. C. Puech's courses on Gnosticism and Manicheism at the École des Hautes Études. (And did Bataille, anyway, during the period of his friendship with Queneau, not perhaps see Hegelianism as a new version of the dualistic cosmogonies of the Gnostics?)

In all these experiences Queneau's attitude is that of the explorer of imaginary universes, carefully picking up their most paradoxical details with the amused eye of the Pataphysicist, but without cutting himself off from the possibility of noticing amongst all this a glimmer of genuine poetry or genuine knowledge. It is with this same spirit, then, that he set out to discover 'literary madmen' and to immerse himself in Gnosticism and Hegelian philosophy acting as both friend and disciple of two illustrious masters of Parisian academic culture.

It is no accident that the starting point for Queneau's (as well as Bataille's) interest in Hegel was his *Philosophy of Nature* (Queneau showing a particular interest in possible mathematical formulations of it); in short, in what comes *before* history. And if what Bataille was interested in was always the irrepressible role of the negative, Queneau would aim decisively at an openly declared point of arrival: the overcoming of history, what happens *after* history. This is already enough to remind us how far removed the image of Hegel is according to his French commentators, and Kojève in particular, from the image of Hegel that has circulated in Italy for over a century now, whether in its idealist or Marxist incarnations, and also from the image endorsed by that side of German culture which has spread and continues to circulate most widely in Italy. If for Italians Hegel will always remain the philosopher of the spirit of history, what Queneau the pupil of Kojève seeks in him is the road that leads to the end of history, and to the arrival at wisdom. This is the motif that André Kojève himself will underline in Queneau's fiction, suggesting a philosophical reading of three of his novels: *Pierrot mon ami* (*Pierrot*), *Loin de Rueil* (*The Skin of Dreams*), and *Le Dimanche de la vie* (*The Sunday of Life*) (in *Critique*, 60 (May 1952)).

The three 'wisdom novels' were written during the Second World War, in the grim years of the German Occupation of France. (The fact that those years, which were lived through as though they were a parenthesis, were also years of extraordinary creative activity for French culture, is a phenomenon which does not seem to have received the attention it deserves.) In a period like that the emergence from history appears to be the only point of arrival one can have, since 'history is the science of man's unhappiness'. This is the definition given by Queneau at the start of a curious little treatise also written at that time (but only published in 1966): *Une Histoire modèle* (*A Model History*). This was a proposal to make history 'scientific', by applying to it an elementary mechanism of causes and effects. As long as we are dealing with 'mathematical models of simple worlds' the attempt can be said to be successful; but 'it is difficult to make historical phenomena referring to more complex societies fit into that grid', as Ruggiero Romano points out in his introduction to the Italian edition.[6]

Let us go back to Queneau's principal objective, that of introducing a bit of order and logic into a universe which is totally devoid of those qualities. How can one succeed in doing this except by 'emerging from history'? This would be the theme of the second last novel published by Queneau: *Les Fleurs bleues* (*The Blue Flowers*). It opens with the heartfelt exclamation uttered by a character who is a prisoner of history: ' "All this fusstory," said the Duke of Auge, "all this fusstory for a few puns and anachronisms: hardly worth it at all. Can we never find a way out?" '

The two ways of looking at history's pattern, from the perspective of the future or the past, meet and overlay each other in *The Blue Flowers*: is history that which has as its point of arrival Cidrolin, an ex-convict who lazes about on a barge moored on the Seine? or is it one of Cidrolin's dreams, a projection of his unconscious in order to fill a past which has been suppressed from his memory?

In *The Blue Flowers* Queneau makes fun of history, denying its progress and reducing it to the substance of daily existence; in *A Model History* he had tried to turn it into algebra, to make it submit to a system of axioms, to remove it from empirical reality. We could say that these are two processes which are antithetical but which are perfectly complementary, though of a different mathematical sign, and as such represent the two poles between which Queneau's researches move.

On closer examination, the operations which Queneau carries out on history correspond exactly to those he effects on language: in his battle for 'le néo-français' he debunks the literary language's claims to immutability in order to bring it closer to the truth of the spoken language; in his (itinerant but always faithful) love affair with mathematics he repeatedly tends to experiment with arithmetical and algebraic approaches to language and literary creativity. 'To deal with language as though it were reducible to mathematical formulae' was how another mathematical poet, Jacques Roubaud,[7] defined the principal preoccupation of the man who proposed an analysis of language through algebraic matrices,[8] who studied the mathematical structure of the sestina in Arnaut Daniel and its possible developments,[9] and who promoted the activities of the 'Oulipo'. In fact it was in this spirit that he became co-founder in 1960 of the Ouvroir de Littérature Potentielle (abbreviation: 'Oulipo'), along with the man who would be his closest friend in his final years, the mathematician and chess expert François Le Lionnais, a delightful personality, a wise eccentric of endless inventions which were always half-way between rationality and paradox, between experiment and play.

Similarly with Queneau's inventions it has always been difficult to draw the line between serious experiment and play. We can make out the two poles I mentioned earlier: on the one hand the fun of giving an unusual linguistic treatment to a given theme, on the other the fun of a rigorous formalisation applied to poetic invention. (Both trends are a nod in the direction of Mallarmé that is typical of Queneau and which stands out from all the tributes paid to that master in the course of the century, because it preserves his basically ironic essence.)

In that first trend we find: a versified autobiography (*Chêne et chien*), in which it is above all the metrical virtuosity that provides the most exhilarating effects; *Petite Cosmogonie portative*, whose declared aim is to put the most rebarbative scientific neologisms into the idiom of poetic verse; and of course the work which is probably his masterpiece, precisely because of the total simplicity of its programme, *Exercices de style*, where a totally banal anecdote reported in different styles produces highly diverse literary texts. Instances of the other trend are: his love for metrical forms as generators of poetic content, his ambition to be the inventor of a new poetic structure (like the one put forward in his final book of verse, *Morale élémentaire*, 1975), as well as, of course, the infernal machine of the *Cent mille milliards de poèmes* (1961). In either trend, in short, the objective is the multiplication or ramification or proliferation of possible works starting out from an abstract formulation.

Jacques Roubaud writes: 'For Queneau the producer of mathematical ideas, his favourite field is that of combinatory systems: combinatory systems come from a very ancient tradition, almost as ancient as Western mathematics. The analysis of *Cent mille milliards de poèmes* from this perspective will allow us to place this book in the context of the shift from pure mathematics to mathematics as literature. Let us remind ourselves of its principle: he writes ten sonnets, each with the same rhymes. The grammatical structure of each is such that, without forcing it, each line in each "base" sonnet is exchangeable with every other line in the same position in each sonnet. There will thus be, for each line of any new sonnet, ten possible independent choices. Since there are fourteen lines in a sonnet, there will be virtually 10^{14} sonnets, in other words one hundred million million poems.

'. . . Let us try, by analogy, to do something similar with one single

Baudelaire sonnet: for instance by replacing one line with another (either from the same sonnet or a different one), respecting what the sonnet "does" (its structure). We will come up against difficulties primarily of a syntactic nature, against which Queneau had immuned himself in advance (and it is for that reason that his structure is "free"). *But*, and this is what the *Cent mille milliards* teach us, *against* the constraints of semantic probability, the sonnet structure creates, virtually, from one sonnet all sonnets that are possible through substitutions which respect the structure.'

Structure is freedom, it produces the text and at the same time the possibility of all virtual texts that can replace it. This is the novelty that resides in the idea of 'potential' multiplicity, implicit in his promotion of a literature that develops from the constraints which literature itself selects and imposes on itself. It has to be said that in the 'Oulipo' method it is the quality of these rules, their ingenuity and elegance that counts in the first place; if the results, the works obtained in this way, are immediately of equal quality, ingenuity and elegance, so much the better, but whatever the outcome, the resultant work is only one example of the potential which can be achieved only by going through the narrow gateway of these rules. This automatic mechanism through which the text is generated from the rules of the game, is the opposite of the surrealist automatic mechanism which appeals to chance or the unconscious, in other words entrusts the text to influences over which there is no control, and which we can only passively obey. Every example of a text constructed according to precise rules opens up the 'potential' multiplicity of all the texts which can be virtually written according to these rules, and of all the virtual readings possible of such texts.

As Queneau had already declared in one of his first formulations of his poetics: 'There are forms of the novel which impose on its subject matter all the virtues of Number,' by developing 'a structure which transmits to such works the last glimmers of universal light or the last echoes of the Harmony of the World.'

'Last glimmers', notice: the Harmony of the World appears in Queneau's oeuvre from a remote distance, in the same way as it can be glimpsed by the drinkers who stare at their glass of pernod with their elbows on the zinc counter. The 'virtues of Number' seem to impose their own brightness on them especially when they manage to appear transparently through the dense corporality of living people, with their unpredictable moods, with the phenomena emitted by their twisted mouths, with their zigzag logic, in that tragic meeting of the individual's dimensions with those of the universe, which can only be expressed through giggles or sneers or jeers or bursts of convulsive laughter, and at best through full-throated hilarity, people dying with laughter, laughter on a Homeric scale . . .

[1981]

Notes

1. In John Cruikshank (ed.), *The Novelist as Philosopher: Studies in French Fiction 1935–60* (London: Oxford University Press, 1962), pp. 79–101.
2. A. Kojève, *Introduction à la lecture de Hegel*, Leçons sur la phénoménologie de l'esprit professées de 1933 à l'École des Hautes Études, réunies et publiées par R. Queneau (Paris: Gallimard, 1947).
3. 'Sur Nietzsche', in G. Bataille, *Oeuvres complètes* (Paris: Gallimard), VI, 416.
4. On this subject see D. Hollier, *Le Collège de sociologie (1937–1939)* (Paris: Gallimard, 1979).
5. *Les Écrivains célèbres*, vol. II. Before editing Gallimard's *Encyclopédie de la Pléiade*, Queneau edited for the publisher Mazenod the three large folio volumes of *Les Écrivains célèbres*, as well as compiling an 'Essai de répertoire historique des écrivains célèbres', published as an appendix. The chapters on each author were entrusted to experts or to famous writers. It is significant which authors Queneau himself chose to write on: Petronius, Boileau, Gertrude Stein. He also wrote the introduction to the final section: 'Twentieth-century masters', where he discusses Henry James, Gide, Proust, Joyce, Kafka, Gertrude Stein. Queneau never included his entries in this work in his collected essays; I have inserted in this Italian translation the pieces on Petronius and on the 'Twentieth-century masters'. Another editorial initiative typical of Queneau was the enquiry *Pour une Bibliothèque idéale* (Paris: Gallimard, 1956), which he organised and edited: the most famous French writers and scholars were each invited to suggest his or her own choice of titles for an ideal library.
6. R. Queneau, *Una storia modello*, ed. by R. Romano (Milan: Fabbri, 1973).
7. J. Roubaud, 'La mathématique dans la méthode de Raymond Queneau', *Critique*, 359 (April, 1977).
8. In *Cahiers de Linguistique Quantitative* (1963).
9. In *Subsidia Pataphysica*, vol. 29.

Pavese and Human Sacrifice

Each one of Pavese's novels revolves around a hidden theme, something unsaid which is the real thing he wants to say and which can be expressed only by not mentioning it. All around it he constructs a tissue of signs that are visible, words that are uttered: each of these signs in turn has a secret side (a meaning that is either polyvalent or inexpressible) which counts more than its obvious one, but their real meaning lies in the relation which binds them to the unspoken theme.

La luna e i falò (*The Moon and the Bonfires*) is the novel by Pavese which is densest with emblematic symbols, autobiographical motifs, and peremptory statements. Perhaps to excess: it is almost as though out of his typical style of narrating, reticent and elliptical, there emerged that profusion of communication and representation which transforms a short story into a novel. But Pavese's real ambition in this work did not reside simply in the creation of a successful novel: everything in the book converges in one single direction, images and analogies bear down on one obsessive concern: human sacrifices.

This was not a passing interest. The linking of ethnology and Greco-Roman mythology with his own existential autobiography and his literary achievement had always been part of Pavese's programme. The roots of his devotion to the works of ethnologists lay in the powerful appeal of a work he had read as a young man: Frazer's *The Golden Bough*, a work that had already proved crucial for Freud, Lawrence and Eliot. *The Golden Bough* is a kind of round-the-world tour in search of the origins of human sacrifice and fire-festivals. These are themes which would resurface in Pavese's mythological reevocations in *Dialoghi con Leucò* (*Dialogues with Leucò*): the passages in this work on rural rites and ritual deaths pave the way for *La luna e i falò*. Pavese's exploration of the theme ends with this novel: written between September and November 1949, it was published in April 1950, four months before the author took his own life, after recalling in one of his last letters the human sacrifices of the Aztecs.

In *La luna e i falò* the first-person narrator returns to the vineyards of his home village after making his fortune in America; what he is looking for is not only his memories of the place or his reintegration in a society or any revenge for the poverty of his upbringing. He is looking for the reason why a village is a village, the secret that links places and names and generations. It is not by accident that this 'io' has no name: he was a foundling in a hospice, brought up by poor farmers as a low-paid labourer; and he grew into adulthood by emigrating to the United States, where the present has fewer roots in the past, where everyone is just passing by, and he does not have to account for his name. Now, back in the unchanging world of his own countryside, he wants to discover the real substance behind those rural images which are the only reality he knows.

The brooding, underlying fatalism in Pavese is ideological only in the sense that he sees it as an inevitable point of arrival. The hilly area of Lower Piedmont where he was born ('la Langa') is famous not only for its wines and truffles, but also for the crises of despair which are endemic, constantly afflicting the peasant families. It could be said that not a week goes by without the Turin newspapers reporting the story of a farmer who has hanged himself, or thrown himself down a well, or (as in the episode at the heart of this novel) set fire to the farmhouse with himself, his family and animals all inside.

Of course Pavese does not seek the reason for this self-destructive despair only in ethnology: the social background of the isolated smallholders in these valleys is portrayed here in the various classes with the sense of social completeness of a naturalist novel (in other words a type of literature which Pavese felt was so much the opposite of his own that he thought he could avoid or annex its territories). The foundling's upbringing is that of a 'servitore di campagna' (country labourer), an expression which few Italians understand except the inhabitants of some of the poorest areas of Piedmont – and we hope that they need not know it for long. On the rung below paid workers, he is a boy who works in a family of smallholders or sharecroppers, and receives only his board and the right to sleep in the barn or the stall, plus a minimal seasonal or annual bonus.

But this identification with an experience so different from his own is for Pavese just one of the many metaphors of his dominant poetic theme: his sense of exclusion. The best chapters in the book narrate his experiences of two different festivals: one as the despairing young boy who had to stay at the farm and miss the fun because he had no shoes, the other when as a young man he had to take his master's daughters to it in the cart. The existential vitality which is celebrated and let loose in the festival, and the social humiliation which now demands revenge, enliven these pages which blend the various levels of knowledge on which Pavese conducts his research.

A thirst for knowledge had driven the protagonist to return to his village; and three levels of this search could be distinguished: the level of memory, the level of history, the level of ethnology. A typical feature of Pavese's stance is that on these two latter levels (the historical-political one and the ethnological) just one character acts as a guide to the narrator. The carpenter Nuto, clarinettist in the local band, is the village Marxist, the one who recognises the injustices of the world and knows that the world can change, but he is also the one who continues to believe in the phases of the moon as essential for various agricultural activities, and in the bonfires on the feast of St John which 'reawaken the earth'. Revolutionary history and this mythical, ritual anti-history have the same face in this book, speak with the same voice. A voice which only mutters through his teeth: Nuto is the most closed, taciturn and evasive figure imaginable. This is the opposite extreme from an open declaration of faith; the novel consists entirely in the protagonist's efforts to get a few words out of Nuto. But it is only in this way that Pavese really *speaks*.

Pavese's tone when he mentions politics is always a bit too brusque and trenchant, as though he were shrugging his shoulders because everything is already clear and it is not worth expending any more words. But nothing really was understood. The point of confluence between Pavese's 'Communism' and his recovery of man's prehistoric and atemporal past is far from clear. Pavese was well aware that he was dealing with the topics which had been most compromised by twentieth-century decadentism: he knew that if there is one thing one cannot joke with, that is fire.

The man who comes back to his village after the war records images, following an invisible thread of analogies. The signs of history (the corpses of fascists and partisans which the river still occasionally brings down to the valley) and the signs of ritual (the bonfires lit every summer on the hilltops) have lost their significance in the frail memories of his contemporaries.

What happened to Santina, the beautiful but careless daughter of his masters? Was she really a Fascist spy or was she on the partisans' side? No one can say for sure, because what drove her was an obscure desire to surrender herself to the abyss of war. And it is pointless to look for her grave: after shooting her, the partisans had buried her in vine shoots and had set fire to her corpse. 'By midday it was all just ashes. A year or so ago the sign of it was still there, like the bed of a bonfire.'

[1966]

Publisher's Note

The essays collected in this volume for the first time were published in the sources listed below. The asterisk (*) indicates that the title is the one used by the author; whereas words in bold print are the bibliographical notes that Calvino himself had prepared with a view to the eventual publication of some of his essays.

'Why Read the Classics?' (*), *L'Espresso*, 28.6.1981.

'The Odysseys within *The Odyssey*' (*), partially published in *la Repubblica*, 21.10.1981. Later in *Risalire il Nilo. Mito fiaba allegoria*, ed. Ferruccio Masini and Giulio Schiavoni (Palermo: Sellerio, 1983).

Xenophon, *Anabasis*, introduction to the BUR (Biblioteca Universale Rizzoli) edition (Milan: Rizzoli, 1978).

'Ovid and Universal Contiguity' (*), **Preface to an edition of the Metamorphoses, 1979.** The only changes Calvino made to this preface written for the Einaudi edition are the change of title, and the addition of the paragraph on p.33, beginning 'This technique of metamorphosis' and ending 'straightening, joining, separating etc.)'.

(Pliny), 'The Sky, Man, the Elephant' (*), preface to Pliny, *Storia naturale* (Turin: Einaudi, 1982).

'Nezami's Seven Princesses' (*), *la Repubblica*, 8.4.1982.

'Tirant lo Blanc', in *Tesoros de España*, published by the Spanish Ministry of Culture for the Exhibition, 'Ten Centuries of Spanish Books', in the New York Public Library, 1985.

(Ludovico Ariosto), 'The Structure of the *Orlando Furioso*' (*). **Text written for the radio, in 1974, on the occasion of the fifth centenary of Ludovico Ariosto's birth**, broadcast on 5.1.1975. Calvino modified the title which had been used when the text was published in *Terzoprogramma*, 2–3 (1974).

(Ludovico Ariosto), 'Brief Anthology of Octaves' (*), *La rassegna della letteratura italiana*, 79:1–2 (January–August 1975).

'Gerolamo Cardano', written on the fourth centenary of the death of Gerolamo Cardano, physician and mathematician, *Corriere della sera*, 21.9.76.

'The Book of Nature in Galileo' (*), written in French, under the title 'Exigences et perspectives de la sémiotique', for *Recueil d'hommages pour A. J. Greimas* (Amsterdam-Philadelphia, 1985). Translated into Italian by Carlo Fruttero.

'Cyrano on the Moon' (*), *la Repubblica*, 24.12.1982.

(Daniel Defoe), '*Robinson Crusoe*, Journal of Mercantile Virtues' (*), in *Libri del tempo* (Turin: Aurora Zanichelli, 1957).

(Voltaire), 'Candide or Concerning Narrative Rapidity' (*). **Preface to an Italian edition of Voltaire's *Candide* with illustrations by Klee**, BUR (Milan: Rizzoli, 1974).

'Denis Diderot, *Jacques le Fataliste*', *la Repubblica*, 25.6.1984.

'Giammaria Ortes', introduction to *Calcolo sopra la verità della storia e altri scritti* (Genoa: Costa & Nolan, 1984).

'Knowledge as Dust-cloud in Stendhal' (*), in *Stendhal e Milano. Atti del 14° Congresso Internazionale Stendhaliano* (Florence: Olschki, 1982), where it appeared under the title 'La conoscenza della Via Lattea (Knowledge of the Milky Way)'.

'Guide for New Readers of Stendhal's *Charterhouse*' (*), *la Repubblica*, 8.9.1982.

'The City as Novel in Balzac' (*). **Preface to a translation of *Ferragus*, written for the Centopagine series** (Turin: Einaudi, 1981).

'Charles Dickens, *Our Mutual Friend*', *la Repubblica*, 11.11.1982.

'Gustave Flaubert, *Trois Contes*', *la Repubblica*, 8.5.1980.

'Leo Tolstoy, *Two Hussars*', preface written for the Centopagine series (Turin: Einaudi, 1973).

'Mark Twain, *The Man That Corrupted Hadleyburg*', preface written for the Centopagine series (Turin: Einaudi, 1972).

'Henry James, *Daisy Miller*', preface written for the Centopagine series (Turin: Einaudi, 1971).

'Robert Louis Stevenson, *The Pavilion on the Links*', preface written for the Centopagine series (Turin: Einaudi, 1973).

'Conrad's Captains' (*), on the thirtieth anniversary of Conrad's death, *l'Unità*, 3.8.1954.

'Pasternak and the Revolution' (*), *Passato e presente*, 3 (June 1958).

(Carlo Emilio Gadda), 'The World is an Artichoke' (*). **Speech delivered at a meeting of the Premio Internazionale degli Editori (International Publishers' Prize), in Corfù, 29 April–3 May 1963, supporting the (eventually successful) candidacy of C. E. Gadda. Translated from the French original. Unpublished.**

'Carlo Emilio Gadda, the *Pasticciaccio*'. Gadda's American publisher asked Calvino to write this introduction to introduce the novel to the new reading public of the paperback edition. Partially published in *la Repubblica*, 16.4.1984. Here we give the full edition.

'Eugenio Montale, *Forse un mattino andando*', in *Letture montaliane in occasione dell'80° compleanno del poeta* (Genoa: Bozzi, 1977). Partially published in *Corriere della sera*, 12.10.1976.

'Montale's Cliff', (★), in memory of Eugenio Montale, *la Repubblica*, 15.9.1981.

'Hemingway and Ourselves' (★), *Il Contemporaneo*, I:33 (13.11.1954).

'Francis Ponge', written on the occasion of the poet's 80th birthday, *Corriere della sera*, 29.7.1979.

'Jorge Luis Borges', speech delivered at the Italian Ministry of Education on the occasion of a visit by the Argentinian writer, partially published in *la Repubblica*, 16.10.1984.

'The Philosophy of Raymond Queneau' (★). **Preface to an Italian edition of *Bâtons, chiffres et lettres* and of other essays by Raymond Queneau** (Turin: Einaudi, 1981).

'Pavese and Human Sacrifice' (★), *Revue des Études Italiennes*, 2 (1966).

Index